ON TIME, ON BUDGET

ON TIME, ON BUDGET

Managing Projects with Limited Time and Resources

JOHN SHOEMAKER, PH.D.

On Time, On Budget: Managing Projects with Limited Time and Resources
First Edition Trade Book, 2024
Copyright © 2024 by John Shoemaker

All rights reserved. No part of this publication may be reproduced, stored in a retrieval system, or transmitted in any form by any means—electronic, mechanical, photocopy, recording, or otherwise—except for brief quotations in critical reviews or articles, without the prior permission of the publisher, except as provided by U.S. copyright law.

To order additional books:
www.amazon.com
www.pmprof.online

ISBN: 978-1-952943-29-4

E-book also available: 978-1-952943-26-3

Editorial and Book Packaging: Inspira Literary Solutions, Gig Harbor, WA
Cover Design: Brianna Showalter

Printed in the USA

TABLE OF CONTENTS

Acknowledgments	xiii
Foreword	xv
Preface	xvii

CHAPTER 1 Introduction — 1
- Why Project Management? — 3
- Projects and Project Management — 6
- What Is Project Management — 8
- Performance Domains — 9
- Project Management Principles — 10
- The Project Life Cycle — 10
- Types of Projects — 13
- Project Management Software — 16
- Traditional Desktop Applications — 17
- Software as a Service — 18
- Summary — 19

CHAPTER 2 Initiating the Project — 21
- Introduction — 21
- Defining the Problem — 22
- Project Concept Document/Project Scope Overview — 23
- Project Selection – Internal Projects — 25
- Project Selection - External Projects — 32
- Real-World Project Selection — 34
- Defining Project Parameters — 40
- Summary — 45

TABLE OF CONTENTS

CHAPTER 3 Project Charter — 47
- Introduction — 47
- Developing a Charter — 48
- Charter Contents — 50
- Project Charter Approval — 62
- Summary — 63

CHAPTER 4 Project Scope Planning — 65
- Introduction — 65
- Advantages of Effective Scope Planning — 66
- Steps in the Project Planning Process — 68
- The Scope Statement — 68
- The Work Breakdown Structure — 70
- Generating the Work Breakdown Structure — 72
- How Far to Break Down the Project — 78
- Bottom-Up Planning — 81
- Project Work vs. Project Management — 82
- Displaying the WBS — 83
- Scope Verification — 85
- Summary — 86

CHAPTER 5 Project Resource Planning — 89
- Introduction — 89
- Estimating Resource Requirements — 89
- Acquiring Resources — 96
- Assigning Resources — 100
- Resource Usage — 108
- Resource Leveling — 109
- Project Cost Planning — 114
    - Estimating Project Costs — 115
    - The Project Budget — 120
    - Summary — 121

TABLE OF CONTENTS

CHAPTER 6 **Project Schedule Planning**   **123**
    Introduction   123
    Duration and Work   124
    Common Methods for Estimating Duration   125
    To Pad or Not to Pad?   129
    Activity Relationships   133
    Summary   140

CHAPTER 7 **Developing the Project Schedule**   **143**
    Introduction   143
    Slack   145
    Constraints   148
    The Project Start Date   152
    Analyzing the Schedule   153
    Forward vs. Backward Pass   157
    Estimating the Project End Date   159
    Finalizing the Schedule   159
    Milestones   160
    Tying Up Loose Ends   161
    Summary   162

CHAPTER 8 **Communications Planning**   **165**
    Introduction   165
    The Communication Plan   168
    Responsibility for Project Communication   172
    Methods of Communication   173
    Summary   184

CHAPTER 9 **Risk Management Planning**   **187**
    Introduction   187
    What Is Risk?   188
    Risk Planning   189

TABLE OF CONTENTS

Risk Identification	189
Risk Documentation	195
Risk Analysis and Prioritization	196
Risk Response Planning	203
Opportunity Response Strategies	207
Selecting a Risk Response Action	208
Inherent Risk vs. Residual Risk	208
Risk of the Project as Opposed to the Project Risks	209
Summary	210

CHAPTER 10 Change Management Planning — 213

Introduction	213
Identifying Environmental Changes	215
Identifying/Evaluating Proposed Project Changes	218
Approving and Implementing Change	221
Communicating Project Changes	225
Changing Goals and Objectives	226
Summary	226

CHAPTER 11 Quality Management Planning — 229

Introduction	229
The Concept of Quality	229
The Quality Management Plan	231
Project Quality vs. Quality of the Project Deliverables	236
Summary	241

CHAPTER 12 The Critical Role of the Project Manager — 243

Introduction	243
Facets of the Project Manager Role	244
Project Manager as Coach	247
Project Manager as Leader	254
Summary	257

TABLE OF CONTENTS

CHAPTER 13 Role of Other Key Stakeholders — 259
- Introduction — 259
- The Project Sponsor — 259
- The Project Champion — 261
- The Project Customer — 262
- Project Support Personnel — 264
- The Project Team — 264
- Stages of Team Development — 268
- Team Quality — 271
- Team-Building Exercises — 272
- Virtual Teams — 272
- Time Management — 274
- The Kick-off Meeting — 279
- Summary — 279

CHAPTER 14 Tracking Project Performance — 281
- Introduction — 281
- What to Track — 282
- Project Review Meetings — 294
- Executive Management Review Meetings — 299
- Customer Review Meetings — 301
- Virtual Meetings — 302
- Meeting Evaluations — 303
- Summary — 303

CHAPTER 15 Project Reporting — 307
- Introduction — 307
- Status Reports — 308
- Progress Reports — 318
- Reporting Bad News — 320
- Summary — 321

TABLE OF CONTENTS

CHAPTER 16	**Controlling the Project**	**323**
	Introduction	323
	Issues	324
	Problem-Solving	324
	Change Management Process	328
	Communication	332
	Conflict Management	333
	When the Project Is Not Going Well	338
	Killing the Project	340
	Summary	342
CHAPTER 17	**Project Closure**	**345**
	Introduction	345
	Project Closure Methods	345
	Contract Closure	348
	Customer Acceptance	349
	Premature Closure	351
	Administrative Closure	351
	Closeout Meetings	360
	Summary	365

Appendices

A *Bibliography*	369
B *Project Tools*	379
C *Diagnostic Surveys*	381
D *Exercises*	409
E *Miscellaneous*	417
F *Project Forms*	435
Project Selection Form	435
Stakeholder Register	436
Project Charter	437
Scope Statement	440

TABLE OF CONTENTS

RAM/RACI Example	442
Project Budget Template	443
Project Control Chart	445
Change Order Request	447
Project Change Control Log	448
Risk Register Template	450
Issues Log	452
Project Team Meeting Agenda	454
About the Author	455
Index	457

ACKNOWLEDGMENTS

I would like to thank the many people who have made this book possible. The participants at the 200+ project management seminars I have given have contributed more than they know. Their feedback and insightful comments have helped me to better understand the nuances of managing projects.

I would also like to thank my students at City University of Seattle, Centro de Enseñanza Técnica y Superior (CETYS University in Mexicali and Tijuana), and the University of International Business and Economics in Beijing who have helped to sharpen my understanding of project management best practices.

Lastly, I would like to thank my wife, Tina, for her patience as this book has evolved into what it is today.

FOREWORD

In the dynamic landscape of today's business world, successful project management is not merely a skill; it is a strategic imperative. As we navigate through the complexities of modern projects, the need for a comprehensive guide that articulates time-tested principles with best practices becomes increasingly apparent.

It is with great pleasure that I introduce this work on traditional project management. In these pages, you will find a rich tapestry of insights, strategies, and practical wisdom that collectively form a compass for project managers in their pursuit of excellence. John Shoemaker has crafted a guide that has drawn on his extensive experience and a deep understanding of the field; he has helped demystify the intricacies of project planning, execution, and control. This book is not just a compilation of theories; it is a roadmap, guiding both novices and seasoned professionals through the challenging terrain of project management. The principles articulated here are universal, offering a framework that can be applied across diverse projects and organizational settings.

I commend John Shoemaker for his dedication to advancing the field of project management and for his commitment to sharing his expertise with a broader audience. These lessons are shared in the classes that he teaches as a professor. Whether you are a project manager, a team member, or an executive overseeing multiple initiatives, the wisdom contained within these pages will undoubtedly enhance your ability to lead and deliver successful projects.

Linh Luong, MBA, MIS, PMP, CSM, CSPO, POPM, SSMC

PREFACE

One of the first questions that one has to ask one's self when contemplating a work like this is, "Why another introduction to project management?" A quick check on Amazon or E-Bay reveals a long list of such works. Some of these books are very good; some are nobut there clearly is no shortage. So, why one more?

Over the years, I have read a few books that, upon completion, I thought to myself, *I wish I had written this book.* What these books had in common is that the authors had taken a complex subject and made it clear, easy to understand, and relevant to my work.

I have read a great number of books on project management. I have found the books by James Lewis, Kim Heldman, Tom DeMarco, Timothy Lister, and Scott Berkun particularly useful and have learned much from them. But none of these books is the book that I would like to have written.

For the last 25 years, I have taught over 200 project management seminars for many of the largest corporations in the United States, Canada, the United Kingdom, and the United Arab Emirates. These seminars have helped me refine my ideas on how projects should be managed and how to communicate these lessons to others. They have also given me much insight into the types of day-to-day problems working project managers face.

I did not start out to write a book about project management. This work began as a series of speaker notes to accompany my seminar slides. Over a period of years, these notes have become rather extensive. Ultimately, they have become the book I would like to have written.

PREFACE

Many project management books are designed for those who manage large, high-dollar, long-term projects with the support of a project management office and Microsoft Project server. This book was for people who have managed projects for a few years with no formal training and limited organizational support and those new to the field of project management.

I read a book review recently in which the reviewer began by stating that whenever he reads a new book or manuscript, he always asks himself the question, "What is the author adding to the state of the art on this subject?" This book does not attempt to break new ground in project management but rather to help project managers, those who aspire to be project managers, and those who do project work to better understand and apply project management best practices.

While this is not meant to be a how-to book in the strict sense of the word, it is designed to help project managers better manage their projects by providing them with practical information about project management tools and techniques and how to apply them to the types of projects they work on.

INTRODUCTION

Although the origins of modern project management are a matter of debate, it is clear that projects have existed since the earliest times. Two of the earliest known projects, Noah's Ark and the Tower of Babel, are described in the Book of Genesis. Other well-known early projects include the pyramids of Egypt, Stonehenge, and the Great Wall of China. These projects required a highly structured process to coordinate the massive amounts of labor and materials necessary to complete such projects.

Although projects have existed since the beginning of recorded history, project management, as we know it today, is a relatively new discipline. Awareness of project management as a discipline did not begin until the 1940s with the Manhattan Project, which is widely considered to mark the beginning of modern project management.

A few of the most widely used project management tools, the Gantt chart, for example, predate the Manhattan Project, but most of the major developments in project management came in the late 1950s. Among the most important of these developments were new methods for planning and controlling projects. One of these methods is called the Critical Path Method (CPM); Program Evaluation and Review Technique (PERT) is another. In recent years, elements of these two methodologies have merged to form what we now call "Project Management."

CPM is a scheduling tool based on a set of mathematical algorithms designed to manage projects with interdependent activities. It was developed jointly by the DuPont Corporation and the Rand Corporation in the late 1950s to manage plant maintenance projects. Based on activities, durations, and dependencies, CPM calculates the critical path, i.e., the minimum amount of time it will take to complete the project.

At about the same time, the Navy, together with Booz, Allen, and Hamilton Consulting developed a set of techniques designed to improve the management of the Polaris submarine program. These techniques were collectively known as Program Review and Evaluation Technique, or PERT for short. PERT utilizes probability estimates to calculate project schedules, making it possible to calculate the probability that the project will finish by a certain date. PERT can also be used to estimate the impact of changes on the project schedule.

Both CPM and PERT focused on schedule control. The U.S. government, the Department of Defense, and NASA soon recognized that effective project management depends on more than just controlling the schedule; it also depends on controlling cost and scope. Refinements in the PERT/CPM methodologies and new tools such as the Work Breakdown Structure (WBS) and Earned Value Analysis (EVA) were subsequently developed to address cost and scope issues.

Project managers applied these tools and techniques using an approach known as *waterfall project management*. The waterfall method is a linear approach to project management that divides projects into phases, which are completed in sequence. Once work has been completed, it cannot be revisited. The flow of the project is unidirectional.

In the mid-1980s, the U.S. Department of Defense formally recognized this approach in DOD-STD-2167. In this standard, the DOD required software vendors to utilize the waterfall approach. ". . . the contractor shall implement a software development cycle that includes the following six phases: Preliminary Design, Detailed Design, Coding, Unit Testing, Integration, and Testing."

INTRODUCTION

Due to low success rates, project managers, especially those in IT, began to look beyond the waterfall method. Within the past 20 or 30 years, many new approaches have been developed, including Agile, Scrum, Rapid Application Development, RUP, and Kanban, to name a few. Agile has become the most widely used of these alternative approaches, although it has limited applicability outside the field of software development.

As a result of these developments, project managers now have a wide assortment of approaches to managing projects. Project success depends on applying the right tools to the right projects in the right way. That is the essence of contemporary approaches to project management.

Why Project Management?

If projects have existed for thousands of years, why has project management only recently been recognized as a distinct discipline? While there are undoubtedly many reasons for the recent emergence of project management as a separate field of study, it is primarily the result of the convergence of two forces. First, projects make up an increasingly large percentage of work. Second, the failure rate among projects has traditionally been quite high.

The work world is becoming increasingly projectized. More and more of what we do these days is project work. There was a time when projects were what people did in addition to their primary work responsibilities. Today it is the reverse; non-project work is what we do when not working on projects. As a result, success in business increasingly depends on one's ability to manage projects. Project management skills have become the key to success. Anyone who aspires to move up in his or her organization must have good project management skills.

There is considerable statistical evidence to support this trend. For example, organizations are spending an increasingly large amount of money on projects. According to PMI, approximately 25% of the world's GDP is now spent on projects. That amounts to almost 10 trillion dollars, 2.3 trillion of that in the United States alone, a trend likely to continue for the foreseeable future.

Given the amount of money currently spent on projects, it is imperative that organizations learn to manage them effectively and efficiently. Success in the marketplace depends on it. Poorly managed projects are a significant source of lost revenue. In extreme cases, poor project management practices have bankrupted organizations.

A second reason for the emergence of project management as a discipline is the high failure rate of projects in the U.S. and worldwide. The Standish Group, for example, has conducted periodic surveys of the IT industry, beginning in 1994. Their surveys have found that the success rates for IT projects are relatively low. Their first survey in 1994 reported that only 44 % of projects finished on time, and that projects took 222% of the planned duration and 189% of the original budgeted cost. In addition, they reported that 70% of projects fell short of their planned scope, and 30% were canceled before completion.

In short, software projects took more than twice as long as scheduled to produce 61% of the functionality at nearly twice the estimated cost. Not an impressive record! While these results were specific to the software industry, there is no reason to believe the results were much different in most other industries.

A more recent Standish Group report made public in 2015 suggests that project performance has improved since their initial 1994 study. According to their most recent report, 35% of all IT projects are successful compared to only 16% in their first study. Critics have pointed out that much of the difference can be attributed to the fact that the Standish Group changed its definition of success between 1994 and 2015.

Some of this improvement, however, is undoubtedly due to improved project management. Traditionally a very small

INTRODUCTION

percentage of people who work as project managers have had any formal project management training. That is beginning to change as more project managers receive formal project management education and training.

The increasing use of project management best practices should improve project performance, and studies seem to bear this out. The Center for Business Practices recently conducted a study of professional project managers. In this survey, they found that using project management tools and techniques improved IT project performance in the following areas by the following percentages:

Schedule Estimating	38.6%
Customer Satisfaction	37.6%
Strategic Business Alignment	37.0%
Cost/Hour Estimating	32.8%
Time/Budget	32.5%
Schedule Performance	32.1%
Quality Improvement	31.9%
Labor Hours Performance	25.6%
Cost Performance	23.8%
Response Time	23.0%
Staff Productivity	22.8%
Time to Market	21.7%

(Source: http://www.information-management.com/specialreports/20030218/6365-1.html)

These results reinforce the findings of the Standish Group. Using the appropriate project management methodologies, tools, and techniques does improve IT project performance. Non-IT projects have obtained similar results. (*PMNetwork*, September, 2006, p. 19)

So, what exactly is "project management"? This question is addressed in the next section.

Projects and Project Management

To apply the principles of effective project management, it is important to understand what constitutes a project and how projects differ from other types of work. The following characteristics differentiate projects from the other type of work:

- Projects are unique endeavors.
- Projects are designed to accomplish a specific goal or set of goals.
- Projects have start dates, end dates, and schedules for completion.
- Projects are carried out through a series of interrelated tasks.

The Project Management Body of Knowledge (PMBOK) describes a project as "a temporary endeavor undertaken to create a unique product, service or result." (*PMBOK*, 7th ed., p. 245) This definition incorporates the characteristics listed above into a single, concise statement.

Figure 1.1 | The PMBOK

The Project Management Institute, the non-profit, professional organization that serves the project management community, has, as a part of its certification program, developed what is called the Project Management Body of Knowledge (PMBOK). It is an attempt to document best practices in project management and serves as the basis for the PMI certification examination.

Some people have difficulty believing that projects are unique endeavors because they work on what they perceive to be the same project on more than one occasion. For example, a person who installs computer systems may not view each new installation as unique. However, each new installation, no matter how similar to previous installations, is unique. Each has a different time frame, a different hardware and software configuration, a different physical location, a different customer, etc. In other words, a project may not be significantly different from other projects, but no two projects are exactly alike. Like snowflakes, they may look alike, but upon closer inspection, we find differences, even though these differences are often very small.

Projects are also different from other kinds of work in that projects have start dates, end dates, and a schedule for completion. Projects do not go on forever. (At least, they are not supposed to.) That does not mean, however, that project start and end dates cannot change. It just means that projects are not ongoing activities.

It is these two characteristics that most clearly differentiate projects from processes. While processes produce repetitive outputs, project outputs are unique. Processes are ongoing while projects have start dates and end dates.

From this perspective, manufacturing an automobile is not a project. Because each automobile is exactly the same (within very narrow limits) as every other automobile that comes off the assembly line, it does not meet the uniqueness test. And, because manufacturing is ongoing, it does not meet the scheduling requirement. In other words, it is neither unique nor temporary.

Designing an automobile, on the other hand, is a project. Setting up the assembly line is a project. Setting up a distribution system is a project. Developing a marketing plan is a project. These are temporary activities that produce a unique deliverable. Manufacturing, on the other hand, is a process. Processes are repeatable and therefore not unique.

A frequently asked question has to do with the difference between projects and programs. A program consists of a set of interrelated projects. For example, the U.S. Space Program of the 1960s was a set of interrelated projects designed to achieve one overarching goal: to put a man on the moon. Because projects are often serial, the life span of a program may be quite long, sometimes lasting several years or longer. The purpose of program management is to manage these related projects more efficiently and effectively than managing each of them individually.

"Portfolio" is another project management term that sometimes causes confusion. As we noted earlier in this chapter, companies are becoming increasingly project-oriented. As a result, most project managers work on multiple projects that may or may not be related, often four or five (or more) at a time. Collectively, these projects make up the project manager's project portfolio.

What Is Project Management?

The *PMBOK* defines project management as ". . . the application of knowledge, skills, tools, and techniques to project activities to meet project requirements." (*PMBOK*, 7th ed., p. 245) It is a collection of tools and techniques designed to produce deliverables that, within time and cost constraints, will satisfy the customer.

From a more cynical, though perhaps more realistic, perspective, Reich Gardner described project management as:

> *"The art and science of doing something that has never been done before by predicting the unknown, developing a plan to deal with it, and implementing it through people who do not report to us using resources over which we have no control."* (Gardner, 1990)

In a similar vein, Kerzner writes, "Project management is the art of creating the illusion that any outcome is the result of a series of predetermined, deliberate acts when, in fact, it was dumb luck." (Kerzner, 1998, p. 4)

INTRODUCTION

Performance Domains

In the 7th edition of the *PMBOK*, the Project Management Institute (PMI) introduced the concept of performance domains. The reason for doing this is to bring a system focus to the practice of project management. PMI has identified eight performance domains, i.e. groups "of related activities that are critical to the effective delivery of project outcomes." (*PMBOK*, 7th ed., p. 7) Though conceptually distinct, they are all interrelated and run concurrently throughout the life of the project. These are:

1. Stakeholders
2. Team
3. Development Approach and Life Cycle
4. Planning
5. Project Work
6. Delivery
7. Measurement
8. Uncertainty

The processes within these domains are addressed in the PMBOK and in the subsequent chapters of this book.

Figure 1.2 | PMI Certification

There are no industry-specific performance domains or principles. That is why PMI offers only one project manager certification test. Project management is project management.

That is not to say that writing software is the same as building a bridge or developing a training course. The application of these knowledge groups, skills, and processes may vary, sometimes significantly, from one industry to another. Yet, the fundamental principles of project management apply to all projects in all industries.

Project Management Principles

The newest version of the PMBOK includes for the first time a set of 12 project management principles:

1. Stewardship – Be a diligent, respectful, and caring steward.
2. Team – Create a collaborative project team environment.
3. Stakeholders – Effectively engage with stakeholders.
4. Value – Focus on value.
5. Systems Thinking – Recognize, evaluate, and respond to system interactions.
6. Leadership – Demonstrate leadership behaviors.
7. Tailoring – Tailor based on context.
8. Quality – Build quality into processes and deliverables.
9. Complexity – Navigate complexity.
10. Risk – Optimize risk responses.
11. Adaptability and Resiliency – Embrace adaptability and resiliency.
12. Change – Enable change to achieve the envisioned future state.

There is a great deal of overlap between these principles of project management and the principles that govern good management. Both sets of principles are designed to deliver value to the customer. Good project managers incorporate these principles into their leadership style.

The Project Life Cycle

Another way to look at project management is to focus on the stages of the project life cycle. Project management activities conceptually fall into phases or stages that collectively make up the project life cycle. According to the *PMBOK* (See Figure 1.3), the project life cycle consists of five stages, sometimes referred to as process groups: initiation, planning, execution, control, and close-out.

Initiation

The key parameters are defined in the *initiation stage,* or *definition stage,* as some project texts call it. The primary objective in this stage is to obtain formal approval for the project. The two primary documents developed in this stage are the *project charter* and the *stakeholder register.*

Planning

Planning revolves around the translation of project requirements and constraints into a work plan. Key processes include defining the scope of the project, scheduling project activities, and assigning work resources. The baseline plan serves as the basis for the project execution processes.

Figure 1.3 | Life Cycle Process Groups

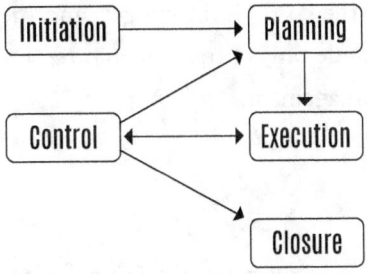

Execution

Good planning is essential to project success, but plans have limited value unless they are implemented. The primary focus of the execution processes is to accomplish the work identified in the project work plan. Key processes include directing and managing the project work, acquiring and developing the project team, and ensuring that the project deliverables meet customer requirements.

Figure 1.4 | A Different Perspective on the Project Life Cycle

1. Project initiation
2. Wild enthusiasm
3. Disillusionment
4. Chaos
5. Search for the guilty
6. Punishment of the innocent
7. Promotion of the non-participants

Control

The primary focus of the monitoring and controlling processes is keeping the project on schedule, keeping the cost within budget, and the work within scope. Key processes include project tracking and reporting, change management, and risk management.

Closeout

Closeout activities bring closure to the project by obtaining formal acceptance from the customer. Additional activities include evaluating project management performance, archiving project records, sharing lessons learned, and recognizing those who contributed to the project.

In large, complex projects, it is common to divide the project into phases, each designed to produce a key deliverable. Typically, these phases include feasibility, requirements, design, build, test, and launch. Each phase becomes a project that goes through an initiation, planning, execution, control, and closeout stage. A performance review is often conducted at the end of each phase to determine if the project should continue to the next phase or stage.

The level of activity varies considerably from one stage of the project to the next. Figure 1.5 shows the activity level within each process group at each stage of the project life cycle. There is considerable overlap though one or two process groups are most prevalent at each stage. As one would expect, initiation activities are most prevalent during the early stages, while execution and control activities are most common during the later stages.

Figure 1.5 | Activity Level by Phase

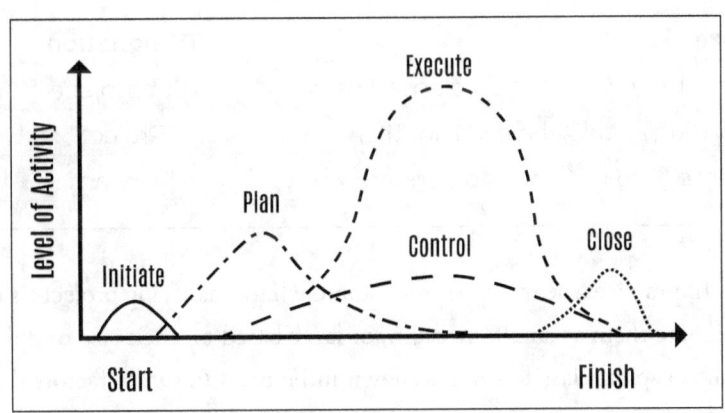

Types of Projects

Projects differ in a surprisingly large number of ways. Because of this, it has been difficult to develop a classification system that helps to simplify the task of determining the appropriate tools and techniques for any given project.

That being said, there have been many attempts to develop a project typology. The reason for classifying projects by type is that no one approach or set of tools and techniques works equally well for all types of projects. A good typology makes it possible to utilize the most appropriate approach to managing the project.

Unfortunately, too many organizations do not differentiate between project types and therefore do not adapt their approach to the needs of the project. This is much like trying to force a square peg into a round hole: the results are predictable. The failure to adapt to the project's needs may have something to do with why so many projects fail.

Figure 1.6 | Project Types by Size

Size	Designation
Small (a few days to 30 elapsed days)	Subproject
Medium (1 to 3 elapsed months)	Project
Large (4 to 12 months or longer)	Program

In practice, the most common approach to classifying projects is to designate them as small, medium, or large based on their size or duration. A typical classification is shown in Figure 1.6. Other factors that have been used to differentiate project types include:

- the amount of risk
- the value of the project to the organization
- the level of technology required to produce the deliverables
- the number of business units within the organization involved in the project
- the cost of the project

Robert Wysocki described another approach in his book *Effective Software Project Management* (Wysocki, p. 8). In this scheme, projects are categorized based on the clarity of goals and the means used to achieve them. These dimensions result in a typology with four project types.

> Quadrant 1 – Clear goals, clear means
> Quadrant 2 – Clear goals, unclear means
> Quadrant 3 – Unclear goals, clear means
> Quadrant 4 – Unclear goals, unclear means

In Quadrant 1 projects, both goals and solutions are clear. The project team knows what to do and how to do it. Success is largely a matter of developing a plan and carrying it out. Traditional project management methods work well for this type of project. Success rates for Quadrant 1 projects are relatively high.

Highly structured, repetitive projects often fall into this category. Quadrant 1 projects include many construction projects (bridges, highways, office buildings), events (conferences, trade shows, festivals), and improvement and maintenance projects, among others.

Quadrant 2 projects present a somewhat greater challenge: the goals are clear, but the means are not. The project team knows what it needs to do but is not clear how to accomplish it. This situation occurs when the project is significantly different from anything the organization has done before, and there are no previous projects from which to draw lessons. The Apollo Moon Project is a textbook example of this type of project. In this case, the goals and objectives were clear, but the project's success depended on technology that did not yet exist. Much of the project was devoted to developing this technology.

Research and development projects are a common type of Quadrant 2 project. Achieving project goals is a matter of trial and error. As a result, it is very difficult to estimate the cost and duration of this type of project. Project risk is, therefore, much higher.

In Quadrant 3, neither the goals nor the means are clear. Much of the work in the early stages of the project must, therefore, focus on clarifying goals and developing strategies for achieving them. The team must be flexible since goals and objectives will frequently change until the stakeholders reach a consensus on the project's scope.

Many software development projects fall into Quadrant 3. In recent years, several new approaches have been developed to deal with this type of project, collectively known as "agile" methods. While agile methods were first used to manage software development projects, a variety of industries now use these. Agile approaches are most useful in projects where means and goals are not clear at the beginning of the project and must, therefore, be clarified in the early stages.

In the real world of project management, there are no Quadrant 4 projects. It is very difficult to solve a problem whose goals are unclear. Without clear goals, there can be no good solution.

While this typology is somewhat simplistic, it is not too simple. Almost all projects fit into one of these four categories, although the fit may not always be perfect. Understanding the project type helps the project manager better select the most appropriate tools and techniques.

Project Management Software

One of the decisions that every project manager has to make is whether to use project management software and, if so, which program or programs to use. The answer to these questions depends on the size of the project, the type of project, the availability of hardware and software, and the project manager's comfort with project management software. Of course, many project managers are not able to choose the software they will use to manage projects. That decision is made for them by their organization.

Microsoft Project is the industry standard and has been for some time. Of course, not all project managers use MS Project. In one survey, project managers were asked what software they used to manage their projects. The number one response was MS Word; Excel was number two. Microsoft Project was the most frequently mentioned project management software program at number 11 on the list. This result is somewhat surprising since the sample consisted of people who make their living managing projects and are generally familiar with project management software.

In some respects, it is not surprising that respondents most often mentioned Word as the program of choice for managing projects by project managers. Many of the tasks that project managers must perform involve filling out forms and writing reports, tasks that word processors handle well.

Excel is also widely used, for similar reasons. The spreadsheet format lends itself well to budgets, lists, and simple database functions frequently used in project management. An added advantage is that it is much easier to create professional-looking graphs and charts in Excel (and other spreadsheet programs) than in Project and most other project management programs.

Since both Word and Excel are widely used, most stakeholders and project team members have access to them and have at least some minimum level of proficiency in using them. This makes it easier to share documents. One cannot make those assumptions about proprietary project management software programs such as MS Project.

It is important to remember that project management software programs are tools designed to make it easier to manage projects. The software can be extremely helpful when correctly applied to the appropriate projects. Unfortunately, many users lack the necessary project management skills and familiarity with the software, making it difficult to use the software effectively. As a result, they often spend more time at the computer than managing the project. Just as using Excel does not make you a competent accountant, no project management software will make you a competent project manager.

Traditional Desktop Applications

There are two categories of project management software packages, one of which consists of traditional commercial software applications such as MS Project 2021. These applications reside on the user's computer or an internal server and range in price from under one hundred dollars to a few thousand dollars. There are, however, some freeware and open-source applications that are available over the internet at little or no charge. While very affordable, many of these programs lack the features of commercial programs, and most offer little or no user support services.

Software as a Service

The second category of project management software is Software as a Service (SaaS), in which traditional software packages are sold to customers to install on their own servers or computers. SaaS software, on the other hand, is installed on the vendor's server, and customers can access it through the internet, usually with a web browser. The customer usually pays a subscription fee for the use of the software, with the fees generally depending on the size of the project and the number of users. For small projects with few users, these fees are relatively low.

The advantage of the SaaS model is that it is usually cheaper, particularly if the software is used throughout the organization. And, of course, users can access the software from any computer with network/internet access. Accessibility is particularly important for teams that are not geographically co-located. Because the software is usually web-based, it is also cross-platform.

Another advantage is that the SaaS software can be updated quickly since the administrator only needs to update the server. It is not necessary to update every workstation. That would be a major task in a large organization.

The web interface, however, also has a downside. Web-based SaaS applications usually have fewer features than comparable commercial desktop software programs; they also tend to be a little slower, though actual speed depends on the speed of the user's internet connection.

INTRODUCTION

And, of course, SaaS applications are not accessible if the internet connection is not active.

Security is another issue. All transactions must pass through the internet to reach the vendor's server, a storage device not controlled by the client organization. This may be a problem for some organizations. Even if transactions are encrypted, the lack of physical control may not be an acceptable risk for those who manage sensitive projects.

Despite the rapid change in project management software, the project management software landscape for desktop applications has not changed much over the last five or 10 years. The number of web-based SaaS applications, however, has grown exponentially and continues to grow at a rapid pace.

In the last few years, some traditional software companies have switched to a web-based, subscription that charges an annual fee to use their software. As a result, the distinction between traditional project management software and SaaS web-based software is no longer so clear cut.

Summary

Although projects have been around since the beginning of recorded history, project management has only recently emerged as a distinct discipline. As organizations become more focused on projects and success rates do not match expectations, the need for good project management becomes even more critical.

The Project Management Institute has developed a project management certification program based on the *Project Management Body of Knowledge*. The *PMBOK* defines a project as "a temporary endeavor undertaken to create a unique product, service or result." These characteristics differentiate projects from processes and other kinds of work.

The *PMBOK* identifies eight performance domains, i.e. "related activities that are critical to the effective delivery of project outcomes." It is the interactions of activities within these domains that drive project results, including integration, scope, schedule, cost, quality, resource, risk, procurement, and stakeholder management. These domains include all the processes necessary to manage projects efficiently.

The life cycle of a project consists of five stages or process groups, as the PMI calls them. These are initiation, planning, execution, control, and closure. The level of activity varies considerably from one stage of the project to the next. While projects begin with the initiation phase and end with closure, there is much back and forth between planning, execution, and control.

Because not all project management tools and techniques work equally well for all projects, it is helpful to categorize projects by type. While there are many ways to do this, one of the most common is to classify projects as small, medium, or large. Grouping projects by size or some other relevant characteristic helps the project manager apply the tools and techniques most appropriate to the type of project.

Nowadays, most project managers use some form of software to help them manage their projects, often Microsoft Word and Excel. Increasingly, project managers are using software specifically designed to manage projects. Some of these are traditional desktop applications like MS Project, Merlin, and Fasttrack Scheduler, among many others. In recent years, web-based subscription software has become increasingly popular.

INITIATING THE PROJECT

Introduction

There is an old (and very apt) saying, "Tell me how your project starts, and I will tell you how it will end." Without a strong foundation, the project is not likely to end successfully.

Project initiation is that group of processes designed to provide a foundation for the successful management of the project. The initiation stage provides the basis for the planning, execution, and control of the project. This stage is also where the organization formally authorizes the project and officially commits the resources. Failure to properly initiate the project has implications for all subsequent project activities.

In a similar vein, James Lewis (Lewis, 2001, p. 107.) wrote that you can almost always trace project failures back to the initiation or planning stages. Although problems may not manifest themselves until much later, the seeds are almost always sown very early on in the project. As one project manager put it, "Projects fail early, not late."

Just as you cannot build a sound structure on a weak foundation, you cannot develop an effective project plan from an unclear or incomplete understanding of the project. Moreover, lack of clarity cannot be made up through good planning and execution any more than good construction can compensate for a weak foundation.

Defining the Problem

Projects often start with a "problem statement"—as a rough idea of what needs to be done to fix a problem or take advantage of an opportunity. A problem statement clearly defines the problem so that stakeholders understand what the project does and what criteria will be used to evaluate its success.

Generally speaking, organizations undertake projects to solve problems or meet needs. For example, a call center manager feels that absenteeism is too high. Data indicate that absenteeism is running at about 10 percent. The manager appoints a process improvement team to study the problem and recommend a solution. After studying the problem, the team develops the following problem statement:

- At the Dallas call center, 9.5 percent of the employees are absent on any given day, increasing call center operating costs by 3 percent.
- Within six months, absenteeism at the call center will be reduced to less than 5 percent, saving the company approximately $125,000 per year.
- To do this, the company will develop an employee rewards program that incentivizes attendance.

The first paragraph above is called the "current state." As part of the problem statement, it describes the existing situation and should make clear why the current situation is a problem or an opportunity. It is also important to describe the financial implications. The example above states that absenteeism is a problem because it costs the company $125,000 a year.

The second paragraph is the "future state"; it describes the desired situation. In the future state, the company has reduced the absenteeism rate to 5 percent. The future state is essentially a statement of the project's goals.

INITIATING THE PROJECT

The third paragraph of the problem statement succinctly describes the solution to the problem identified in the current state, describing the steps that need to be taken to get from the current state to the future state.

Figure 2.1 | Einstein on Problem-solving

Albert Einstein is reported to have said, "A problem well stated is a problem half solved." He also said that "If he only had an hour to save the world, he would spend 55 minutes defining the problem and only 5 minutes solving it." Defining the problem is critical.

This problem statement is an example of a top-down project designed to improve the efficiency and profitability of the organization. In large companies, the source of many projects is the strategic plan, the capital planning budget, or another document that outlines the organization's long-term plans. These plans outline the initiatives needed to achieve the organization's strategic objectives.

Project Concept Document/Project Scope Overview

Once a potential project has been identified, some important questions need to be answered before deciding whether or not to proceed. *What are the project goals and objectives? What resources will be needed? How long will it take? How much will it cost? How much risk is involved?* The project overview answers these and other important questions. Some organizations have formalized this process using a project concept document (PCD) or project scope overview (PSO).

Many sources of information are used to develop the project concept document. These include a product/service description, the organization's strategic plan or related documents, project selection criteria, and relevant historical information. These may or may not be helpful to your project, depending on its size and complexity.

The project concept document consists of four parts:

1. Product/Service Description

The product description outlines the characteristics of the product or service the project is designed to create. For an internal project, the product description may be a simple request from the customer, a conversation, or a memo. It may take the form of a Request for Proposal (RFP) or Request for Quote (RFQ) for external projects.

2. Strategic plan

Projects are the means by which organizations carry out strategic initiatives. Since resources are limited, it is important to focus on projects whose goals best meet the organization's strategic objectives.

3. Project Selection Criteria

Since organizations always have more projects than resources, it is necessary to select the right projects. Many organizations use a project selection methodology that prioritizes projects based on criteria important to the organization.

4. Historical information

It is a good idea to review any relevant historical data before beginning a new project. Previous projects are an important source of information about project costs and timeframes. Historical documents may also be an important source of information about "best practices."

The project concept document explains what the project—if initiated—is designed to accomplish. It involves an in-depth understanding of why the organization would want to use its limited resources to undertake the project and should include the project's name, the purpose of the project, the project's customers, and their needs and requirements.

The project concept document is usually very short, often just a page or two. It provides just enough information to make it possible for the sponsor or project selection committee to decide whether to pursue, defer or kill the project. For any project in which there is a great deal of uncertainty concerning the scope, this is an appropriate step—especially for large, complex projects—but its usefulness is determined more by the clarity of the scope than the type of the project. If the organization has already decided to pursue the project, developing the project concept document may not be necessary.

Senior management is responsible for developing the project concept document, but they will often delegate this responsibility to the project manager. This assumes, of course, that the project manager has already been appointed. In some organizations, the project manager is not appointed until the project has been approved.

Project Selection (Internal Projects)

Most organizations have more projects than resources. As a result, they must decide which projects to accept, which to defer, and which to reject. The failure to select the right project mix can strongly impact the organization's bottom line. In fact, a company's success depends not only on how well it executes projects but which projects it selects. Good decisions depend on an effective approach to project selection.

Some of the most common errors in selecting projects include:

- Selecting projects no one cares about
- Selecting a solution without analyzing the problem
- Selecting something in transition
- Selecting projects whose goals are too ambitious

Organizations that are most successful in avoiding these problems are the ones with a systematic process for identifying, selecting, and managing projects, a process known as "portfolio management."

Project selection begins with the development of a pool of potential projects. There are many ways to develop the project pool. In some organizations, senior leaders compile the list based on input from department heads—a bottom-up approach. In a top-down approach, senior leaders select the project portfolio based on strategic considerations. Smaller projects tend to result from bottom-up approaches. Conversely, larger projects are usually the result of top-down approaches.

A quick and dirty approach involves the use of a PICK chart, which divides projects into categories based on the ease of implementation and the value of the deliverables. (PICK is an acronym for Possible/Implement/Challenge/Kill.)

The Implement cell consists of projects that are easy to accomplish and result in significant benefits. These are high-priority projects that provide the biggest bang for the buck.

Figure 2.2 | The Pick Chart

	Low Benefit	High Benefit
Easy	Possible	Implement
Difficult	Kill	Challenge

The Kill cell includes those projects that are difficult to implement and provide little benefit. They would, of course, be the lowest priority projects. The remaining projects would fall somewhere in between based on their assigned priority.

There are some more rigorous approaches to project selection. One such approach used by many successful organizations uses the Baldrige Criteria for Performance Excellence, in which the organization is assessed against a set of validated business criteria. When the assessment has been completed, the organization receives a feedback report that identifies its strengths and opportunities for improvement. A typical feedback report identifies 40 to 60 opportunities for improvement, or OFIs, as they are commonly called. The organization develops the pool of potential projects from the list of OFIs.

The advantage of this approach is that the pool consists of projects aligned with the company's strategic goals and objectives. This alignment helps focus resources on what is most important to the organization and avoid those projects which contribute little or nothing to its long-term success.

The next step is to prioritize the list of potential projects, which involves the use of a project selection model. There are two general approaches to project selection. One is to rank projects using predetermined criteria, approving only those with the highest priority. In this approach, organizations select projects once a year, often in conjunction with the organization's budgeting process.

Another approach is to make a go/no go decision on each project. Most organizations select projects using a combination of these approaches. Smaller projects are evaluated on a go/no go basis, while larger projects, because of their higher cost and a greater commitment of resources, are approved through the annual budgeting process.

The two most common project select methods are Benefit Measurement and Weighted Scoring models.

Benefit Measurement Methods

There are three widely used benefit measurement methods used to evaluate projects. These are Return on Investment, Payback Analysis, and Net Present Value. A brief explanation of each method follows.

1. Return on Investment (ROI)

Return on Investment is a method for determining if a project will return the required rate of return on the money invested in the project. ROI is defined as the total discounted benefits minus total discounted costs divided by the discounted costs.

(Total Discounted Benefits - Total Discounted Costs)/Total Discounted Costs

ROI as calculated in the above formula results in a percentage. Presumably, those projects with the largest ROI will be selected while those with a lower ROI will not. Many organizations have set minimum ROI thresholds, often in the range of 8 to 10 percent. They rank projects by ROI, and those failing to meet the minimum requirement are deferred or rejected.

2. Payback Analysis

Another benefit-based approach to project selection is payback analysis. This method calculates the amount of time needed to reach the project break-even point. In other words, at what point do the benefits of the project equal the amount of money spent on it? Again, there are no universally accepted standards for what constitutes an acceptable payback period, but it is in the range of one to three years for many businesses.

Since this method does not consider the time value of money, it is not often used for larger, long-term projects.

3. Net Present Value

Net Present Value (NPV) is used in capital budgeting to analyze the profitability of an investment or project. Organizations frequently use this method to prioritize large-scale, long-term projects where the time value of money is important. It is seldom used for small projects since they tend to have smaller budgets and shorter durations, making the time value of money a much less significant factor.

Net Present Value compares project costs and benefits. Presumably, organizations select projects whose benefits outweigh the costs and reject or postpone those that do not. The problem is that project costs usually occur early in the project, while benefits are often not received until the project has been completed. This makes it difficult to compare the relative value of costs and benefits.

INITIATING THE PROJECT

For example, if a business owner were considering a building project, he or she would first estimate the future cash flows that the project would generate. In the example in Figure 2.3, the amount is $325,000. The cost to construct the building is $250,000. Future cash inflows outweigh the construction costs by $45,000, but this number does not account for the relative time value of both costs and benefits. Net Present Value discounts the value of both costs and benefits in years two and three by 8 percent to come up with a net benefit expressed in Year 1 dollars. The Net Present Value of the project is $36,746.12 for the three-year period of the analysis.

The benefits outweigh the costs by $45,000, but because the costs are incurred early in the project and the benefits later in the project, the discounted value of the benefits less the cost is only $36,746.12.

Generally speaking, projects with a positive should NPV be undertaken, while those with a negative NPV should be postponed or rejected. Because resources are limited, projects with higher NPVs should be considered first. There may, of course, be other factors to consider when making the project selection decision, but a positive NPV suggests that the project makes good sense from a financial perspective.

Figure 2.3 | Net Present Value Analysis

Project A	Year 1	Year 2	Year 3	Total
Benefits	$0	$175,000	$150,000	$325,000
Cost	$250,000	$20,000	$10,000	$28,000
Cash flow	-$250,000	$155,000	$140,000	$45,000
NPV	$36,746.12			
Discount rate	.08			

Spreadsheets such as Excel and Numbers have a built-in NPV function that makes it very easy to calculate a project's Net Present

Value. There is also an online NPV calculator on the Investopedia website. (http://www.investopedia.com/calculator/NetPresentValue.aspx)

Weighted Scoring Models

The benefit measurements approach is based solely on financial measures and does not take into account non-financial considerations. Weighted scoring models, on the other hand, often incorporate both financial and non-financial factors. In this approach, organizations prioritize projects using a set of predetermined selection criteria. The first step is to develop the criteria. In some organizations, these criteria are established by senior management and used to evaluate all project proposals, with some organizations preferring to develop project-specific criteria. Common evaluation criteria include cost, time frame, type of project (cost reduction, revenue generation, etc.), ROI, cost-benefit ratio, availability of personnel, and strategic importance.

The second step is to assign a weight to each of the selection criteria. Typically, these weights vary between one and five, representing the relative importance of the criteria in the evaluation process. High scores represent high priority, and conversely, low scores indicate low priority.

Once the criteria and the weights have been established, each project is assigned a score on each criterion. Scores are multiplied by their respective weights and summed across all the selection criteria, yielding an overall priority score for each project.

Many project managers do this in a spreadsheet with which they can determine project priorities by sorting on the priority scores column. This sort yields a prioritized list of projects ordered from most important to least important. The selection process begins with the highest-rated project and moves down the list as far as the budget allows.

By the way, managers often use weighted scoring models to facilitate decision-making in a variety of situations. For example, they are often used to evaluate job candidates and to select suppliers.

Benefit Measurement and Weighted Scoring methods can be used with any project but are more commonly applied to large, complex projects because of their higher levels of risk. The amount of effort involved makes it difficult to justify using these methods for smaller, low-risk projects, though there is no conceptual reason why these methods cannot be used with these types of projects as well.

Other Approaches to Project Selection

The project selection methods discussed in the previous sections assume that decisions are made by rational people using relevant data. That is not always the case. Project selection almost always includes some political and psychological considerations. The most common of these types of selection processes include squeaky wheel, sacred cow, and expert judgment selection methods.

Squeaky Wheel

A common method for selecting projects in many organizations is called the "Squeaky Wheel Method." Those who make the most noise are more likely to get their projects approved irrespective of their merits. Just as the squeaky wheel gets the grease, senior managers sometimes approve projects to get the project manager (or whoever requested the project) off their backs. This method is also known as the "volume method of project prioritization."

Expert Judgment

Some projects are championed by subject matter experts within the organization. Because of the credibility their expertise creates, the projects they propose are often not subjected to the same kind of scrutiny that many other projects are. These projects are often approved without much discussion of the benefits or quantitative data on their contribution to organizational goals.

Sacred Cow

This method is similar to the expert judgment method just described. A sacred cow project has the support of one or more persons high up in the organization, so no one openly questions whether or not it should be done. These projects are often approved irrespective of their strategic importance or return on investment.

Project Selection (External Projects)

The discussion of project selection methodologies has, up to this point, assumed that potential projects are internal to the organization. This is not always the case. The mission of many work units is to provide products and services to external customers.

Projects for external customers are usually initiated by a Request for Proposal (RFP). In this situation, the organization has to decide whether to respond, i.e., bid on the project. This decision is a go/no go, with the primary selection criteria being the organization's current capacity, its expertise, the expected benefit, and the likelihood the bid will be accepted. Sometimes political considerations also play a role.

The form in Figure 2.4 represents an example of a systematic approach to project bidding. Factors influencing the bid/no-bid decision are weighted and summed to produce a bid score. Some organizations may use slightly different selection criteria; others may weight the criteria differently to produce a score that more accurately reflects the organization's priorities. This form is a variation of the weighted scoring model described in the previous section.

So how high does the score have to be to merit a bid on the job? The answer depends on the organization, its resources, and its willingness to accept risk. The answer will be different for each organization. Over time, organizations will find that bids above a certain score are more likely to lead to successful projects than those with scores below that point.

Figure 2.4 | Bid/No Bid Selection Form

Project Title	
Customer	

Rate each factor from 1 to 10 with 1 representing the lowest score and 10 the highest.

Factor	Score	Comments
Alignment with vision and mission		
Likelihood of winning the bid		
Expected ROI		
Risk		
Availability of personnel		
Total Score		
Strengths		
Weaknesses		

You could also use a form like this to prioritize and select internal projects as well, particularly those not addressed in the strategic planning or budgeting process. The use of a formal selection process like this helps to ensure that tactical projects support strategic goals, which is not always the case in many organizations.

Real-World Project Selection

There is not much research on what project selection methods organizations actually use, but in a national survey of CIOs reported in *PM Network* (July, 2005, p. 18), 53% said that their IT project prioritization is politically driven. The implication is that "expert judgment" and "sacred cow" projects are relatively common. This finding should not be surprising since 60% reported that their organization did not use a portfolio management approach to IT projects. These percentages have probably not changed dramatically in the last few years; most other industries are probably similar in this respect.

In many organizations, project selection does not involve the project manager. In these organizations, projects are approved and then assigned to a project manager for implementation. It is, however, important to involve the project manager and the project team in the project as early as possible. As a general rule, those charged with carrying out the project (stakeholders) should also help to define and plan it.

What Is a Stakeholder?

A stakeholder is someone who has a vested interest in the outcome of the project. Their interest in the project stems from the fact that the project impacts them in some way. For some, the impact may be positive. For others, it may be negative. Either way, it is important to identify the project stakeholders and their needs, wants, expectations, and concerns.

It is important to remember that not only are stakeholders impacted by the project, but some stakeholders may also impact projects. For this reason, the project manager needs to make a distinction between key stakeholders and other stakeholders. Key stakeholders can significantly impact the project's success, so it is critical to earn and maintain their trust and support.

Managing stakeholders involves the following activities:

INITIATING THE PROJECT

- Identifying stakeholders
- Analyzing stakeholder needs and requirements
- Prioritizing stakeholders
- Managing stakeholders

Identifying Stakeholders

The identification of stakeholders should begin as early in the project as possible. For most projects, this will be the initiation stage. If, as in some organizations, the project manager is not assigned until the planning stage, the stakeholder analysis should be one of the project manager's first priorities.

For some projects, the number of stakeholders may be rather large. For example, a project to build a nuclear power plant might have millions of stakeholders. It will not be possible to include all of them in the analysis, at least not individually. It is critical, however, to include all key stakeholders or stakeholder groups. Overlooking a key stakeholder can have serious consequences for the project.

The project manager will have identified some of the key stakeholders in advance of the project. When developing the list, start with those listed in the inset box in Figure 2.5, which are stakeholders common to most projects. Next, think about the scope of the project. That may suggest others who might not otherwise come to mind. Talk with the sponsor, team members, and other stakeholders who have already been identified; they might be able to suggest others who may have been overlooked.

For smaller, less complex projects, particularly those in which the project manager is familiar with many of the key stakeholders, this process can be done very quickly and informally. For larger projects, the project manager will probably have to identify key stakeholders using a more thorough and systematic method.

As a part of this process, the project manager should begin to develop the stakeholder register. This register should include information about each stakeholder, their interests, their role in the project, and any other information of importance to the project. Figure 2.6 contains a simple stakeholder register.

Figure 2.5 | Common Stakeholders

Project manager
Project team members
Customers
Suppliers
Management
Regulators
The public/Community
Sponsors
Owners

Analyzing Stakeholder Needs and Requirements

Since stakeholders, especially key stakeholders, can impact the project's success, it is important to know which stakeholders support the project and why. Knowing the "why" has helped many project managers avoid making decisions that might cost them the support of a key stakeholder. For example, I was once involved in a project that initially had the support of the company's IT Director. His support was lost when the project manager decided to outsource some of the IT work. Better communication between the project manager and the IT Director might have resolved this issue and maintained his continued support.

The project manager will also want to know if any of the key stakeholders are less than fully supportive of the project. Good project managers will seek them out to learn why they are not more supportive and what positive steps the project manager could take to earn their support.

Next, the project manager must translate stakeholder needs, wants, expectations, and concerns into appropriate product/service requirements. These are the requirements the project deliverables must meet to satisfy the customer and other key stakeholders. These requirements are, in essence, the project's key success criteria.

Other items sometimes included in the stakeholder register include involvement with the project, ability to influence the project, stakeholders' project expectations, and anything else the project manager wants to include.

Like many other aspects of project management, there is no one right way to conduct a stakeholder analysis. Many project managers like to visit with each of the key stakeholders face-to-face, if possible. Others prefer to talk with stakeholders over the phone or communicate via e-mail. The choice comes down to what is most appropriate for the circumstances.

Face-to-face meetings are probably the most effective, particularly if the project manager is unfamiliar with some of the key stakeholders. Face-to-face meetings with key stakeholders make it easier for project managers to get to know them and develop relationships with them. As one experienced project manager once said, "I don't want to meet a key stakeholder for the very first time when we have to discuss a problem." It is always easier to talk about problems with people with whom you have a good working relationship.

Prioritizing Stakeholders

Conducting the stakeholder analysis often reveals that key stakeholders have different perspectives on the project. As a result, they often have different expectations with respect to project goals and objectives, making it difficult—if not impossible—to develop a set of stakeholders' requirements that will satisfy all key stakeholders.

Situations involving conflicting stakeholder requirements test the project manager's people skills, as he or she must forge a consensus

Figure 2.6 | Sample Stakeholder Register

Stakeholder Register

#	Name	Organization	Phone	E-mail	Role	Level of support	Must do	Must not do	Comments

among key stakeholders on the goals and objectives of the project. Failure to achieve a consensus usually creates conflict among the key stakeholders and can cause the project to fail. When the project manager is unable to develop a consensus, he or she, in conjunction with the project sponsor or customer, must determine which stakeholder needs and requirements will take priority. In other words, the project manager must prioritize the stakeholders. The Power/Interest Grid is a common tool used for this purpose.

Figure 2.7 | Power/Interest Grid

Power/Interest	Low Interest	High Interest
High Power	Keep satisfied	Manage closely
Low Power	Monitor (minimal effort)	Keep informed

The most important of these key stakeholders are the ones who have high power and high interest in the project. They can make or break a project.

Managing Stakeholders

Stakeholder management has two primary purposes. The first is to develop and maintain buy-in among key stakeholders. Since the project's success depends largely on the stakeholders' support, it is critical to obtain their support at the earliest point in the project.

It is amazing how many projects experience difficulties because of a lack of consensus among the key stakeholders on critical project requirements. In the absence of a thorough stakeholder analysis, the lack of consensus often goes unnoticed until the implementation is well underway. By then, it may be too late to avoid serious problems, including project failure.

Even when the project manager realizes there is no consensus, it is frequently dismissed as unimportant. You may hear someone say, "That's just a small detail. We can work it out later." Yet later, the project manager finds it is more than a small detail. There were fundamental differences among key stakeholders on important aspects of the project.

These misunderstandings do not only happen to inexperienced project managers lacking professional training and expertise. Safeco Field (now T-Mobile Park), home of the Seattle Mariners, is a good example. It cost $517 million to build, $100 million over the original estimate of $417 million. The Seattle Mariners attributed $70 million of the additional cost to "unanticipated capital costs." The Public Facilities Department (PFD) attributed much of the additional $100 million to cost overruns. Cost overruns are additional costs incurred as a result of errors, omissions, or inefficiencies. The Mariners, on the other hand, argued that the majority of these additional costs were not overruns but the necessary costs of completing the facility as originally designed. When asked to pinpoint blame for the additional cost, the mayor replied, "Let the lawyers duke it out." (*Seattle Times*, December 23, 1999)

Could the cost overrun have been prevented? There is, of course, no way to know. However, it is likely that if the two major stakeholders had taken more time upfront to discuss critical design issues, the final cost of the project would have been much closer to the original estimate.

This example illustrates the importance of communication. According to a recent survey, 55% of project managers believe that effective stakeholder communication is the most critical factor in managing projects successfully. (*PMNetwork*, Dec. 2014, p. 17)

Defining Project Parameters

A constraint is anything that restricts the actions of the project team or requires them to act in a specific way; all projects are subject to many constraints. The three universal constraints—known as the "triple constraints"—are time, cost, and scope.

While all projects must deal with the triple constraints, there are many other constraints that can significantly impact the management of the project as well. These include technology constraints, political constraints, legal and ethical constraints, and risk constraints, to name just a few. To the extent that they are important, they must also be addressed in the project initiation stage.

The triple constraints are often displayed in the shape of a triangle, as shown in Figure 2.8. This triangle is variously referred to as the Triple Constraint Triangle, the Project Triangle, the Eternal Triangle, the Iron Triangle, or the Golden Triangle. Regardless of what you call it, an understanding of the triple constraints is critical to effective project management. The failure to understand the interrelationship of these constraints contributes directly or indirectly to many if not most, project failures.

Figure 2.8 | The Triple Constraints

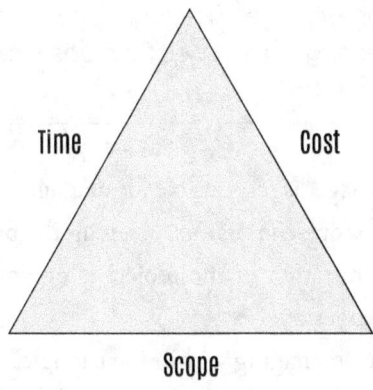

These constraints are rather simple. The time constraint is the amount of time available to complete the project. For example, the project must be completed within three months. This time frame constrains the team's actions, i.e., the project must be completed within three months.

Cost is the amount of resources that the project team is authorized to use for the project. Cost is a constraint in that the project manager may not exceed the authorized amount for the project. It is usually expressed in dollars, euros, or some other unit of currency, though some industries prefer to use person-hours or person-days.

The scope side of the triangle is variously labeled "Quality," "Performance," or "Features." Regardless of the term used, this is what the project has to accomplish, i.e., the work that must be done to achieve project goals and objectives. Scope is a constraint in that the project team must restrict its efforts to those activities that contribute to achieving the project's goals. Anything that does not directly contribute to the achievement of project goals and objectives is outside the project's scope.

Figure 2.9 | Scope Definition

Scope refers to the work required to produce a deliverable that meets the customer's specifications. Any work that does not contribute to meeting these specifications is considered out of scope.

The project manager is responsible for managing the project within the time, cost, and scope constraints. Keeping the project within these constraints for the duration of the project is one of the project manager's biggest challenges.

The first step to "managing within the triangle" is to define each of the project constraints as precisely as possible. It is difficult to manage the project within the constraints when the boundaries are not clear.

Time and cost are easy to define, as there are universal measures for both. For cost, it might be dollars, euros, or some other unit of currency. For time, it might be days, weeks, months, or years. These measures make it easy for the project manager to document the limits for the time and cost sides of the triangle.

Defining the scope side of the triangle, however, is more problematic. There is no universal measure of scope. The scope of each project is unique and must, therefore, be defined in some detail. Not surprisingly, the project scope is often inadequately defined and is at the root of many project conflicts and failures.

The reason for using a triangle to represent the project constraints has to do with the structural properties of triangles. The sides of a triangle are interdependent. A change in any one of the sides impacts the other two sides. Time, cost, and scope are likewise interdependent. Any change to one of them affects the other two.

However, the use of the triangle metaphor does not mean that all three constraints are equally important. The relative importance of each of these constraints will vary from project to project. For example, the cost will almost certainly be the most important constraint on a low-bid project. For other projects, it may well be time or scope. It is important to understand that it is the project sponsor or customer who decides their relative importance.

The most important constraint is called the "driver," while the least important of the three constraints is the "weak" constraint. The remaining constraint is the "middle" constraint. When faced with decisions that involve constraints, decisions should always be made in favor of the driver. Because this constraint is the most important to the sponsor/customer, it has the least flexibility.

Some experienced project managers have suggested that the sponsor should determine the value of the driver and the middle constraint, and the project manager should determine the value of the weak constraint. For example, if the sponsor determines the cost and the timeframe, the project manager should determine the scope. Doing this would help to ensure that the constraints are balanced. In the real world of project management, however, this rarely happens. Perhaps that is why most projects exceed one or more of their project constraints.

Karl Wiegers (Wiegers, 2007) suggests a slightly different way of looking at this issue. Writing about software development, he says there are five dimensions to each project: features (scope), quality, staff, costs, and schedule. To successfully manage the project, the project manager must understand how much flexibility there is in each of these dimensions. This can be done using a flexibility diagram, also known as a spider or radar diagram, as shown in Figure 2.10.

Figure 2.10 | Flexibility Diagram

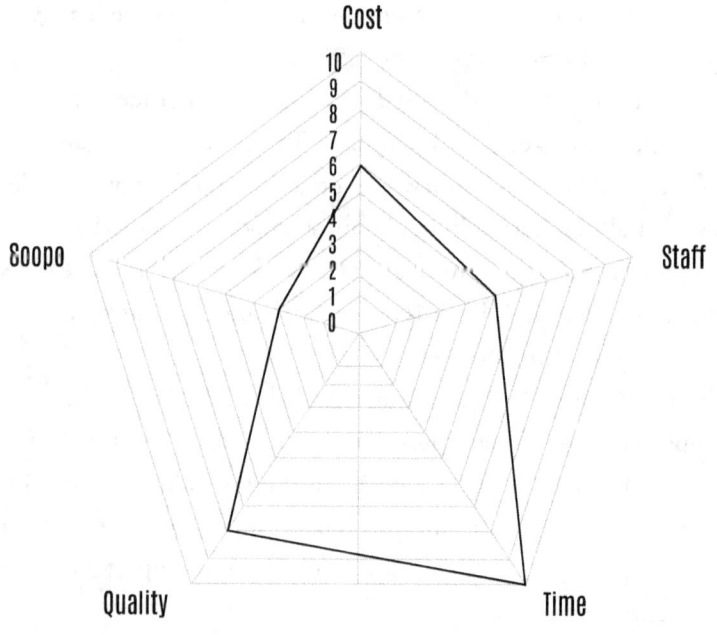

Each of the five dimensions is rated from 0 to 10, with high scores reflecting high degrees of flexibility. Conversely, low scores represent dimensions with little or no flexibility. When you need to adjust the constraints to rebalance the triangle, it is important to know which constraints have the most flexibility and are, therefore, most easily renegotiated.

In this example, the project manager has the most flexibility on the time and quality dimensions, and the least flexibility on scope and staff. This lack of flexibility will have important implications for managing the project as the project manager works to keep the project within its constraints.

Regardless of which view one takes, it is extremely important to understand the sponsor's priorities. The project manager will make decisions throughout the project that will involve trade-offs. A project manager who does not know the project sponsor's priorities risks making decisions that will ultimately cause the project to fail.

What if the project manager is not clear about the relative importance of the constraints? The answer is simple. Ask! A project manager should never begin a project without a clear understanding of the sponsor's priorities. However, the problem with asking is that sponsors tend to say something like, "They are all important." In such situations, the project manager must force a choice. What if the project can't meet both the time and cost constraints? Would it be more important to bring the project in on time, or would it be more important to finish it within the project budget?

Summary

Project initiation processes are critical to the success of the project. Since they form the foundation for the project, the failure to clearly define the project and its constraints has serious consequences throughout the life of the project.

To ensure that the project manager can successfully carry out the project, it is important to have the support of key stakeholders. It is also vital to include all key stakeholders, particularly those who may be skeptical of the project. If there are conflicting views, it is the responsibility of the project manager to negotiate a consensus among the key stakeholders on the goals and objectives of the project and maintain their support throughout the life of the project.

Organizational success, however, depends not only on managing projects right but also on managing the right projects. Selecting the right projects helps ensure that the organization uses its resources for projects designed to achieve strategic goals. Poor project selection wastes both time and money. The best way to ensure the right projects are selected is to develop and implement a systematic approach to project evaluation.

All of the activities described in this chapter lead up to the primary purpose of the initiation stage: the development of the project charter, which is described in the next chapter.

THE PROJECT CHARTER

Introduction

Many projects fail because key stakeholders do not reach a consensus on the time, cost, and, scope constraints at the beginning of the project. Worse yet, they may not be aware that there is no consensus.

In the absence of written documentation, stakeholders may assume they have reached a consensus on these constraints when there is no consensus. Not until much later in the project do the stakeholders realize that no such agreement ever existed. Therefore, an important step in the initiation process is to document the constraints so the project manager can be sure there is agreement on them before moving on to the planning stage. Often these project parameters are described in a document called the "Project Charter" or "Project Initiation Document." The project charter is a written document that has two primary purposes:

- to define the scope of the project and the resources needed to achieve project goals and objectives
- to formally authorize the project manager to expend organizational resources on the project

As such, the project charter forms the basis for all subsequent work on the project. It is the project's guiding document.

Developing a Charter

PMI defines the project charter as "a document issued by the project initiator or sponsor that formally authorizes the existence of a project and provides the project manager with the authority to apply organizational resources to project activities." (*PMBOK*, 7th ed., p. 245)

In theory, senior managers develop the project charter. After it has been approved, they hand it off to the project manager for implementation. In most organizations, however, it is the project manager who develops the project charter. He or she begins the implementation after formal approval by the approving authority—usually a project steering committee, senior manager, or external customer.

Project charters include information from one or more of the following documents: a project feasibility document, a project selection matrix, a project concept document, and a formal business case. It may also include information from any other documents generated to identify a need and establish a senior management commitment.

Some project managers resist the idea of a written project charter because it holds them accountable for producing the deliverables within the constraints outlined in the charter document. They may not want to be held accountable for a variety of reasons (e.g., goals are unclear or constantly shifting, lack of support from upper management, etc.). They may perceive the charter as an attempt to make them accountable for an outcome they cannot control.

The charter, however, is an agreement. As in any agreement, both sides have responsibilities. The project manager promises to deliver the project deliverables on time and within budget, and the sponsor promises to make the necessary resources available for that purpose. The project manager cannot be held accountable if the sponsor fails to provide the agreed-upon time and resources.

THE PROJECT CHARTER

Figure 3.1 | Project Charter Components

- An overview of the project
- Project goals, objectives and key success criteria
- Project deliverables
- Business case or need for the project
- Risks and assumptions
- Resource and cost estimates
- Feasibility study results if one was performed
- Human resources needed and any special skills required
- Roles and responsibilities of key team members and resources

That does not mean the project constraints cannot or will not change. The project manager working with key stakeholders will frequently adjust the time, cost, and scope constraints throughout the implementation and control of the project. When this happens, the project manager and the sponsor must renegotiate the constraints to ensure the project can be successfully completed.

In many environments, projects are so loosely defined that it is difficult to hold anyone accountable for project outcomes. Project failures result in finger-pointing and blame but rarely lead to improved project management performance. The project charter helps to avoid this by ensuring that all stakeholders know the purpose of the project, what resources the organization has allocated to it, and how long it will take to complete. And, the project manager knows what he or she has to do to satisfy key stakeholders.

It is surprising how many organizations have no formal chartering process. In these organizations, projects are often poorly defined, roles and responsibilities are unclear, and everyone blames everyone else for the project's failure. Moreover, without a systematic process for managing projects, there is little hope for improvement.

Charter Contents

What goes into the project charter? There is no simple answer to this question. It depends on the organization and the types of projects they undertake. Over time, organizations discover what works and what does not. Figure 3.1 identifies a list of issues often included in the project charter, which you may adapt for your own situation.

The following discussion is a generic example describing the sections of the project charter form shown in the appendix. With some modifications, most organizations can use this form for most projects.

Business Problem/Opportunity

Organizations undertake projects to solve problems or fulfill needs. The first step in defining any project is to develop a clear understanding of the problem or opportunity it is designed to address. A project that does not solve a problem or meet an important need will probably not satisfy the customer and will ultimately be considered a failed project by key stakeholders.

This is why it is so important to develop a clear problem statement, as discussed in the previous chapter.

Too often, however, problems or needs are defined in terms of solutions rather than causes. For example, a local credit union decided to develop a website to facilitate online financial transactions. They viewed the lack of a functional website as the problem when, in fact, that was the solution to a problem they had not clearly defined.

Subsequent analysis revealed that the real problem was twofold: the high cost of processing financial transactions and the loss of customers to financial institutions that made it possible to transact business from home at any time of day or night. The e-commerce website was not the problem; rather, it was the solution to these problems. Had the project team gone through the process of developing a problem statement, this confusion might have been avoided.

THE PROJECT CHARTER

Goal Statement

Once we have a good understanding of the problem or the opportunity, we have to decide what action to take, if any. How are we going to fix the problem or take advantage of the opportunity? We have to clearly but briefly describe what we are going to do and how it addresses the problem.

The description in this section of the charter defines the scope of the project and is necessarily a very high-level description of the project scope. Since the purpose of the charter is to obtain approval to begin the project, this description must include enough detail to enable the sponsor/customer to decide whether or not to authorize the project.

While it is important to describe clearly what the project will do, it is sometimes equally important to describe what it will not do. A list of exclusions can help stakeholders avoid making incorrect assumptions about the scope of the project. For example, a project to develop a software program may or may not include training for end-users. If training is beyond the project's scope, it should be included on the list of exclusions. This removes all doubt.

If the project customer/sponsor is an external client, the list of exclusions can be used as an opportunity to cross-sell. For example, training could be added to the list of deliverables as an added service for an additional fee. Listing exclusions has the potential to significantly increase revenues from the project.

Lastly, the more clearly the scope is defined, the easier it is to develop accurate cost and duration estimates. Many delays and cost overruns are the results of a poorly defined project scope. An inadequately defined scope also increases the likelihood of "scope creep"—an incremental expansion of the project beyond its original objectives without a commensurate increase in time and/or resources. Scope creep is one of the contributors to project failure and, for this reason, it is important to be as clear as possible when defining the project's scope.

Key Success Criteria

A successful project is one that satisfies key stakeholders. What will it take to satisfy them? Key Success Criteria, sometimes called Key Performance Indicators (KPI), are financial and non-financial measures used to help an organization measure project success. The trick here is to select a set of metrics that reflect the extent to which the project deliverables meet customer requirements.

Selecting the right metrics, of course, assumes you have determined the customer's requirements and that the project addresses these requirements. Without appropriate metrics, it will not be possible to determine if the project meets these requirements when completed.

No project manager wants to be in the situation of having to debate the success of a completed project. Specific success criteria must be developed as a part of the charter so there can be no doubt about whether or not the project has succeeded. When completed, it meets the criteria—or it does not. The project is successful, or it is not.

Assumptions

This seems to be one of the more difficult project concepts to grasp. Assumptions are often confused with risks. Perhaps this is because assumptions are risks, but risks are not necessarily assumptions. This distinction will become clear shortly.

The dictionary defines an assumption as something "that is accepted as true or as certain to happen, without proof." Similarly, the *PMBOK* defines an assumption as "a factor in the planning process that is considered to be true, real or certain, without proof or demonstration." (*PMBOK*, 7th ed., p. 235) Project teams never have all the facts. In the absence of complete information, it is necessary to make assumptions. Without assumptions, no project would ever get started.

Project assumptions should meet the following criteria:

- Assumptions must be about things that we cannot know, i.e., they are unknowable. They are unknowable because they deal with future events or the resources are not available to verify their veracity.
- Assumptions must be relevant to the success of the project. If one or more of the assumptions turn out to be untrue, the project's success will be seriously jeopardized.

For example, the project manager of a construction project might assume there will be no weather-related delays during the course of the project. As a result, the schedule does not include any time for such stoppages, nor does the budget include money to cover any additional costs caused by weather-related delays. If there is a weather-related delay in work on the project, the project probably will not finish on time nor finish within the budgeted cost.

This assumption meets both criteria. Firstly, it is unknowable. Weather forecasts do not provide sufficiently specific information, and this is particularly true for longer-term projects. Secondly, if this assumption turns out to be false, it could significantly impact the project. Depending on the nature of the delay, it could delay the project by weeks or months, causing significant cost overruns.

Suppose the project manager of a software project assumes that the features specified in the product description will satisfy end-users. This assumption is certainly relevant to the success of the project, but is it unknowable? A survey of potential users could determine the features end users want. Because customer preferences are not unknowable, this would not be a valid assumption. On the other hand, assuming a construction project will not be delayed because of supply chain issues might be a valid assumption given that such issues are hard to predict, particularly for projects that may take a year or two to complete.

Unfortunately, project assumptions are rarely discussed and seldom documented. The failure to document project assumptions may obscure the fact that there is no consensus among stakeholders on key project assumptions. The failure to recognize divergent views can cause serious problems, potentially causing the project to fail.

This is why the project charter should include a list of important assumptions, and why the project manager should ensure that key stakeholders review this list and discuss any differing views. This review will help ensure that everyone has the same understanding of the assumptions upon which the success of the project rests.

It is possible the project sponsor might reject one or more of the assumptions listed in the charter, potentially refusing to sign the charter until the project manager has reworked the list to eliminate the assumption(s) in question. For this reason, the project manager and his or her team should give some thought to what they would do if any of the assumptions are not acceptable to the approving authority.

In large projects, assumptions should be documented in a log and tracked, just like issues, risk events, and change orders. Many project managers keep an assumptions log that they regularly review throughout the project. This log should also include information about what the team will do if any of the assumptions are no longer valid.

Risks

Since every project entails some risk, it is important to make the project stakeholders aware of these risks and their implications for the project. While a thorough analysis of risk is usually not undertaken in the initiation stage, project sponsors must have some basic knowledge of project risks to decide whether or not to approve the project. For this reason, the project charter should contain a list of known risks and the actions, if any, necessary to address them.

For large, complex projects, the risk section of the charter might be quite substantial. In such cases, it is common to document the risks in a separate risk management plan. For most smaller projects, risk still needs to be addressed, though it may be just a few paragraphs in the work plan.

THE PROJECT CHARTER

Chapter 9 has a more detailed description of risk management planning.

Exclusions

Sometimes it is important to list work that is not within the scope of the project—particularly true for those activities that customers might reasonably expect to be within the scope of the project as defined in the charter. For example, customers might expect that a project to develop a customized software product would include user training on the new product. If the project does not include such training, it should be specifically excluded. Some organizations list excluded items together with the cost of adding them to the project.

Constraints

This section contains information about the priorities of the triple constraints (see page 41). Listing them in the project charter helps ensure agreement between the project manager and the project sponsor or customer on their relative importance. Too often, no one documents the relative importance of the triple constraints, and differences among key stakeholders are not discovered until much later in the project.

Time

An estimate of the project duration is an essential part of the project charter. It is unlikely that a sponsor would sign off on a project without knowing how long it will take to complete.

Time is usually rather easy to estimate, though a literature review suggests it is often not done very well. The Standish Group studies referenced in Chapter One have documented this very persuasively over the last 10 or 15 years. Most projects do not finish on time. Meeting deadlines will be addressed in more detail in later chapters, where we will examine some techniques for refining estimates of duration.

At this point, we are only concerned with the initial estimate that must go into the project charter. The importance of this estimate depends on the relative priority of time as a constraint. Where time is the driver, the time estimate is often given to the project manager, who must then figure out how to do it within that time frame. For example, a hotel improvement project must be completed before the Memorial Day weekend when the summer travel season begins.

For projects where time is less critical, the completion date will depend on when the project begins and how long it takes to complete the scope of work. It may be difficult to estimate how long it will take to complete the project since the scope of work has only been identified at a very high level at this point.

Cost

The project charter must, of course, include an estimate of the cost of the project. Who would approve a plan without knowing in advance what it is going to cost? That is equivalent to giving the project manager a blank check, which senior managers are understandably reluctant to do. The project charter must, therefore, include an estimate of the total project cost.

Developing a project cost estimate at this stage of the project, however, is somewhat problematic. For this reason, most project managers develop cost ranges rather than point estimates. Typically, these ranges are as low as ±5% but might be as high as ±25% or more in high-risk projects. (There may be some exceptions to these guidelines based on the type of project.)

A former consultant at Arthur Anderson (now Accenture) once said he routinely estimated costs at ±85%. The reason for such a large range was that it was neither time- nor cost-effective to develop a more accurate estimate of project costs. Instead, he simply added a large

THE PROJECT CHARTER

contingency reserve to each project. That is great if the client is willing to accept such a wide range but many clients will not.

For routine projects, i.e., projects similar to previous projects, cost estimation is usually not too difficult. It is simply a matter of identifying any differences that might affect the cost of the current project and factoring in the differences. This information is often available in the organization's project archives, assuming the organization keeps such information.

Where such records are not available, experienced project managers may be of some help. If they have managed similar projects, they can probably estimate the project's cost to an acceptable degree of accuracy. Industry associations may also be a good source of information about project costs.

For projects that are not routine, estimating cost is often more difficult. The problem is that it is difficult to identify the costs of a project when the project scope has only been defined at a very high level. Another challenge is coming up with precise estimates in the absence of detailed information about the scope of the project, making it necessary to do extensive research on project costs. This research may involve getting bids from vendors or subcontractors and may even require the development of a preliminary budget. All of this can be very time-consuming and may add considerable expense to the project.

When time and resources are short, Order of Magnitude Estimation may be the most appropriate estimation technique. Order of Magnitude Estimation (sometimes called Analogous Cost Estimation) is a cost-estimation technique developed specifically for projects that are difficult to estimate because they are unlike any other project the organization has undertaken. Order-of-magnitude estimates start with the cost of the most similar project for which cost information is available. That estimate is increased or decreased based on the perceived difficulty of the project relative to the comparison project.

For example, in the 1960s, NASA was faced with estimating the cost of sending a man to the moon. No one had ever done this before, so there were no records to review and no project managers to consult. The only project that even remotely compared with this was the Mercury Project, which put an astronaut into orbit. NASA experts decided that putting a man on the moon was approximately four times more difficult than putting a man into orbit. Their final cost estimate for putting a man on the moon was, therefore, four times higher than the cost of putting a man into orbit.

Order-of-magnitude estimates should be used only when there is insufficient information to use any other estimating procedure. It is the procedure of last resort because it produces results that are less accurate than other estimating procedures (experience suggests that order of magnitude estimates are no more than ±75% accurate). Such a range is unacceptably large for most project sponsors, particularly for projects where cost is the driver.

Because project cost estimation is difficult, project managers will often advise stakeholders that the estimate is just that: an estimate, simply a forecast of what the project will cost, given the information available at the time the estimate was made. During the course of the project, however, stakeholders tend to forget this and hold the project manager to the initial estimate. Ballpark estimates have a way of becoming project expectations.

There are several ways the project manager can avoid this problem. First, he or she should indicate the level of accuracy. Estimates should, as we noted earlier, be reported as ranges. Point estimates often imply more accuracy than is warranted because precision is often confused with accuracy. For example, most people will assume an estimate of $34,583.44 is more accurate than an estimate of $25,000 when, in fact, the opposite might well be true.

Second, the project manager should make clear how much confidence he or she has in the accuracy of the estimate. Is it based on experience with previous projects? Have the components been costed out? Estimates should always be reported as ranges. The size of the range depends on the confidence you have in the accuracy of the estimate; the higher the confidence, the narrower the range.

Lastly, the project manager should indicate how the estimate was made, which helps stakeholders determine how much confidence to put in them, and helps project managers better manage stakeholder expectations.

Return on Investment

Another issue the charter may need to include is the return on investment. In other words, why should the organization undertake this project? What benefits will the organization receive for the time and money spent on the project? The answers to these questions constitute the business case for the project. They provide a business rationale for the project.

The business case is essentially an investment proposal, identifying the costs, benefits, and risks associated with the proposed investment and offers reasonable alternatives. It provides the return-on-investment information the sponsor needs to make an informed go/no-go decision on the project. The level of detail required will depend on the size and complexity of the project. Larger projects will require more detail.

The business case puts the decision into a strategic context. Does the project help move the organization toward one or more of its strategic goals? Does it accomplish something of strategic importance?

The business case should answer some if not all, of the following questions:

- What is the opportunity/problem you are trying to solve?
- What is the desired result you are looking for?
- What is the nature of the improvement?
- What must be invested to get the desired result?
- What are the new production operational costs?

- What are the spending reductions, revenue improvements, or profit improvements?
- What are the benefits, such as customer satisfaction, strategic value, cycle time improvements, etc.?
- What are the concerns or risks?
- What is the exit strategy if an initiative is not returning investment?

The ROI section of the charter is particularly important in situations where the project manager or some other key stakeholder has to sell the project to upper management. When the project is mandated by management or requested by an external customer, the business case is usually unnecessary and is often omitted from the charter.

If the charter includes the business case, it should be reviewed and re-validated periodically, particularly when there is a significant change to the project or the business function. If the business case changes during the course of the project, the project may need to be re-approved. Some additional topics often included in the charter are business deadlines, deliverables, resource requirements, and a high-level budget.

Business Deadlines

The project charter will, of course, include a timeline with a completion date or estimated project duration. Some projects, however, are driven by a business deadline that has little or nothing to do with the amount of work necessary to complete the project. Sometimes for business reasons, the project must finish by a specified date. This section of the charter should include the reasons why the deadline must be met and perhaps the consequences of not completing it by the deadline.

Deliverables

The project charter often contains a list of key deliverables to be generated by the project. The project manager may be able to avoid unrealistic expectations and the anger and disappointment that inevitably follow by including a list of tangible deliverables together with a short description of each of them.

Resource Requirements

Some organizations include a list of people and other resources needed to carry out the project. There are several reasons for doing this. Perhaps the most important is to make sure stakeholders are aware of the resources that will be used to carry out the projects. Doing this helps to avoid any future surprises that may negatively impact resource availability.

High-Level Project Budget

Some project managers prefer to develop the budget as a part of the planning process, but there may be reasons for including a high-level project budget in the project charter. Including this information probably increases the comfort level of some project sponsors, making it more likely they will sign off on the project.

If the customer is an external organization, the charter should contain the financial information developed while preparing the bid.

Related Projects

Some projects are components of larger projects, and this has implications for both projects. If a project is related to one or more other projects, it should be noted in the charter together with their interdependencies.

Documenting related projects is particularly helpful in larger organizations where these interdependencies might otherwise be overlooked.

Executive Summary

Some project managers like to include a one-or-two-page summary of the project in the project charter. If the charter has been clearly and succinctly written, this is probably not necessary for many projects.

Project Charter Approval

When the project charter has been completed, it must be approved. In an organization with a project management office, the approving authority is usually a member of the project steering committee. In organizations that do not have a PMO, the approving authority is usually the project sponsor.

If the project sponsor is external to the organization, i.e., an outside customer, the contract between the project manager's organization and the customer may serve as the project charter. Depending on what the contract includes, it may be necessary to supplement it with information that would have been included in the project charter had one been developed.

One frequently asked question has to do with the length of the project charter: How long should it be? The answer is simple. As long as it needs to be and as short as possible. If it is too short, it may lack important project details. If it is too long, no one will read it. Some organizations put a five-page limit on project charters. I think that is reasonable for most projects. Small projects may not need that much. Larger projects may require more.

Does every project require a charter? My answer to this question is, "Yes." For large, complex projects, the charter will probably be very detailed. For smaller, relatively straightforward projects, it will probably be very short. For a very simple project, it may just be an e-mail outlining what the project should accomplish and the deadline for completion. However, all projects require a document that contains the information necessary to complete the project successfully.

What if the project sponsor refuses to sign the charter? This does happen occasionally. The solution is to negotiate changes in the charter to make it acceptable to the approving authority. The project cannot begin until it has been approved.

The signing of the project charter marks the end of the initiation stage and the beginning of the planning stage. At this point, the project is usually handed off to the project manager and his or her team if they were not already involved in the drafting of the charter.

Summary

All projects should begin with a project charter. The charter helps to ensure that all of the stakeholders, particularly the project sponsor and the project manager, agree on the goals and objectives of the project and the resources used to accomplish them. For larger, more complex projects, the charter will probably be a rather detailed document. For smaller and less complex projects, it will be much less detailed, perhaps just a short e-mail outlining the essential elements of the project.

When the project manager and the project sponsor have signed the charter, the initiation stage is complete and the planning stage begins. Chapter 3 through Chapter 11 deal with the various aspects of project planning.

PROJECT SCOPE PLANNING

Introduction

The planning stage is considered by many, if not most, professional project managers to be the most critical stage in the project lifecycle. Time spent upfront developing a comprehensive plan based on realistic goals and objectives prevents much confusion and rework during the execution and control stages of the project. The tighter the deadline, the more important it is to thoroughly plan the project work.

The project planning phase begins when the project initiation phase has been completed; the approval of the project charter marks the end of this first stage. All planning activities are based on the project charter and any supporting documents developed in the initiation phase, including resource planning, scheduling, budgeting, risk management, and any other planning activities appropriate to the project. The primary purpose of the project plan is to provide a blueprint for the implementation of the project as defined by the charter.

Unfortunately, some project managers view the planning stage as something to get through as quickly as possible so they can begin the implementation. I think there are several reasons for this. First, most project managers work on projects with tight deadlines. There is constant pressure to complete projects quickly. Defining and planning activities generate little visible progress toward the completion of the project work. "Real" progress first becomes apparent in the execution stage. For this reason, there is a natural tendency to want to get the paperwork out of the way and "get down to work."

Second, many project managers do not fully understand the importance of the planning process. This lack of understanding may be due to the fact that plans always change during the implementation of the project. Why waste time developing a document that will inevitably change as the project progresses? This view is, however, flawed.

As Eisenhower once said, "No battle was ever fought according to plan, but no battle was ever won without one." This idea is just as relevant for project management as it is for war. The plan forms the basis from which changes are made. Just as a poorly drafted project charter, or worse yet, no charter at all, puts the project at risk, failure to adequately plan the project creates problems for the implementation that may be difficult to overcome.

Comparative studies of American and Japanese project management have found that Japanese project managers spend more time planning than their American counterparts. As a consequence, Japanese project managers can execute project work more quickly, resulting in shorter project durations. This emphasis on planning explains, at least in part, why Japanese companies have been able to bring new products to the marketplace faster than their American competitors. They are able to do this even when using American technology.

Advantages of Effective Project Scope Planning

Effective planning helps minimize uncertainty, increase efficiency, clarify objectives, and provide a basis for monitoring and controlling the project.

Minimize Uncertainty

Project scope planning helps to bring predictability to the project. It does this by providing a schedule demonstrating what resources are needed and when. This predictability helps ensure the resources are available when and where they are needed and that the work gets done on time.

Increase Efficiency

Project resources are always limited. Project managers seldom have the time or money they would like to have or feel they need. For this reason, it is important to make the best use of available resources. Project scope planning helps ensure that project managers achieve project goals and objectives using the fewest resources.

Clarify Objectives

The development of the project plan has another important benefit. It forces the project manager, the project sponsor, and other key stakeholders to think through their approach and clarify project goals and objectives. This clarification helps avoid the communication issues that plague many projects and the problems resulting from them.

Effective planning has implications for all stages of the project lifecycle. Since the project plan is the blueprint for implementing the project work, it determines what activities will be performed, monitored, and controlled in the execution stage.

The project plan makes it possible to control the implementation of the project. Control consists of keeping project performance consistent with the project plan. Without a plan, there can be no control.

Steps in the Project Planning Process

There are four primary steps in the development of the project management plan. These are:

- Define the scope of the project (Chapters 3–4)
- Staff the project (Chapter 5)
- Develop the project schedule (Chapter 6–7)
- Develop ancillary plans (Chapters 8-11)

In Chapter 3 and Chapter 4 of this book, we describe the scope management planning activities. This plan describes the steps required to identify the work necessary to achieve project goals and objectives, i.e., the scope of work. Chapters 5, 6, and 7 deal primarily with resource planning and scheduling. Chapters 8 through 11 describe ancillary planning activities such as communications, change management, risk management, and quality assurance.

Note that some project managers prefer to develop the project schedule (step 3) before assigning resources (step 2). The order of these two steps is, however, somewhat arbitrary. In practice, project planning is more iterative than linear. Changes in the project schedule impact the allocation of resources and vice versa so each step must be continuously reviewed and revised. This issue is discussed in more detail in Chapter 5, which addresses project staffing issues.

The project scope plan consists of three components: the project scope statement, the work breakdown structure, and the work breakdown structure dictionary.

The Scope Statement

While the project charter describes the project's scope, it is a high-level description that lacks detail. It is designed to gain approval for the project, not to provide a detailed description of the project scope. The scope statement is designed specifically for this purpose. The PMBOK (7th

PROJECT SCOPE PLANNING

ed., p. 246) defines it as "The description of the project scope, major deliverables, and exclusions." As such, it describes the project scope with enough detail that stakeholders can agree on what the project will do and what it will not do before planning it in detail.

The scope statement is a short document, a few paragraphs to a few pages, that describes the project goals, deliverables, and requirements. It communicates to stakeholders exactly what the work of the project will produce and what resources will be needed to make it happen. As such, it helps to ensure a common understanding of the project's goals and objectives. It also serves as the basis for the work breakdown structure, a planning tool discussed later in this chapter.

Much of the information in the project scope statement may have already been obtained while developing the project charter. If the charter is well written, developing the scope statement may be largely a matter of cutting and pasting. The scope statement is not, however, simply a duplication of the project charter. It builds on the project charter and provides the basis for the development of the project plan.

Since the project scope statement is a working document that guides the project team's day-to-day activities, it is continuously updated as changes are made to the scope of the project. If there are any questions concerning the scope as described in the scope statement, the project manager may want to interview some of the key stakeholders to ensure that he or she understands the intent of the project.

All key stakeholders should have a copy, and the project manager should keep a copy with the project files. Some project managers store the project scope document on a shared drive together with all other important project documentation where it is accessible to everyone who needs access to it.

Once consensus has been reached on the project's scope, it is necessary to determine in more detail what needs to be done to produce the project deliverable(s). The work breakdown structure, or WBS as it is commonly called, is the tool project managers use to do this. It was developed by the U.S. Navy in the late 1950s as part of the Program

Evaluation and Review Technique (PERT) methodology which the Navy had developed for the Polaris missile program.

The Work Breakdown Structure (WBS)

The second element of the project scope plan is the work breakdown structure (WBS).

What Is the WBS?

Since most projects are too large and too complex to manage effectively, it is necessary to break them down into smaller, more manageable work units. This is what the WBS is designed to do. It helps identify the activities needed to produce the project deliverables. This process is sometimes referred to as project disaggregation or decomposition.

PMI defines the WBS as "a hierarchical decomposition of the total scope of work to be carried out by the project team to accomplish the project objectives and create the required deliverables." (*PMBOK*, 7th ed., p. 253)

The WBS has two goals. The first is to identify the work needed to complete the project successfully. The second is to ensure the project plan does not include any unnecessary work. Project resources are scarce. Most organizations do not have the luxury of being able to perform non-value-added work.

While the project scope is defined in the initiation stage through the project concept document and the project charter, these are relatively high-level descriptions. The WBS, by breaking the project into smaller, more specific activities, serves to further clarify the scope of the project. It sets the boundaries for what is within the project's scope and what is outside the scope of the project. Setting scope boundaries makes the WBS one of the project manager's best defenses against "scope creep." If it is not in the WBS, then it is outside the scope of the project—assuming, of course, it has not been overlooked.

Figure 4.1 | Scope Creep

"Scope Creep" is a term used to describe a situation in which the scope of the project is incrementally expanded with no corresponding change to the time and cost sides of the Triple Constraints Triangle. This can seriously jeopardize the success of the project.

It is critical that the WBS includes all the activities necessary to produce the project deliverables. Activities that are left out will not be scheduled. No resources will be assigned to them. Sooner or later, someone will discover the oversight, and the project manager will have to figure out how to get these activities accomplished with limited resources on short notice. Getting this work done can cause significant disruption to the project budget and the schedule.

In reality, no WBS is ever perfect. People are human, and they make mistakes. Sometimes we overlook important work activities. That is why it is so important for the team to work together to develop the WBS. Working as a team helps to minimize the likelihood of omitting important work activities. It is also a good idea to review the lessons learned from previous projects, and existing templates, if any, and to visit with project managers who have worked on similar types of projects.

The WBS is one of the most under-appreciated project management tools. James Lewis wrote in *Project Planning, Scheduling, and Control*, "... I consider the WBS to be the most valuable tool of project management because it ties the entire project together. This position is contrary to the popular belief that project management is just scheduling." (Lewis, 2001, p. 203) For this reason, it is surprising that so few organizations have a formalized process for developing Work Breakdown Structures.

Projects sponsored by Federal agencies, the Department of Defense, in particular, often require the development of a WBS under MIL-STD-881 (Work Breakdown Structures for Defense Material Items). Using a standardized procedure helps to ensure sufficient detail in the WBS and that the WBS serves as the basis for acceptable time and cost estimates.

Generating the Work Breakdown Structure

There are two general approaches to the development of a WBS. The first is a top-down approach. This process starts with the project and decomposes it into specific activities or deliverables. The other is a bottom-up approach which starts with the individual activities that make up the project and groups them into increasingly higher-level categories.

Regardless of the approach, it is important to remember that developing the WBS is a team activity. The team working together will do a better job than any team members can do working individually.

Top-Down Planning

The top-down approach is the most common method. It starts at the top with the project deliverable and decomposes it into increasingly smaller work units. There are two general approaches to this decomposition process. One is to start with the project deliverable, breaking it down into its primary components. This process is repeated for each level of deliverables until the desired level of detail has been achieved. In this approach, each deliverable is the product of its primary components. For example, if we were designing an automobile, we might start by breaking it down into its primary components: body, engine, fuel system, transmission, etc. This approach works well when the project deliverables are made up of clear and distinct components.

Another approach is to break the project deliverable into the major activities that make up the project. For example, the top-level or primary subprojects for a project designed to set up a conference might include functional areas such as facility, logistics, program, and marketing.

Figure 4.2 is an example of this approach.

Figure 4.2 | Top Level WBS

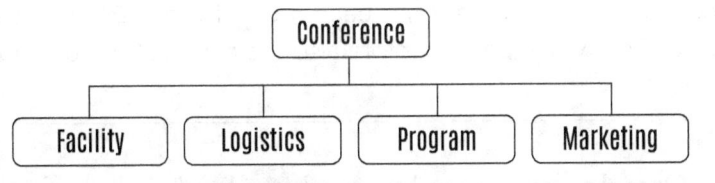

Still, another approach is to break the project into phases. The conference project shown in Figures 4.2 and 4.3 could be broken into a conceptual phase, a planning phase, an implementation phase, and a wrap-up phase. These phases are chronological. This approach works well for projects with a clearly defined time sequence, but not all projects lend themselves to this approach.

Figure 4.3 | Work Breakdown Structure Example

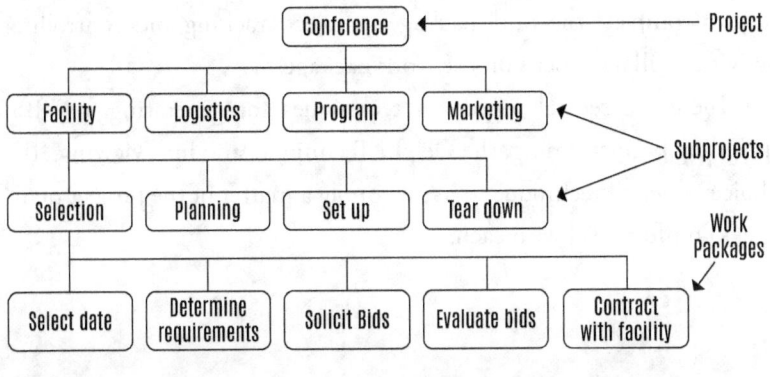

It is important to include all project work in the top-level subprojects. If any work necessary to complete the project is not included in any of the subprojects, then a new subproject must be added. Subprojects at all levels must include 100% of the work at the next higher level. This is the 100% rule.

Figure 4.4 | The 100% Rule

The sum of the elements at each level of the WBS represents 100% of the work (and therefore also the cost) at the next higher level.

Once the team is confident they have identified all the first-level subprojects, they can begin the second round of decomposition. In other words, the first level includes all the work that needs to be done to achieve project goals and objectives. The decomposition process continues until the project has been broken down into sufficiently detailed work units. The work units at the lowest level of each branch, i.e., those that have not been decomposed, are called work packages.

Work packages are the key building blocks of the project plan and serve as the basis for its implementation. Resources are assigned to the work packages. Schedules are based on the duration and the sequence of the work packages. Costs are estimated based on the resources necessary to complete the work packages. Project tracking and controlling activities will also focus on the work packages.

There are several top-down techniques for generating a WBS, including brainstorming, the Delphi Technique, and interviewing. The choice of which technique to use is simply a matter of the project manager's comfort level with each.

Brainstorming

Each technique has its strengths and limitations. Some project managers use a combination of these methods. All can and do produce good results.

Brainstorming, or whiteboarding as it is sometimes called, is probably the most common method for generating WBSs. Brainstorming is a creative method for generating a large number of ideas in a short amount of time. It may be either structured or unstructured, depending on the situation.

Many project managers and team members want to assign resources or durations to activities while developing the WBS. It will be necessary to do this at some point, but this is not the time to do it. The WBS does one and only one thing. It identifies the work that needs to be done to complete the project. The work packages in the WBS constitute the scope of the project.

Most people are familiar with the concept of brainstorming, but few know how to do it effectively. Many teams discuss the scope of their projects and think they have brainstormed it when in reality they have merely discussed it. Discussion is a form of analysis; it is not brainstorming. For a more detailed description of brainstorming and how to do it effectively, see the *Team Handbook* (Scholtes, Joiner, and Streibel, 2018).

One common variation on this technique involves the use of sticky notes. The project manager identifies the primary subprojects and writes each of them on a separate pad. These pads are attached to the wall or set of easels. Team members individually write all of the relevant activities that come to mind on sticky notes, one on each sticky. They then paste their stickies under the appropriate subproject. When this process has been completed, the team works together to arrange them into hierarchical order. The result is a completed WBS.

Mind Mapping

An alternative to brainstorming is a technique called "mind mapping." Essentially, mind mapping is a form of structured brainstorming that visually depicts the relationships between project elements, popularized in the 1970s by Tony Buzan. While project managers use mind mapping for many purposes, project managers often use it to generate project work breakdown structures.

Figure 4.5 | Mind Mapping Laws

1. Start in the centre with an image of the topic, using at least three colours.
2. Use images, symbols, codes, and dimensions throughout your Mind Map.
3. Select key words and print using upper- and lower-case letters.
4. Each word/image must be alone and sitting on its own line.
5. The lines must be connected, starting from the central image. The central lines are thicker, organic, and flowing, becoming thinner as they radiate out from the centre.
6. Make the lines the same length as the word/image.
7. Use colours – your own code – throughout the Mind Map.
8. Develop your own personal style of Mind Mapping.
9. Use emphasis and show associations in your Mind Map.
10. Keep the Mind Map clear by using Radiant hierarchy, numerical order, or outlines to embrace your branches.

Source: www.mind-map.com

Mind mapping has become a sufficiently popular method for generating work breakdown structures that recent books on project management have included discussions of it in the descriptions of WBS generation. As a result of this increased interest, some recent project management software releases have also included a mind-mapping feature.

Figure 4.6 | Mind Map Example

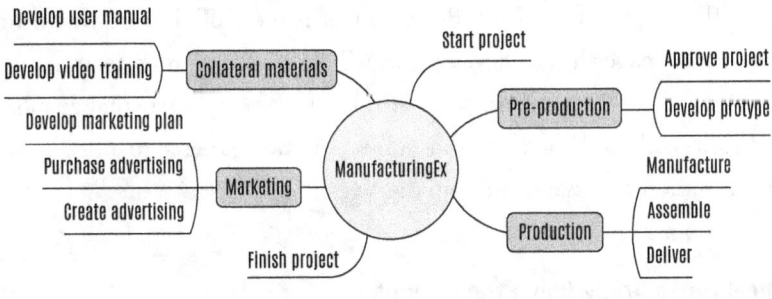

The Delphi Method

The Delphi Method was developed in the 1950s by the Rand Corporation to forecast trends based on the independent input of subject matter experts. Project managers have used the Delphi Method to develop the WBS, particularly when the team comprises members who are not co-located.

In this method, the project manager develops the first draft of the WBS based on his or her knowledge of the project, records from similar projects, etc. This draft is sent to team members who make revisions and return it to the project manager. The project manager consolidates the responses and sends out a revised WBS to team members. This process is repeated until there is agreement among team members that the WBS is complete.

Interviewing

Lastly, the project manager or whoever is responsible for developing the WBS might begin by interviewing key stakeholders and others with relevant project knowledge. These conversations will hopefully lead to the development of an initial WBS. Follow-up conversations will help to refine it. Like the Delphi Process, this approach can be repeated until the project manager, the sponsor, and other stakeholders are satisfied that the WBS is sufficiently detailed.

This approach to WBS development is most often used when the project manager has to develop the WBS before assigning team members. Without input from team members, the project manager must consult with stakeholders and subject matter experts to obtain the information necessary to create the WBS.

How Far to Break Down the Project

Knowing how far to break down the project is a difficult question to answer. The decomposition process can be carried on ad infinitum. At some point, additional decomposition becomes counterproductive. The project manager needs a certain amount of detail to exercise control over the project. However, too much detail causes the project manager to become bogged down in minutiae and lose control over the project. The goal is to break down the project just far enough. It is not always easy to strike that balance.

Although there are no hard and fast rules, there are some guidelines designed to help achieve the optimum level of detail. These include:

1. **The project should be broken down to the level at which the amount of time it will take to complete the work can be estimated with some degree of accuracy.** Some project managers use the "8-80 Rule" to help them do this. Ideally, activities should consist of between eight and 80 hours of work. Similarly, activity durations should also be short. Two weeks is a common limit. While these guidelines work well for many smaller projects, it is often unworkable for large projects. In a

large project, using this rule results in too much detail and, as a result, it becomes almost impossible to manage.

On the other hand, if activity durations are too long, measuring progress is difficult. By shortening activity durations, the completion of activities will be sufficiently frequent to serve as a good indicator of project progress.

2. **Project work should be broken down to the level at which the cost of accomplishing the work can be estimated with some degree of accuracy.** If it is difficult to estimate an activity's cost, you may need to break it down into smaller units whose cost can be more easily estimated. Additional decomposition may clarify the scope making it easier to estimate the cost of accomplishing the work.

Figure 4.7 | WBS vs. Activity List

While these terms are sometimes used synonymously, there is a distinction. A WBS is a hierarchical listing of project work or deliverables that results from the decomposition of the project. It includes the summary activities and the work packages.

An activity list, on the other hand, is simply a listing of project activities or work packages. The activity list is made up of those activities at the lowest level of the WBS, i.e., the terminal elements in each branch of the WBS. It does not include the summary activities.

---

3. **Work should be broken down to the level at which the work packages provide sufficient detail for budgeting purposes.**
4. **While projects are almost always cross-functional, activities at the work package level should not be.** There may be some exceptions, but the work should be decomposed down to the level at which a single person or small workgroup can accomplish the work. If assigned to a workgroup, someone

within the group must be designated as the activity owner. Every activity has to have one and only one person who is accountable for it.

5. **Similarly, projects should be broken down to the level at which the activities are specific enough that qualified persons would know how to accomplish them with a minimum of guidance.** Activities should consist of a single type of work and a single deliverable with clear and measurable completion criteria. If the scope of an activity is too broad or too vague, you may need to break it down further.

6. **Projects should be broken down to the level of detail that you want to track.** Remember that every work package has to be scheduled, resources have to be assigned, costs have to be estimated, and performance must be tracked. Too much detail will make these administrative activities simply overwhelming.

These are guidelines and, as such, do not work equally well in all instances. Other considerations might take precedence. For example, you should break down high-risk work further than work with less risk. By breaking high-risk activities into smaller, more specific activities, the project team can focus their attention on those with the highest risk.

Activities with shorter durations also result in greater flexibility in scheduling. This issue is discussed in more detail in the section on resource leveling in Chapter 5.

Some project managers like to attach checklists to activities as an alternative to further decomposition. The advantage of doing this is that the checklist items provide additional detail, but this detail is not included in the WBS. As a result, no additional resources are assigned, no additional costs are incurred, and there are no additional tracking or reporting requirements.

Not all branches of the WBS need to be broken down to the same level of detail. Some branches may have to be broken down further than others to reach the optimum level of detail.

Sometimes, it is impossible to specify the work in later phases of the project until the work in earlier phases has been completed. Because this type of planning occurs in waves, it is often referred to as "Rolling Wave Planning."

In real-world project management, most branches are broken down to between three to six levels. It is unusual to find projects in which any branches have been broken down into more than six levels. In programs or large, complex projects, however, it is not possible to break a project down to meet the previously described guidelines within six levels. For many of these projects, it would take many times more than that to come even close to achieving the desired level of detail.

So, how do we handle these situations? The solution is quite simple. In very large, complex projects, and perhaps some that are not quite so big or complex, the project manager breaks the project down into its primary subprojects. A project manager is assigned to each subproject and breaks his or her part of the project down another three to six levels. This process continues until the WBS elements at the bottom level meet the guidelines for project decomposition.

In this scenario, project managers are only concerned with the levels immediately above and below them. Project managers who actively involve themselves in work that is more than one level below them are micro-managing. The irony is that this degree of control is neither desirable nor effective.

Bottom-Up Planning

As its name would suggest, the bottom-up approach to developing a WBS starts at the bottom. Work packages are aggregated to form subprojects which are in turn aggregated to form higher-level subprojects.

The most common method for generating a bottom-up WBS is to start with the top-level subprojects. Team members are then given sticky notes and asked to place the work packages under the appropriate subproject. When this has been accomplished, the work packages are then aggregated to form the subprojects under each top-level subproject.

In practice, the development of the WBS is often a combination of bottom-up and top-down approaches.

Project Work vs. Project Management

One final issue in this discussion is about managing the project as distinct from managing the project work. The WBS, as described in this section, consists of all the work necessary to produce the project deliverables. It does not contain the work necessary to manage the project. For example, it does not include the time spent defining and planning project work. Nor does it include the numerous team meetings or status reports written during the implementation of the project plan.

Project management activities must be done, but it is easy to overlook them because they are usually not included in the WBS. As a result, project management activities may not be planned, budgeted, or scheduled. There are two ways to avoid this. First, some project managers add a top-level subproject to the WBS called "Project Management." Other project managers prefer to develop a separate WBS for project management activities. In this approach, the project becomes two projects: the project and the project to manage the project. While this may seem somewhat unwieldy, it has the benefit of keeping work and administrative activities separate. Since there are no direct dependencies between project activities and administrative activities, this approach seems quite logical.

Displaying the WBS

There are several ways to present the results of the work breakdown process. The discussion has, up to this point, used the graphical method to display the WBS (See Figures 4.2 and 4.3). This view of the WBS is sometimes called the organizational or graphic view. In this approach, the project is at the top of the chart, with each successive level representing an increasing level of specificity.

Most project management software programs, including MS Project, do not support the graphical view, although plug-ins can be purchased to add this capability. A tree diagram is a similar approach. It is a variation of the graphical method.

The graphical approach has one significant drawback. It is not well suited for most large, complex projects, i.e., projects with a large number of activities. Even a relatively simple project displayed graphically may take up multiple pages, making it somewhat unwieldy to use.

A more common approach is the outline format in Figure 4.8. The major heading at the top represents the project. The subprojects or summary activities are the major subheadings with sub-activities and activities represented by increasing indentation levels.

Up to this point, we have assumed that the WBS must be developed from scratch for each project. That is not always the case. While every project is unique, many projects are similar to previous projects. In such instances, there is no need to "reinvent the wheel." The use of templates makes the development of the WBS much quicker and easier.

Many organizations archive projects so they can serve as templates for future projects. When a project truly is unique to an organization, it may be necessary to look for templates outside the organization. Fortunately, there is a variety of readily available sources. A Google search for "WBS templates" returned a list of over 100,000 items. Many of these contained links to free downloads.

Figure 4.8 | The WBS in Outline View

WBS Code	Title
0	**Conference**
1	**Facility**
1.1	**Selection**
1.1.1	Select Date
1.1.2	Determine Requirements
1.1.3	Solicit Bids
1.1.4	Evaluate bid
1.1.5	Contract with Facility
1.2	**Site Setup Planning**
1.2.1	Develop conference facility plan
1.2.2	Determine room setups
1.2.3	Develop AV needs
1.2.4	Select menus
1.2.5	Contract for breaks
1.3	**Site Setup**
1.3.1	Set up displays
1.3.2	Set up registration table
1.3.3	Set our registration packets
1.3.4	Set up examiner gift table
1.3.5	Confirm site setup

One of the most frequently asked questions is whether every project needs a WBS. People who manage small to medium-sized projects often ask this question. Many of them see this as an unnecessarily time-consuming step for a small project. My answer is almost always,

"Yes." If the project is large and complex, it is critical. If the project is smaller and less complex, then it will not take long to do it.

Are there projects for which a WBS would be unnecessary? The answer is, "Probably." For some small projects, a WBS may not be necessary. A simple checklist list, if even that, may be sufficient. But, if there is even the slightest chance that you might overlook important activities, then it is advisable to develop a formal WBS.

Scope Verification

When the WBS is complete, and the project manager is confident that it accurately represents the project's scope as described in the project charter and the scope statement, he or she may want to share a copy of it with key stakeholders to review. Doing this gives the stakeholders one more opportunity for input. It also helps to achieve buy-in from those whose support may be critical to the project's success. If any of the key stakeholders have objections to the WBS, it is better to find out during the planning stage than later in the project when options are much more limited.

A secondary benefit of this review is that it helps avoid surprises. Surprises usually take the form of an unexpected event that negatively impacts the project. Keeping stakeholders updated throughout the project is important. The project manager can minimize the likelihood that one of these unpleasant surprises will come from one of the stakeholders by keeping them well-informed. For example, stakeholders cannot claim during the execution stage that they were not aware of the team's approach to the project. Ideally, they were involved in the development of the project charter. They might have reviewed the scope statement if there was one. After reviewing the WBS, they should have few questions about the project's scope or the team's approach to implementing the project.

While acceptance of the WBS is an important part of scope verification, it is not by itself sufficient. It is also advisable for all stakeholders to review the project deliverables, quality standards, and other issues that potentially affect the completion of the project to the satisfaction of the customer.

The WBS is complete once key stakeholders have approved it. This WBS serves as the baseline scope. In practice, however, the WBS is never finished until the project is over. Every time there is a significant change in the project's scope, the project manager must update the WBS. We will revisit this issue in Chapter 10 in the discussion on change management.

Summary

Good planning is essential to project success; it is the foundation upon which all project activity takes place. Nothing happens in the later stages of the project that can fully compensate for a flawed implementation plan.

Initial planning activities focus on clarifying the scope of work. A well-written project charter includes a high-level description of the project scope, but it does not identify the individual activities necessary to produce the project deliverables. So, initial planning activities focus on specifying the scope of the project in more detail.

For many projects, the first step is the development of the project scope statement. This is a working document used by the project manager to manage the project. It also serves as the basis for subsequent planning activities. For routine projects where the project's scope is clear to all stakeholders, a scope statement may not be necessary.

The primary output of the scope planning process is a detailed activity list that includes the project, subprojects, and work packages. The tool used to do this is the WBS, or work breakdown structure.

There are two primary approaches to developing the WBS; the top-down, and the bottom-up with the former being the most common.

PROJECT SCOPE PLANNING

The project is decomposed into increasingly smaller units of work until the duration and cost of the work can be estimated with some degree of accuracy. The work packages should be such that a single person or small group can do the work. Generally, work package durations should not exceed two weeks.

The final draft of the WBS should be reviewed by all key stakeholders, especially the sponsor, to ensure that all important activities have been included. Once it is approved, it becomes the baseline WBS.

PROJECT RESOURCE PLANNING

Introduction

The primary purpose of resource planning is to develop a resource management plan that allocates project resources most efficiently and effectively. This plan addresses project staffing, training needs, safety requirements, compliance issues, and any other resource issues that may affect the project's success.

"Resource" is a generic term referring to people, equipment, materials/supplies, tools, and facilities. In discussions of project management, these resources are often lumped into two categories; work resources and material resources. Work resources are those resources responsible for doing the work. Material resources are those resources consumed during the course of the project.

Project managers are generally most concerned with two key aspects of resource planning and management: the availability of the necessary resources and their cost to the project. The following sections address these issues.

Estimating Resource Requirements

Human Resource Requirements

The first step in resource planning is to identify the project's resource requirements—in other words, identifying the people, equipment, material, and facilities and how much of each will be needed to complete the project. The *PMBOK* refers to this as "activity resource estimating."

To determine the necessary work resources, project managers should develop a list of the skills required to complete the work identified in the WBS, i.e., the work packages. This process is sometimes called a "skills audit." The Project Skills Audit Form below (Figure 5.1), or something like it, is often used to facilitate this process.

Figure 5.1 | Skills Audit Form

WBS Code	Activity	Required Skills	Level of Experience
1.0	Data Processing		
1.1	Data Entry		
1.1.2	Login returned surveys	Basic clerical skills	Novice
1.1.3	Review for completeness	Basic clerical skills	Novice
1.1.4	Assign to entry personnel	Basic clerical skills	Novice
1.1.5	Enter questionnaire responses	Data entry skills	Proficient

The second step is to determine if the team has the skills and experience to do the work. If the project manager is not familiar with some team members or is unsure of their skills and experience, it may be helpful to do a skills inventory, which is simply a listing of all project team members and their skills, abilities, experience, and interest. If team members have already been assigned, it might still be worth doing a project skills audit and a team skills inventory to determine if there are any gaps between team members' skills and the skills required to complete the work to which they have been assigned.

Lastly, it is necessary to determine how much of each resource will be needed. Identifying what resources are needed is a relatively easy task. Determining how much of each resource is much more difficult.

For human resources, this is generally a matter of estimating how many person-hours/days will be needed for each work package. This can be difficult because staffing levels are dependent on the amount of work it takes to complete the activity, the skills required to do the work, and the activity durations.

Estimating work resources is very different from estimating equipment and materials. Bricks are bricks, but 10 person-hours might be one skilled mason working 10 hours, two apprentices working five hours each, etc.

To effectively staff the project, it is necessary to understand the relationship between resources (also called effort), duration, and work. In Figure 5.2 they are shown as the three sides of a triangle indicating that they are interdependent. Just as with the Triple Constraints, any change to one impacts the other two. For this reason, you cannot estimate resource requirements for an activity without knowing the amount of work needed to complete it and how long it will take to complete it. Longer durations require more resources. However, to calculate durations, we need to know the level of resources assigned to the work. In other words, you cannot estimate staffing levels without knowing the duration of the activity and you cannot estimate the duration without knowing the staffing levels.

So, what is a project manager to do? The answer is, as it so often is in project management, "It depends." Staffing and scheduling project work is an iterative process because work, duration, and resources (effort) are interrelated.

The relationship between them is expressed in the following set of equations.

Figure 5.2 | Staff, Work, and Schedule

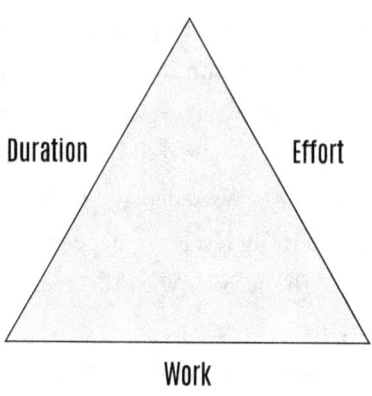

Duration

Duration is defined as the amount of time that elapses between the beginning of an activity and its completion. It includes time spent working on the activity, time spent working on other activities or projects, and any work interruptions.

(1) duration = work ÷ effort

In the first equation, duration is equal to the amount of work divided by the effort. For example, if two people are assigned full-time (effort) to a two-day activity (work), the duration will be one day (1 = 2 ÷ 2)—the more resources assigned to the activity, the shorter the duration. So, four people would take half a day to complete that same work. To decrease duration, you must increase effort or decrease work.

Keep in mind, however, that some activities are not resource-sensitive. It takes two and a half hours to fly from Seattle to San Francisco. Adding more pilots does not shorten the duration. Unless it is possible to divide the work into pieces that can be worked on concurrently, adding resources does not shorten the duration. In other words, both work and duration are fixed. Adding resources does not change the amount of work or the length of the duration; rather, it decreases the effort required from each resource. See Figure 5.5 for an example.

Work

Work is the amount of active time it takes to complete an activity. The difference between work and duration is the difference between active work time and clock time.

Figure 5.3 | Note

Adding resources does not always reduce the duration proportionately. In other words, doubling the resources does not always reduce the duration by half. This is because the additional resources are not always as productive as those initially assigned to the activity. And, the increase in the number of resources adds to the ad-ministrative work of the activity.

Work is usually a given. In other words, the amount of work is usually independent of the resources assigned to it or the amount of time in which it needs to be completed. Work is fixed; duration and effort are variable.

(2) work = duration x effort

Work is the product of duration and effort. For example, if two people are assigned full-time to an activity with a duration of four days, the amount of work will equal eight days (8 = 4 x 2). If two people had been assigned half-time, the amount of work would be four days.

The only time we might need to calculate work is when effort and duration have been specified.

Figure 5.4 | Outsourcing

Outsourcing is the assignment of a project activity or a set of activities to an outside vendor. Generally, when work is outsourced, work and duration are specified. The vendor determines how much effort is needed to complete the work on time, i.e., within the expected duration.

Resources/Effort

Effort is the amount of resources assigned to do the work. It is usually expressed in person-hours or person-days. Generally, adding more resources (effort) reduces the duration.

(3) effort = work ÷ duration

In equation number three, we can see that effort results from dividing work by duration. For example, to complete four days of work in two days would require two resources working full time (2 = 4 ÷ 2). Be sure to use the same unit of measurement, i.e., days, weeks, etc., for all three.

This is illustrated in Figure 5.5. If Doug Jones is assigned to a four-day task, he will need to spend 100% of his time for four days to get it done. If we assign Dave Smith to help him, they will each have to spend 100% of their time on it for two days. Adding the additional resource shortens the duration by two days.

If the duration is fixed, we get a different result. To complete the activity, Doug Jones will spend 100% of his time working on it for four days. When we add Dave Smith, they will each spend 50% of their time for four days. Duration stays the same but the effort for both resources is cut in half.

Figure 5.5 | Resource Utilization

Work = 4 days, Effort = 4 days, Duration not specified

Title	5/10/20				
	11	12	13	14	15
▸ 👤 Doug Jones	100%	100%	100%	100%	
👤 Dave Smith					

Title	5/10/20				
	11	12	13	14	15
▸ 👤 Doug Jones	100%	100%			
▸ 👤 Dave Smith	100%	100%			

Work = 4 days, Duration = 4 days, Effort not specified

Title	5/10/20				
	11	12	13	14	15
▸ 👤 Doug Jones	100%	100%	100%	100%	
👤 Dave Smith					

Title	5/10/20				
	11	12	13	14	15
▸ 👤 Doug Jones	50%	50%	50%	50%	
▸ 👤 Dave Smith	50%	50%	50%	50%	

So, how do we use these equations to help us determine staffing needs? Since the amount of work necessary to complete an activity is usually known, you can estimate effort by specifying a duration in equation number three. The result is the level of resources needed to complete the activity within the specified duration.

Material and Equipment Requirements

Estimating material resource requirements is much easier than estimating the need for human resources because, unlike work resources, equipment, material, tools, and facilities do not go home at the end of the day, and they do not take sick days or vacations. This difference greatly simplifies estimating and scheduling material resources.

On the other hand, equipment does require fuel and maintenance and often needs a trained operator to perform the work. Material resources are consumed during the implementation of the project and may need to be replenished periodically. All this must be taken into consideration when estimating equipment, materials, and facility needs.

Perhaps the best method for estimating material resource requirements is to examine the records from previous projects. For some types of resources, the project manager can estimate the required level from industry standards or calculations based on previous experiences. For example, highway construction contractors know almost exactly how much asphalt they will need per mile of highway construction.

Acquiring Resources

Estimating resource requirements is an important first step in staffing the project, but there is a big difference between estimating resource needs and acquiring them. It is often a major challenge to acquire the necessary resources, and the project's success may depend on how well the project manager can negotiate for the necessary resources.

Acquiring the necessary resources involves two processes: staffing and procurement. Staffing has to do with human resources acquisition, usually the project team and any outside resources that may be needed to complete the project. Procurement is the process by which equipment, tools, materials, supplies, and facilities are acquired. Staffing and procurement are discussed separately in the next two sections.

Project Staffing

The resource acquisition process is used to assign human resources to project teams. There is no one right way to do this, and the number of different ways organizations assign people to teams varies greatly. The variation revolves around the team acquisition process and the point in the project at which it occurs.

When Are Staffing Decisions Made?

There is no one answer to this question. In some organizations, team members are assigned as soon as the project has been authorized. In others, the team may not be assigned until the project plan has been developed and the project manager and team together take responsibility for the implementation of the project.

It is uncommon to find situations where team members are appointed before the approval of the charter. Until the charter has been approved, the goals and objectives are subject to change, and the skill sets required to do the project work may not be entirely clear. This lack of clarity makes it difficult to develop the selection criteria. Sometimes an initial team is appointed and then augmented after the development of the WBS when it becomes clear what additional skills will be needed.

Most experienced project managers believe earlier is better as the people who are responsible for implementing the project plan are the ones who know the most about it, and therefore should play an active role in defining project parameters and developing the project plan. Assigning team members early in the process helps to avoid many problems. It also contributes to building team member buy-in to the project.

In highly projectized industries, permanent teams are common. When the team completes a project, they are reassigned to another project. This process works well when the projects are repetitive. It does not work so well when each new project presents a new and different challenge.

Who Makes Staffing Decisions?

Because organizations vary so widely in how they manage projects, there is no standard for making project staffing decisions. Typically, staffing decisions are made by one of the following:

- project manager
- senior management/project sponsor
- project management office
- self-selection

Understandably, most project managers would like to be able to staff their own projects. After all, if the project manager is accountable for the project's outcome, shouldn't he or she be able to assemble his or her own team? In many organizations, project managers do have much control over the selection of project team members.

Of course, all project managers want the best possible team. Since every project competes with every other project for resources, it is often difficult to get the best people. The project manager may have to negotiate with a functional manager or another project manager for the people he or she wants. Success depends in large part on the project manager's negotiation skills.

When internal resources are not available, the project manager may have to look elsewhere for the needed resources. Adding resources may involve hiring new employees, hiring temporary employees, hiring consultants, or contracting out. Of course, the project manager's flexibility is always limited by the Triple Constraints.

In some organizations, particularly those that are relatively large and highly projectized, it is not unusual to find that resources are assigned to a pool, which is often managed by the project management office if the organization has one. Assignments to individual projects are made from the pool. When projects are completed, team members are released back to the pool.

The primary advantage of a resource pool is that it makes it easier to share resources among multiple projects and avoid scheduling conflicts. It also makes it easier to track resource usage and helps to identify over- or under-allocations across projects.

In some organizations, team members may be self-selected. By staffing projects with volunteers, team members are more likely to be motivated to work conscientiously and to meet project deadlines. The downside is that self-selection does not guarantee that the team is staffed with the right people possessing the right skills.

Regardless of how staffing decisions are made, the available pool of potential team members is often so small there are few real choices. The project manager has to make do with the available resources. In such situations, the project manager must ensure that team members can accomplish the work identified in the WBS. If not, the project manager may have to seek additional resources.

Equipment, Material, and Facility Procurement

Acquiring material resources is more straightforward than project staffing. Many larger organizations have a formalized procurement process to acquire the equipment, tools, material, and facilities needed to complete the project. The project manager needs to understand how this process works and allow sufficient time since it is often a long and sometimes complex process.

Like work resources, material resources are also limited. For this reason, the project manager may have to negotiate for these resources as well.

Assigning Resources

Assigning resources to project activities is often called "resource loading," a term referring to the amount of resources assigned to an activity during a given time period. All resources are assigned at the activity/work package level. Resources are not assigned to summary activities because summary activities are roll-ups, not work activities. Nor are resources assigned to milestones. Since they have no duration, there is no work to be performed.

Getting the right people on the bus, to use author Jim Collins' terminology, is important. Still, even competent and motivated team members must understand their roles and responsibilities to work effectively as a team. The project manager's responsibility is to make sure that team members know what is expected of them.

Roles and Responsibilities

One tool often used to ensure that team members know and understand their roles and responsibilities is the responsibility assignment matrix, often referred to as the RAM chart, which links work to resources and documents the roles each team member plays. The RAM chart is also used to determine staffing needs and individual work requirements.

There are several roles that team members and other stakeholders can play. Assigned roles will depend on the project manager and the nature of the project. However, the most commonly used roles include the following:

- Responsible Need to make this parallel structure
- Accountable
- Consult
- Inform

This variation of the RAM chart is sometimes referred to as a RACI chart. Figure 5.6 is an example of a completed RAM/RACI chart.

Responsible

First, someone must be responsible for doing the work. Effort, i.e., man hours, is assigned only to those who are responsible for doing the work. There must be at least one person responsible for each activity. Otherwise, no work would get done. There is no limit on the number of people you can assign to be responsible. For activity 1.1, the project manager and team members 1, 2, and 3 are responsible. Each has been assigned to work on the activity for one day, i.e., effort equals one day.

Accountable

Someone must have primary responsibility for ensuring that the activity is completed on time and within the budgeted cost. That person is said to be "accountable." Each activity should have one and only one person accountable for its successful completion. In Figure 5.6, the project manager is the one who is accountable for all of the work packages.

Consult

The risk for errors is generally greater when a work package is complex or when the assigned team members have not done this type of work before. In such circumstances, it is advisable to require team members to consult with a more experienced person before beginning work on the activity. That person is designated by entering a "C" in the appropriate place in the RAM. Team member 3 has been designated as the consultant for item 4.1. He or she has also been assigned responsibility with team members 1 and 2 for completing the work on this item.

Figure 5.6 | Responsibility Assignment Matrix

Project Name: Website Development Project

		Project Manager		Team Member 1		Team Member 2		Team Member 3		Total
Activity ID	WBS	RACI	Effort	RACI	Effort	RACI	Effort	RACI	Effort	
0	Web Project		2		43.5		49		20	114.5
1.0	Requirements		1		8		6		1	16
1.1	Review charter	AR	1	R	1	R	1	R	1	4
1.2	Verify requirements	A		R	4	R	2			6
1.3	Develop SOW	A		R	3	R	3			6
2.0	Contents		0		0		18		0	18
2.1	Identify required content	AI				R	5			5
2.2	Acquire/develop content	A				R	10			10
2.3	Transfer content to vendor	A				R	3			3
3.0	Vendor		0		9.5		2		0	11.5
3.1	Bidding		0		5		0		0	5

PROJECT RESOURCE PLANNING

ID	Task										
3.1.1	Develop bidding list	A			3						3
3.1.2	Develop RFP	A		R	1						1
3.1.3	Send RFP	A		R	1						1
3.2	Selection		0		4.5		2			0	6.5
3.2.1	Develop selection criteria	A	0	R	1	R	1				2
3.2.2	Review bids	A	0	R	1	R	1				2
3.2.3	Select winning bid	A	0	R	0.5	R	0				0.5
3.2.4	Contract with vendor	A	0	R	2	R	0				2
4.0	Development		1		12		12		12		37
4.1	Create design	A	0	R	5	R	5	RC	5		15
4.2	Develop prototype	A	0	R	5	R	5	R	5		15
4.3	Review prototype	A	0	R	2	R	2	R	2		6
4.4	Approve design	AR	1								1
5.0	Implementation		0		14		11		7		32
5.1	Obtain domain	A	0	R	1	R	1				2
5.2	Select host	A	0	R	4	R	4				8
5.3	Upload files to server	A	0	R	1	R	1				2
5.4	Test site	A	0	R	5	R	5	R	5		15
5.5	Train users	A	0	R	3			R	2		5

Inform

Inform is similar to consult. In this case, however, the person responsible for doing the work informs the more experienced person when they have completed the work. Team members are trusted to complete the work independently, but the notification gives the more experienced person an opportunity to review their work.

Many organizations have developed a proprietary form, which combines elements of these and other forms. Ultimately every organization has to find what works best for them. The choice comes down to what best fits the needs of the organization.

Team members are not the only ones who may be assigned roles and responsibilities. Some stakeholders may also play an active role in one way or another, and it is also important to identify their roles and responsibilities. For larger projects, it may be necessary to assign activities to departments or work units rather than individuals.

Note that the RAM/RACI in Figure 5.6 also includes a column to capture the estimated effort to which the responsible resources are assigned to work packages. This information provides the basis for determining the labor cost of the project.

Second, assigning resources by skill set or job title focuses on the required skills to complete the project. Assigning skill sets helps ensure the best fit between activities and resources and highlights any gaps between resource requirements and the team members' skills. As the baseline plan is finalized, the project manager will replace the skill sets and job titles in the RAM (and/or RACI) with the names of those responsible for the work.

A frequently asked question is whether the project manager should be assigned activities other than those directly associated with the management of the project. Assigning project work to the project manager is a common practice, but most project managers do not believe it is a good one. The problem is that it often puts the project manager in a conflicted position. As activity deadlines approach, the project manager becomes focused on his or her assigned activities at the project's expense. Work takes precedence over management. While a lack of staffing may force many organizations to do this, it should be avoided whenever possible.

For large, complex projects, it is often helpful to develop a project organization chart. This chart provides a clear overview of the project personnel and forms the basis for determining project roles, responsibilities, and reporting relationships. It can also help to clarify project reporting roles.

One of the issues specific to assigning human resources is the criteria used in making the assignments. People are not interchangeable. Their interests, skills, and experience may vary considerably. It is essential to get the right people into the right positions.

Assignment Criteria

There is no standard method for assigning people to activities. In many organizations, senior managers make the project team assignments based on criteria established by the organization's policies and procedures. These criteria often include availability, skills, personality, and experience.

- *Availability*
  Availability simply means that the resource has some unscheduled time during which the project work is scheduled. Since activities may not yet have been scheduled, there is no guarantee that the assigned resources will be available on the actual date the work will be performed. This is a scheduling issue the project manager must resolve before the baseline plan is finalized.

- *Skills/Ability*
  Presumably, you assign team members to a project in large part because of their skills and ability to perform the work.

Nevertheless, it is often advisable to do a skills audit, if one has not already been done, before assigning resources so the project manager knows which skills the team will need to complete the project successfully.

A form like the one shown in Figure 5.7 can be used to aid in this process. This form lists the names of the people assigned to the project, their primary skills, secondary skills, and interests.

Figure 5.7 | Team Skills Audit

	Team Members/Stakeholders				
	1	2	3	4	5
Skills	1			1	3
Business Analyst					
Interface Designer	2				
System Analyst		1		3	
Programmer		2	1		1
1=Primary skill, 2=Secondary skill, 3=Interest					

In this skills inventory, it is clear that the project manager has a staffing issue: none of the team members have interface design skills. Moreover, none of them have an interest in interface design. It would appear that the project manager's best options are to augment the team with an interface designer or contract out that part of the work.

The skills inventory can be very helpful when the project manager is not familiar with the skills and abilities of his or her team members. For smaller projects or projects where team members have often worked together, a skills assessment may not be necessary. Don't do it if you don't need to. There is already enough to do without making additional, unnecessary work.

- *Experience*

    Project managers want the most experienced people they can get. More experienced people tend to be more skilled and can therefore often finish the work more quickly. Unfortunately, the pool of available resources may be very limited. More often than not, the project manager must take whoever is available.

    It is important to keep in mind that the experience level of team members will impact the duration of the activities and the quality of the work. Lack of experience will make it necessary to supervise project team members more closely and require additional training to ensure that they possess the requisite skills. It is also important to remember that an inexperienced project team is a risk factor, and that risk must be considered in risk management planning.

- *Interests*

    Those responsible for appointing project teams often overlook this criterion for resource selection. Availability and ability are essential. Experience is desirable. But these may be of little value if the people assigned to the project are not interested in working on it. It is the project manager's responsibility to motivate the team to want to do the project and do it well. This issue is discussed more fully in Chapter 12.

- *Personality*

    Team chemistry is critical to the success of the project. It is important to select members, to the best extent possible, that work well with others. There is an old project management saying that you can teach skills, but you have to select for attitude.

- *Cost*

    Cost refers to how much of the project budget will be required to pay for the resources. While project managers always want the most skilled and experienced people, they also know that these are the most expensive resources. The project manager often has to settle for less than what he or she would ideally like to have because there is not enough money, person-hours, etc., in the project budget.

Resource Usage

When assigning resources, it is important to remember that you should never fully schedule work resources. When resources are assigned to their full work capacity, there is no reserve. What happens when something unexpected occurs? Who is going to deal with it? If team members have no reserve, they will have to stop what they are doing to attend to it. Whatever they were working on will be delayed. This delay will have scheduling implications if it delays subsequent activities and perhaps the project itself.

A good rule of thumb is that you should never schedule any resource to more than 85% of its availability. That works out to just over six and a half hours a day for a full-time person. Just because a resource is only scheduled for six and a half hours does not mean that they are idle for the remaining one and a half hours of the day. It just means that they can deal with the unexpected events that inevitably occur during every project.

Work Distribution

The distribution of work within a duration is commonly referred to as the work contour. In the early stages of planning, we assume that the work contour will be flat, i.e., evenly distributed across the duration.

For example, eight hours of work within a duration of four days would result in a work distribution of two hours per day. In reality, that is seldom the case. For various reasons, often having to do with resource availability, the workload varies from day to day, causing utilization peaks and valleys. With additional information, we can adjust the work contour to fit the expected distribution of work.

Higher-end software packages such as MS Project and Primavera include quite a few built-in work contours. MS Project, for example, includes:

- Flat
- Back loaded
- Front-loaded
- Double peak
- Early peak
- Late peak
- Bell
- Turtle

While the use of work contours gives the project manager considerable flexibility in scheduling resources, most project managers prefer to schedule resources manually. Computer-generated work contours are handy, but they do not always conform to the project manager's needs.

Because the initial project schedule is often developed before the resource assignments, durations may be estimated without reference to resource levels. As a result, durations may need to be adjusted to reflect resourcing decisions. This is where resource leveling comes into play.

Resource Leveling

Before completing the project resource planning, it is important to review the work assignments to ensure that project resources have been used effectively and efficiently. To obtain the best utilization of resources, particularly human resources, it may be necessary to use a technique called "Resource Leveling." Resource leveling is "an optimization technique in which adjustments are made to the project schedule to optimize the allocation of resources. (PMBOK, 6th ed., p. 719.) It deals with three primary issues; resource over-allocations, resource conflicts, and workload optimization.

Resolving Resource Over-Allocations

One of the unintended consequences of the planning process is that both work and material resources may become over-allocated or over-committed. This happens when resources are assigned work that exceeds their availability. For example, an over-allocation would occur when a team member not authorized for overtime is assigned more than eight hours of work in a 24-hour period. In short, an over-allocation occurs when work exceeds availability.

Most project management software programs will flag resource over-allocations. In projects where project management software is not used, the project manager must identify these over-allocations manually. If the number of resources is not too large, this is relatively easy to do but when the number is larger, this can be very difficult and time-consuming.

Figure 5.8 lists the resources assigned to the project together with their utilization by day and by week. A chart like this makes it easy to identify over- and under-allocations. In this example, allocations greater than 100% of the maximum authorized workload are considered over-allocations. Allocations greater than 25% but less than 100% help the project manager achieve the optimum distribution of the workload.

Allocations less than 25% may indicate an under-allocation.

In this example, 200% of Dave Smith's time is allocated to the project on May 15th. He is flagged as over-allocated for that day. He is not, however, over-allocated for the week. If we were to look at the weekly allocations only, we would not see that he was assigned more work than authorized on May 15th.

Figure 5.8 | Resource Utilization Chart

Resource Utilization by Day

Title	5/10/20					5/17/20		
	11	12	13	14	15	18	19	20
▸ 👤 Doug Jones	50%	50%	50%	50%				
▸ 👤 Craig Stevenson	50%	50%	50%	50%		100%	100%	100%
▸ 👤 Dave Smith					200%	100%	100%	
▸ 👤 Jane O'Brien					100%			

Resource Utilization by Week

Title	5/10/20	
	11	12
▸ 👤 Doug Jones	40%	
▸ 👤 Craig Stevenson	40%	60%
▸ 👤 Dave Smith	40%	40%
▸ 👤 Jane O'Brien	20%	

(Created using Merlin Project by Project Wizards)

Over- and under-allocations must be resolved before the project plan can be finalized. Under-allocations are usually relatively easy to deal with. Over-allocations, on the other hand, are more problematic.

There are several ways to resolve over-allocations. These include:

- **Adding resources**

    Adding additional resources may eliminate the over-allocation. By dividing the work among a greater number of resources, the amount of work assigned to each individual resource is reduced. This assumes, of course, that the activity is resource sensitive and that the additional resources are sufficient to reduce the workload of the assigned resources to within their authorized limits.

- **Reassigning the over-allocated resource**
  Another solution is to reassign the over-allocated resource. This is a simple and straightforward way to resolve the over-allocation. Unfortunately, scheduling constraints often make this solution impossible.

- **Rescheduling the conflicting activities**
  If the over-allocated resource cannot be reassigned, it may be possible to reschedule one of the conflicting activities. There are a number of ways to do this. For example, one of the activities can be rescheduled within the available slack. If there is insufficient slack, resolving the conflict in this manner may delay the completion of the project.

  Another way to resolve the conflict is to change the dependencies of the conflicting activities. If the conflicting activities are not dependent on each other, it may be possible to reschedule one of them by overlapping one or more upstream activities. If there is a dependency between them, changing it, i.e., removing the overlap might resolve the conflict.

- **Splitting one of the conflicting activities**
  Splitting an activity into two or more smaller activities is sometimes the best way to handle a resource over-allocation. Splitting an activity gives the project manager additional flexibility with respect to scheduling. An activity can be split by dividing it up into several smaller activities or by simply dividing its duration into one or more segments.

Some project management software packages will automatically resolve these conflicts based on the leveling score assigned to them by the project manager. When there is a scheduling conflict or over-allocation, the software splits or delays the activities with the lowest priority. While some project managers see this as an essential feature, most prefer to level the resources manually.

Keep in mind that any actions that affect critical activities may also affect the completion date of the project. Since there is generally no slack on the critical path, rescheduling a critical activity may delay the completion of the project. If time is the driver, the sponsor will undoubtedly view this as an unacceptable solution.

Assigning a resource to two simultaneous activities does not necessarily create an over-allocation. As long as the combined amount of work is less than the amount of work the resource is authorized to perform, an over-allocation will not occur. As the amount of work approaches the amount authorized, however, scheduling becomes increasingly difficult and over-allocations become increasingly difficult to resolve.

The issue of resource over-allocation does not apply to material resources. They are generally available until the supply is used up. While overcommitments are generally not an issue, it is important to allocate material resources in such a way that they are available when and where they are needed in order to ensure that the work gets done and the project finishes on time.

Resolving Resource Conflicts

A conflict occurs when a work or material resource is assigned to an activity that prevents its use in another activity. For example, when a resource is assigned to two or more activities that are scheduled to be performed at the same time, a conflict may occur. A conflict can also occur if two activities are scheduled to be performed at different locations not in close proximity to each other. Travel time may make it impossible to use the resources for both activities. A more common instance of resource conflict occurs when resource assignments on one project conflict with those on another project.

Conflicts are resolved in much the same way as over-allocations. The range of options includes adding resources, reassigning the conflicted resource, and rescheduling or splitting one of the conflicting activities.

Optimizing the Workload

The absence of overcommitments and conflicts does not guarantee a schedule that makes the best use of project resources. While the initial schedule may be workable, it is unlikely that it will make optimal use of the resources available to the project. Resource leveling is used not only to reduce over- and under-allocations and resolve resource conflicts but also to staff the project in such a way as to best utilize project personnel.

Initial schedules will often include periods of intense activity followed by periods of relative inactivity. A more even distribution of the workload is less likely to burn team members out while continuing to keep them engaged in the project. While it is seldom possible to develop a workable schedule with an even distribution of work, it is often possible to spread work assignments more evenly across the duration of the project using resource-leveling techniques.

Project Cost Planning

The initial project cost estimate is developed in the initiation stage of the project. This estimate is included in the project charter and approved by the project sponsor and the project manager. Although it is based on the best information available, these initial estimates tend to be very rough and subject to considerable error. As the scope of the project is refined, it becomes possible to develop a more accurate estimate of the project cost.

The development of the WBS makes it possible to refine the initial cost estimates. A more accurate estimate of the total project cost can be obtained by estimating the cost of the work packages identified in the WBS and adding them together. This estimate is likely to be more accurate than the original estimate in the project charter. There are two reasons for this:

- The WBS provides a more detailed description of the project scope
- It is easier to estimate the cost of smaller chunks of work (work packages) than larger chunks (projects)

Because work package estimates tend to be more accurate than estimates of the overall cost of the project, adding the estimated cost of the resources needed to complete the work packages yields a more accurate estimate of the project's total cost.

Estimating Project Costs

After assigning resources to each work package, the next step is to estimate work package costs. The major cost of most work packages is labor. Labor costs are usually expressed in units of currency (e.g., dollars, euros, or yen). However, it is common in some industries—software development, for example—to estimate labor costs in person-hours or person-months.

If the project manager has developed a RAM/RACI chart like the one in Figure 5.6, he or she would simply multiply the effort times the charge rate for the resource. For example, Team Member No. 2 has been authorized to spend 10 hours working on item 2.2. If his charge rate is $75 per hour, then the labor cost for item 2.2 would be $750. If other team members had been assigned to this activity, the cost of their labor would have to be added to obtain a total labor cost.

Note that resources are assigned to work packages only. Subprojects are only groupings of work packages; they are not work. The amount of effort assigned to a subproject can be calculated by adding up its constituent work packages.

What if the cost (in dollars, euros, person-hours, etc.) of the work identified in the WBS adds up to more than the amount approved in the project charter? If exceeding the project budget is not a good thing, then a plan to exceed it is certainly not a good thing. The project manager needs to resolve this discrepancy. The most obvious solution is to request more resources. In this era of tight budgets, that may not seem like the obvious strategy, particularly if cost is the driver. While success is far from guaranteed, it is usually worth the attempt.

Figure 5.9 | Project Cost Components

- Labor
- Equipment
- Materials/Supplies
- Facilities
- Permits
- Fees
- Travel
- Adjustments for inflation
- Currency fluctuations
- Cost of contingency plans

Requesting more resources should be the first option because the estimate derived from the WBS is likely to be much more accurate than the initial estimate. As noted earlier, initial estimates may be nothing more than a SWAG. A newer, higher, and probably more accurate estimate makes a persuasive case for the additional resources. If the needed resources are not forthcoming, the project may be at risk.

A newer and probably more accurate estimate does not, however, guarantee the additional resources. One reason may be that there are no additional resources available. It may also be that the project's priority is not high enough to warrant any increases beyond the amount approved in the charter. For whatever reason, requests for more resources are often turned down.

At this point, the project manager must go to Plan B. Working together with key stakeholders, he or she must come up with a revised WBS that does not require resources beyond the amount approved in the project charter. This involves reworking the Triple Constraints Triangle described in Chapter 2.

Even if the project manager does not get the additional resources, the request alerts management that the project may be under-resourced and is likely to experience delays. He or she must monitor underfunded projects closely, particularly if cost is the driver. In some cases, it may be better to delay or even kill the project rather than accept the high risk of long delays and cost overruns.

Some organizations often exclude labor from their project cost estimates. They do not track labor costs and sometimes do not even include them in post-project cost calculations. This practice is particularly common when the people assigned to project teams are salaried and the project owner is an internal customer. On these projects, labor is considered overhead rather than a direct cost and is therefore not charged to the project.

The rationale for this approach to cost planning and management is that labor is free, at least to the project. Salaried employees are a cost to the organization regardless of the projects they are assigned to if assigned to any projects at all.

The failure to include the cost of labor in project cost estimates means that the organization cannot accurately estimate the project's full cost. In fact, for projects in which labor is a major component, the failure to include labor results in a gross underestimation of the project's actual cost. Organizations have more projects than resources, and without accurate cost information, it is difficult to prioritize projects.

It is not uncommon for an organization to do a project in-house because they mistakenly believe the bids from outside vendors were too

Figure 5.10 | Project Budget

WBS Code	WBS	Type of Cost					
		Labor	Equipment	Materials	Facilities	Other	Total
0	BS Web Project	$24,150	$0	$8,000	$0	$100	$32,250
1	Start Project						
2	Requirements	$1,250	$0	$0	$0	$0	$1,250
2.1	Review charter	$500	$0	$0	$0	$0	$500
2.2	Verify requirements	$250	$0	$0	$0	$0	$250
2.3	Develop SOW	$500	$0	$0	$0	$0	$500
3	Contents	$5,350	$0	$7,500	$0	$0	$12,850
3.1	Identify required content	$2,100	$0	$0	$0	$0	$2,100
3.2	Acquire/develop content	$3,000	$0	$7,500	$0	$0	$10,500
3.3	Transfer content to vendor	$250	$0	$0	$0	$0	$250
4	Vendor	$3,700	$0	$0	$0	$0	$3,700
4.1	Bidding	$1,700	$0	$0	$0	$0	$1,700
4.1.1	Develop bidding list	$300	$0	$0	$0	$0	$300
4.1.2	Develop RFP	$1,200	$0	$0	$0	$0	$1,200

PROJECT RESOURCE PLANNING

4.1.3	Send RFP	$200	$0	$0	$0	$200
4.2	Selection	$2,000	$0	$0	$0	$2,000
4.2.1	Develop selection criteria	$750	$0	$0	$0	$750
4.2.2	Review bids	$1,000	$0	$0	$0	$1,000
4.2.3	Select winning bid	$250	$0	$0	$0	$250
5	Development	$6,000	$0	$500	$0	$6,500
5.1	Create Design	$1,500	$0	$500	$0	$2,000
5.2	Develop prototype	$3,500	$0	$0	$0	$3,500
5.3	Review prototype	$750	$0	$0	$0	$750
5.4	Approve design	$250	$0	$0	$0	$250
6	Implementation	$7,850	$0	$0	$100	$7,950
6.1	Select host	$150	$0	$0	$0	$150
6.2	Obtain domain	$200	$0	$0	$100	$300
6.3	Setup website	$2,500	$0	$0	$0	$2,500
6.4	Test website	$2,000	$0	$0	$0	$2,000
6.5	Train users	$3,000	$0	$0	$0	$3,000
7	End Project					

high. They underestimated the cost of doing it internally because they did not include the full cost of the labor and occupancy required to complete the project.

Cost is also an important measure of efficiency. Without good cost information, it is difficult for an organization to determine how efficiently it manages its projects. And, of course, the organization has no way to know if it is improving its efficiency if it does not track costs.

Computing labor costs is a relatively easy task: it is simply a matter of multiplying the number of hours, days, or months that each resource has committed to the project by their hourly rate. Most project management software programs will compute these costs automatically once you enter the resources and their costs.

While labor is often the largest component of project cost, it is not the only component. In addition to labor, estimates must also include materials, equipment, and facilities. It may also include fees, permits, and the cost of contingency plans. (See Figure 5.10) These costs are just as real as labor costs and, therefore, should not be overlooked. For long-term projects, cost projections may also include adjustments for the increased cost of materials, inflation, or currency fluctuations.

While many project managers are primarily concerned about what and how much, they must consider other resource issues as well. These include training needs, recognition, and safety. The importance of these issues varies widely between projects.

The Project Budget

The WBS represents the project's scope. The estimated cost of the work identified in the WBS represents the total known costs of the project. There are also unknown costs, including the cost of the work and rework necessitated by issues that arise during the project, which is why managers usually add what is called a "management reserve" to cover these expenses. The management reserve must, of course, be approved by those who have authorized the project, particularly if it puts the budget over the amount approved in the charter. Estimating the size of the management reserve is described in the section on risk exposure in Chapter 9.

Another item that needs to be considered is the cost of project management. Many organizations do not include these activities in the WBS. In these organizations, project management costs are considered overhead but doing so results in underestimating the true cost of the project.

Summary

At the risk of oversimplifying, resource planning is about identifying the resources necessary to accomplish the work, estimating the amount of each resource needed, staffing the project team, and assigning team members to activities in such a way as to ensure the project is successfully completed.

Estimating material resource requirements is relatively easy. Estimating the need for work resources, project staffing, in particular, is often much more difficult. The problem is that staffing needs are dependent not only on the amount of work but also on the availability of the resources with the appropriate skills. A skills audit of the project work packages will help determine the types of resources necessary, and an inventory of team skills will help reveal gaps between what the project requires and what the team can accomplish.

Acquiring the necessary resources is a rather straightforward process, though not always easy to accomplish. Since the demand for project resources is usually greater than the supply, project managers often have to negotiate with functional managers for the resources they need. Some human resources are acquired through a staffing process. Other resources may be obtained through a procurement process.

Resource assignments are based on skills/ability, experience, interest, personality, and cost. Ideally, the project manager would like to have the most experienced and skilled team. Realistically, he or she may have to settle for what is available or what they can negotiate with functional managers.

Initial resource assignments seldom result in a workable schedule. A quick analysis of the initial schedule often reveals resource over-allocations, resource conflicts, and a less-than-optimum use of project resources. Project managers can resolve these problems through the use of a technique called "resource leveling."

Resource leveling is an iterative process designed to produce a schedule that represents the best possible use of project resources and the highest level of customer satisfaction. Resource leveling resolves the over-allocations, resource conflicts, and inefficient use of resources by increasing staffing levels, reassigning project personnel, and adjusting activity start dates and end dates.

Resource cost estimation is an important part of resource planning, estimating the cost of the resources assigned to the work packages that make up the WBS. Hopefully, the total cost of the work packages is less than the amount authorized in the project charter. If it exceeds that amount, the project manager must obtain additional funds, reduce the project scope, or find a way to work with fewer resources.

PROJECT SCHEDULE PLANNING

Introduction

Once the scope of the project has been identified and resources assigned, the team can begin work on the project schedule. Some project managers prefer to develop the schedule before allocating resources. In either case, the project manager will have to review the project work plan to ensure that all activities are assigned to people who are available and qualified to perform the work. It is an iterative process that may take several passes before a workable schedule can be achieved.

Scheduling is the process that transforms the work identified in the Work Breakdown Structure (WBS) into a timetable for completion. Schedules are estimates based on an analysis of the project scope and experience from past projects. As such, schedules are targets. The likelihood of hitting the target depends in large part on how well the schedule is estimated.

Some project managers tend to confuse the project schedule with the project plan. The schedule is an essential part of the project plan, but it is only a part. The plan includes all the documents used to initiate and plan the project work, including the documents used to define the project's scope, assign the resources, schedule the activities, manage stakeholder communications, and assess the risk.

While the schedule is an important part of the plan, particularly for projects where time is the driver, we should never lose sight of the fact that the schedule is simply the means to an end. Project management is about delivering value to the customer. The schedule is a means of delivering that value within a time frame that meets the customer's requirements.

The project schedule serves several additional purposes. First, it commits resources to work assignments at an agreed-upon date and time. It communicates to stakeholders when the work will be started and when it will be completed. It also serves as the basis for tracking activity progress.

Tracking will be addressed in Chapter 14. The remainder of this chapter deals with the issues involved in developing the project schedule.

To develop the schedule, it is necessary to determine:

- The duration of each activity
- The relationship between activities (dependencies and constraints)
- The project start date

Each of these is discussed in the following sections.

Duration and Work

When projects are resource-driven, i.e., durations are determined by resource availability, durations are calculated using the formula discussed in Chapter 5 (duration = work ÷ effort). If a project is schedule-driven, i.e., the project has to be completed by a specific date, the project manager is more likely to specify durations and calculate the effort needed to meet activity deadlines (effort = work ÷ duration). The previous chapter discussed the impact of resources on scheduling. This chapter deals with scheduling projects based on activity durations.

Figure 6.1 | Duration vs. work

Duration is often confused with work. Work is the amount of effort that is needed in order to complete an activity. Duration is the time period within which the work takes place. For example, it might take two days to complete a three-hour activity because the person assigned to the activity is working on multiple projects and has work commitments outside the project.

Recall that we defined duration as the elapsed time between the beginning of the activity and its completion. It is the period within which the work takes place. Duration includes work, distractions, time spent on other projects, etc. It does not include non-working times such as weekends (unless scheduled), vacations, or other non-working times.

Estimating duration is often difficult. The failure to accurately estimate activity durations is in part why so many projects do not meet their planned completion dates. One reason for this is that estimates are frequently too optimistic. Sometimes estimates reflect only the work without considering the distractions and competing priorities to which every project is subject. As a result, project teams may find they cannot complete activities within the estimated durations.

Another reason why activity estimates tend to be unrealistic is that activities are often not clearly defined. It is challenging to estimate the amount of time it will take to complete an activity when its boundaries have not been clearly established. As a result, the activity may ultimately include work never anticipated when the team initially estimated its duration.

Common Methods for Estimating Duration

There are many sources of information available to help estimate activity durations. These include:

- Historical information obtained from previous projects with similar goals and objectives
- Estimates from people who have previous experience with the work
- Project managers who have managed similar projects
- Professional or trade associations that compile data on project performance
- Successful scheduling efforts drawing on most, if not all, of these sources of information

Project managers can use this information to estimate activity durations using a variety of methods including wags and swags, expert judgment, the three-point estimate, and Planning Poker.

Wags and Swags

In the absence of good information, project managers often resort to WAGs. In polite circles, this acronym stands for "Wildly Aimed Guess" and refers to a rough estimate based on the best available information. A more refined version of the WAG is the SWAG or "Scientific Wildly Aimed Guess." This technique is relatively common, as evidenced by the following quote from a newsletter article on the allPM website a few years ago:

> "A common technique for estimating activity duration is the SWAG. Some of you may not be familiar with this term, but I 'estimate' that most of you will recognize this as a 'Scientific Wild A** Guess.' Yes, that's right and it's more common than you may think. The WAGNER is something I picked up at UCF. It's a Wild A** Guess Not Entirely Realistic. The BONSOP is my favorite. I learned this from engineers in a company in Michigan that designed aircraft. It's the Back of Napkin Seat of Pants approach."

WAGS and SWAGS are generally not very accurate, although they are sometimes the best available estimates. However, it is essential to remember that even rough estimates have a way of becoming firm expectations. It is, therefore, important to consider this when developing the project schedule.

Expert Judgment

Expert judgment is probably the most common method for estimating activity durations. Subject Matter Experts (SMEs) are often tasked with making activity estimates. Sometimes this is a person assigned the activity. The people who do the work know best how long it takes to do it.

Experience indicates, however, that expert estimates tend to be overly optimistic. First, experts often base their estimates on the amount of work involved in the activity and overlook the fact that there is usually a difference between how long it should take and how long it actually takes. Second, experts are experts because they have extensive experience and are therefore highly proficient at the activity. The person or persons assigned to do the work are probably less experienced and may take longer.

The Three-Point Estimate

Another standard and generally the more accurate method used to estimate activity durations is the three-point estimate or PERT estimate, as it was originally called. This method, developed by the U.S. Navy and Booz, Allen, and Hamilton Consulting in the late 1950s, is based on three estimates of duration: an optimistic (To), a most likely (Tm), and a pessimistic (Tp) estimate. The three-point estimate is a weighted average of these three.

$$\text{Duration} = (To + 4(Tm) + Tp)/6$$

In this equation, the most likely time (Tm) is given a weight of four. Weighting the most likely time prevents an extremely pessimistic duration from skewing the estimate. Experience has demonstrated that the weighted average provides a more accurate estimate of activity duration than a simple average of the three estimates.

For example, we might estimate that an activity takes 10 days to complete. As a result of discussions with colleagues, we come up with an optimistic estimate of four days and a pessimistic estimate of 30 days. The three-point estimate for these values is 12.3 days. Note that the three-point estimate is slightly greater than the most likely time (12.3 vs. 10 days). This is usually the case. That is because the most likely time is almost always closer to the optimistic estimate than it is to the pessimistic time.

This method has several advantages over a WAG or SWAG. First, it forces team members to give the estimate some thought. It is hard to provide a quick answer when asked to give an optimistic, pessimistic, and most likely estimate of activity duration.

Second, many events that cause project schedules to slip are unpredictable. A pessimistic estimate offsets the optimistic estimates that project managers and subject matter experts are prone to make.

Planning Poker

A newer estimating technique developed by practitioners in the agile community is "Planning Poker." It is used primarily for estimating duration, ideal days, or story points in software development projects. This technique, a variation of the Delphi Technique discussed in Chapter 3, is beginning to find advocates among project managers outside the field of software development.

In Planning Poker, participants are given numbered cards. The numbers correspond to days, weeks, or months. After a brief discussion, participants lay the card corresponding to their estimate face down on the table. When all participants have laid their cards face down on the table, they turn them over to reveal their estimates.

If estimates differ, as they probably will, the high and low participants explain their estimates. Participants then discuss the rationale for their estimate. The discussion must focus on the activity and not the estimates themselves. When participants finish their discussion, each participant re-estimates the activity duration by selecting another card and repeating the process until they reach a consensus.

In many cases, the estimates will converge by the second round. It rarely takes more than three rounds. Everyone doesn't need to arrive at exactly the same estimate. If the second-round estimates are 7, 7, 7, and 5, for example, the project manager might ask the low estimator if he or she is okay with an estimate of 7. Again, the point is not absolute precision but an estimate that everyone can live with.

Research indicates that the Planning Poker method may be more accurate than many other estimation methods. Planning poker estimates may be more accurate because the planning poker process uses the same logic underlying The Wisdom of Crowds. (See Figure 6.2) The average of a large number of independent estimates is often more accurate than the estimates of a few experts.

Planning Poker is difficult with virtual teams because virtual teams are rarely, if ever, able to meet face to face. However, the Planning Poker website (www.planningpoker.com) makes it possible for dispersed teams to do this online in real time.

(For a good discussion of the advantages and disadvantages of using the planning poker method see https://www.atlassian.com/blog/platform/a-brief-overview-of-planning-poker.)

To Pad or Not to Pad?

Because it is hard to estimate activity durations with any degree of certainty, project managers often tend to pad their estimates. The purpose of padding is to provide a measure of protection against activity slippage. The fact that most projects do not finish on time casts doubt on the effectiveness of this strategy.

Figure 6.2 | The Wisdom of Crowds

It was common at English county fairs in the 18th century to have contests to guess the weight of an ox. Sir Francis Galton noted that the most accurate estimates were obtained by averaging the individual estimates of the crowd. This average was closer to the ox's actual weight than the estimates of most crowd members, and even closer than any of the separate estimates made by the cattle experts.

The wisdom of crowds refers to the fact that the average of independent estimates is more accurate than the estimate of most individuals and often those of the experts.

For a detailed discussion of this concept, see *The Wisdom of Crowds* (Surowiecki, 2004). A full reference can be found in the bibliography.

A three-point estimate is an average. Because it is an average, the probability of finishing within the estimated time frame is approximately 50 percent. In other words, half the time the activity will take less than the estimate, and half the time it will take longer. Over the course of the project, the early and late activity completions will even out so that the project will meet its expected completion date. In practice, however, this seldom happens. The problem is that delays, i.e., late finishes, are passed on, and early completions are not.

Figure 6.3 | Duration vs. Elapsed Duration

Sometimes it is necessary to distinguish between duration and what is called "elapsed duration". For example, suppose a work crew has been assigned the activity of pouring a concrete drive.

Once the concrete has been poured it will take 24 hours to dry. If the assigned duration is 24 hours, then, according to the work schedule, it will take three days for the concrete to dry (assuming an 8-hour work day). But the concrete will continue to dry even after the work crew has gone home for the day. To resolve this problem, we could assign the activity an elapsed duration of 24 hours.

Most project managers would prefer an estimate that ensures an 80 or 90 percent probability of an on-time completion. To do this, many project managers add a substantial amount of padding or "safety" to activity estimates.

While padding is intended to protect the project from the inevitable delays that plague many if not most, projects, it may also have unintended consequences, and most of them are negative. If project managers suspect that team members are padding their estimates, they may reduce those estimates by 10 to 15 percent. If they do, team members will often add an extra 10 to 15 percent to future estimates. And, padding extends the completion date of the project.

Figure 6.4 | Activity Durations

A general rule of thumb is that activity durations should not exceed two weeks elapsed time. This is a good idea for several reasons. First, it provides more flexibility in scheduling. Second, it permits a high level of control over the project.

In large projects, however, this may prove to be impractical. Breaking down the work to that level of detail may go beyond the project manager's ability to exercise sufficient control over the project.

Ironically, padding the project does not increase the likelihood of meeting the scheduled completion dates because of what has been called the "School Effect." Students are notorious for waiting until the last minute to study for tests. Postponing the test another week does not give them more time to study. It simply means they have another week until they have to begin studying. Likewise, padding project activities does not mean the team members assigned to the activity will start earlier or spend more time on the activity. It may just delay the actual activity start date. Therefore, the probability of finishing the activity on time remains unchanged. So, if padding does not work, what is a project manager to do?

An alternative approach is to add a "dummy" activity at the end of the project. This dummy activity is sometimes referred to as a "Management Reserve." As long as delays are shorter than the duration of the "dummy" activity, the project will finish on schedule. Creating a buffer works as long as the team understands that the buffer is a reserve and is not to be used to offset routine schedule slippage.

So how long should the buffer be? Unfortunately, there is no simple answer to this question. It should probably be in the range of 5 percent to 15 percent of the project's total duration. Examining the expected and actual completion dates of previous projects may provide some guidance on this issue.

Another approach is to set it equal to the project's schedule risk exposure. DeMarco and Lister, in *Waltzing with Bears* (2003), wrote, "When a project strays from the schedule, it's seldom because the work planned just took longer than anyone had thought; a much more common explanation is that the project got bogged down doing work that wasn't planned at all." In short, most project managers do a reasonably good job of estimating the duration of the activities in the WBS but a relatively poor job of estimating the amount of time they will have to spend on the unexpected activities that inevitably arise during the project implementation.

In other words, the project duration is the total amount of time it takes to complete the work identified in the WBS (known work) plus the time it takes to complete the unexpected work (unknown work) that arises during the implementation of the project plan. The buffer should be equal to the length of the unanticipated work estimated in the risk analysis. This issue is discussed in some detail in the section on risk exposure in Chapter 9.

While duration, whether estimated or calculated, is an important component, the project manager will need additional information to develop a project schedule. These include the relationship between the activities (sequences, dependencies, and constraints) and the project start date.

Activity Relationships

The second item of information needed to establish the project schedule is the relationship between activities. Activity relationships consist of three parts; the sequence of the activities, their dependencies, and associated time constraints.

Sequence

Sequence and dependencies are often confused. Although similar, they describe different aspects of the relationship between activities. Sequence is the order in which the activities are performed. Activity A must precede Activity B. This is sometimes called the order of precedence. In this case, Activity A is the predecessor, and Activity B is the successor.

The project team generally determines the order of precedence based on their knowledge and experience. Some sequences, however, are mandatory. The three types of sequences:

- Mandatory
- Discretionary
- External

Mandatory sequences are dictated by the nature of the activities themselves. For example, you have to write a proposal before you can submit it. No other sequence is physically possible. This sequence is mandated by the logical and physical nature of the relationship.

Some sequences may be legally mandated; building permits are an example of this. Construction cannot legally begin until a building permit has been issued. Other required sequences result from company policies and customer requirements. In these cases, the nature of the work dictates the sequence.

The project manager or the project team usually determines discretionary sequences, with decisions being driven by goals, resource availability, or other process-related considerations. For example, when purchasing a new computer system, the project team will have to decide whether the hardware requirements will drive the software selection or vice versa.

Events outside the project impose external sequences. For example, equipment purchases may depend on budgetary approval, an activity outside the project's scope.

Activity sequence can be displayed visually in a network diagram. The network diagram, also known as a "precedence diagram," "dependency diagram," or "PERT chart," is a flowchart that illustrates the flow of the work within the project. It consists of three basic elements; activities, dependencies, and milestones.

Dependencies

The second aspect of activity relationships is the concept of dependency. A dependency exists between two activities when the deliverable produced by one is necessary to complete the other. Dependencies determine the sequence of the activities. There are four common types of dependencies between activities. They are listed in Figure 6.5 together with a brief description.

PROJECT SCHEDULE PLANNING

Figure 6.5 | Dependency Types

Dependency	Gantt View	Description
Finish-to-start	May 10, days 10–16	Activity A must finish before Activity B can start. Activity B may start any time after Activity A has been completed.
Start-to-start	May 10, days 10–16	Activity A must start before Activity B can start. Activity B may start any time after Activity A has started.
Finish-to-finish	May 10, days 10–16	Activity A must finish before Activity B can finish. Activity B may finish any time after Activity A has finished.
Start-to-finish	May 10, days 10–16	Activity A must start before Activity B can finish. Activity B may finish any time after Activity A has started.

1. **Finish-to-Start**

    By far, the most common dependency is the Finish-to-start. This dependency is common because most project activity sequences are serial; something must be finished before something else can begin. For example, you cannot submit a grant application before you have finished writing it. Most project management software programs use this as the default dependency.

    Because the Finish-to-start dependency describes a serial relationship, activities linked by this type of dependency require fewer resources than dependencies characterized by parallel activity, but this means they take longer to complete.

2. **Start-to-Start**

   Start-to-start and Finish-to-finish dependencies result in overlapping activities. In a start-to-start relationship, Activity B can start immediately after Activity starts. Activity B does not have to wait for Activity A to finish. It can start any time after Activity A has started. In practice, there is often a lag between the start of Activity A and the start of Activity B. This lag is often inherent in the process but may also be due to manpower or scheduling issues.

3. **Finish-to-Finish**

   Finish-to-finish dependencies are used when one activity cannot finish until another has finished, i.e., the completion of the second activity is dependent on the completion of the first. For example, installing a computer network cannot be completed until the last computer in the network has been installed.

   Note that in the finish-to-finish example in Figure 6.6, the two activities do not finish simultaneously. Depending on the start dates and durations, they may finish simultaneously, but the requirement is simply that the successor activity cannot finish before the predecessor finishes.

   The start-to-start and finish-to-finish dependencies are very similar and, in many situations, work equally well. These dependencies are not entirely interchangeable, however. Look at the example in Figure 6.6. The first Gantt chart shows the relationship between manufacturing and assembly as a start-to-start dependency. In the second Gantt chart, this relationship is a finish-to-finish dependency. While, theoretically, both would work, the problem with the start-to-start dependency is that assembly finishes before manufacturing is completed. For this reason, the finish-to-finish dependency is the more appropriate way to overlap these activities in this situation.

Figure 6.6 | Start-to-Start vs. Finish-to-Finish

Start-to-Start							
May 2020				June 2020			
May 3	May 10	May 17	May 24	May 31	June 7	June 14	June 21

Manufacturing
Assembly

Finish-to-Finish							
May 2020				June 2020			
May 3	May 10	May 17	May 24	May 31	June 7	June 14	June 21

Manufacturing
Assembly

4. **Lags and Leads**

   You can use lags and leads when the relationship between activities is more complicated than can be expressed in a simple dependency. Adding a lag inserts a delay between activities while a lead overlaps them, providing the project manager additional flexibility in the scheduling of project activities.

   The nature of the successor activity may dictate a lag. The primer, for example, has to dry before the second layer of paint can be applied. Without the lag, the project manager might schedule the next coat of paint to begin before the primer has dried. A lag of 12 hours will ensure that the primer is dry before painting resumes.

   A lag may also help to resolve scheduling issues arising from the lack of available resources. For example, Activity

A and B have a finish-to-start relationship. Still, Activity B cannot begin immediately upon completion of Activity A because the team member assigned to Activity B will be on vacation and will not return until two days after Activity A has been completed. You could insert a lag here to ensure that Activity B is not scheduled to begin until the team member returns to work.

There are at least two ways to incorporate lag time into a project schedule. The first is to specify the amount of lag in the dependency. The use of project management software makes this option very easy.

A second way is to create a dummy activity with a duration equal to the length of the desired lag. A dummy activity is an activity with a specified duration but no resources assigned to it. Both methods work. The choice is a matter of personal preference.

While lags are common, leads are much less frequently used. A lead is often referred to as a negative lag. A lead of three days is equivalent to a lag of minus three days. In either case, Activity B would start three days before Activity A finishes, assuming a finish-to-start dependency.

So, when would you use a lead? Let's say that Activity A has a duration of four days, and Activity B needs to start two days before Activity A is finished. In Figure 6.7, Activity A finishes on December 14th, so Activity B needs to start on the 13th.

One solution is to create a start-to-start dependency with a lag of two days. This dependency works fine as long as Activity A is completed in four days as planned. But if Activity A slips an additional day, then Activity B will begin three days before Activity A is completed, not two days as originally scheduled.

A better solution is to create a finish-to-start dependency between Activity A and Activity B with a lead of two days (a

Figure 6.7 | Lags and Leads (One day)

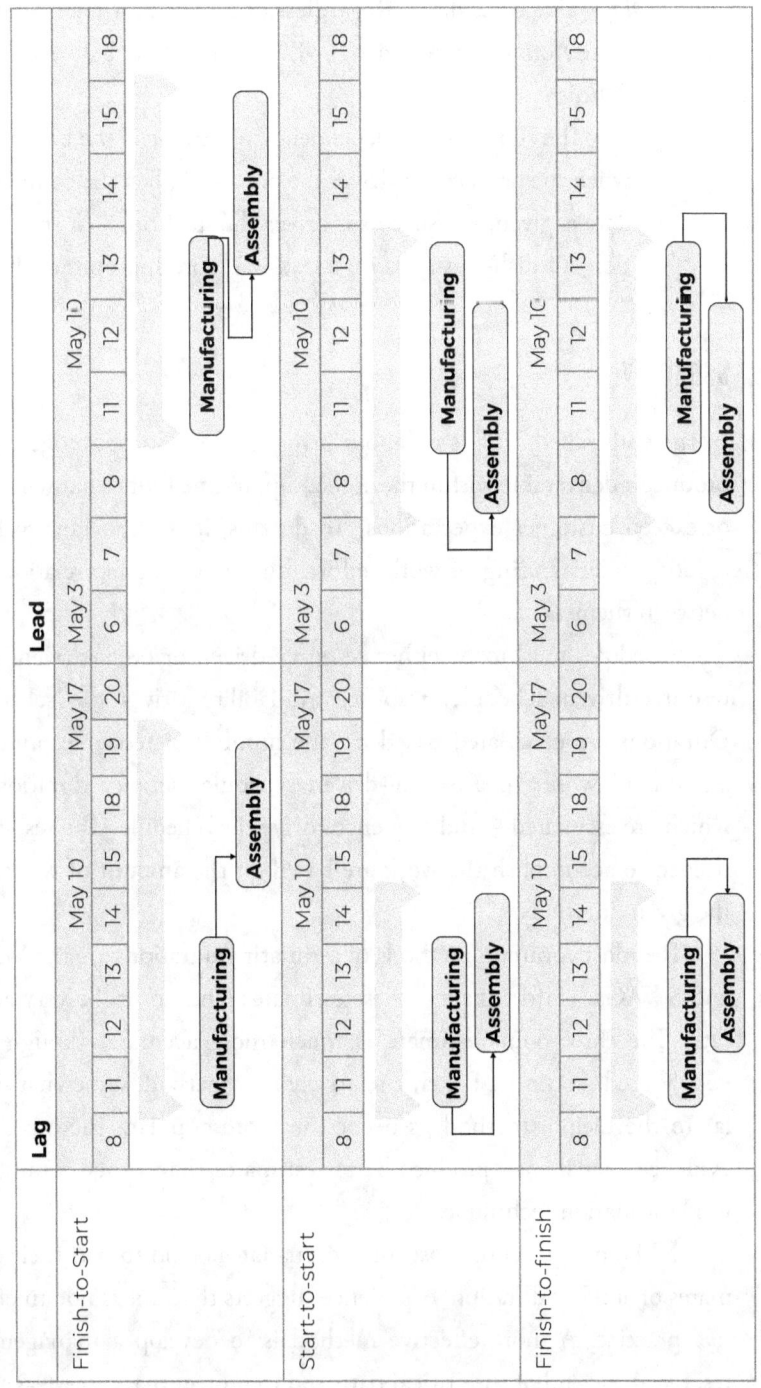

lag value of -2 days). Regardless of how long it takes to complete Activity A, Activity B will start two days before Activity A finishes.

The start-to-start dependency with a lag is the best choice when the predecessor drives the process. When the completion date is given, the successor drives the start time. In this situation, a finish-to-start with a lead is a more appropriate choice.

Summary

In the end, scheduling is all about bringing the resources together to produce a deliverable within the agreed-upon time frame that will meet or exceed customer expectations. To do this, it is important to have a good understanding of work, effort, duration, and the relationship between them.

Schedules tend to be either resource-driven or event-driven. In a resource-driven schedule, resource availability drives the schedule. Durations are calculated based on the number of resources and the amount of work. In an event-driven schedule, activity durations—which are estimated—and sequences drive the schedule. The resources needed to accomplish the work are based on the amount of work and the given durations.

The most common methods of estimating durations are the WAGs and SWAGs. Unfortunately, these estimates tend not to be very accurate. The three-point estimate is much more accurate, though less widely used. Planning Poker, a relatively new method, somewhat similar to the Delphi method, is becoming more popular. There is some evidence that it may produce better estimates than other commonly used estimation techniques.

While many, if not most, project managers tend to pad their estimates of activity duration, experience suggests that this is not an effective practice. A more effective method is to develop a management reserve at the end of the critical path and to protect that reserve against attempts to use it unless absolutely necessary. As a rule of thumb, the management reserve should be about 10 percent of the project's duration as a whole. A method for calculating a more precise estimate of the management reserve is discussed in Chapter 9 in the discussion on schedule risk estimation.

Once durations have been estimated, activity relationships must be established. Relationships between activities are defined by their sequence and their dependencies. Sequence is usually rather straightforward, dependencies less so. There are three common types of dependencies: finish-to-start, start-to-start, and finish-to-start.

Project schedules are determined by activity durations, relationships, and the project start date. Activity relationships and the start date are addressed in the next chapter.

DEVELOPING THE PROJECT SCHEDULE

Introduction

Every project contains one or more paths. A path is simply a series of activities linked by one or more dependencies. The number of paths is the number of different routes linking the first activity to the last activity in the project. In the Network Diagram in Figure 7.1, there are four paths. Note that some of the activities fall on more than one path.

The critical path is the longest path, i.e., the path with the longest total duration. Since the critical path is the longest, the project's duration is equal to the duration of the critical path.

The activities on the critical path are referred to as critical activities. It is important not to confuse the terms "critical" and "important." A "critical" activity is one that, if not completed on time, potentially delays the completion of the project. "Critical" relates to on-time completion of the project. An "important" activity, on the other hand, may or may not fall on the critical path. Activities are important because they have a significant impact on customer satisfaction with the project, regardless of whether or not they are critical.

To effectively manage a project, it is important to know which activities are on the critical path, particularly if the project has a tight deadline. The critical path identifies the activities the project manager must manage most carefully since any delay in completing these activities will potentially extend the project's completion date. If a critical

Figure 7.1 | Project Paths

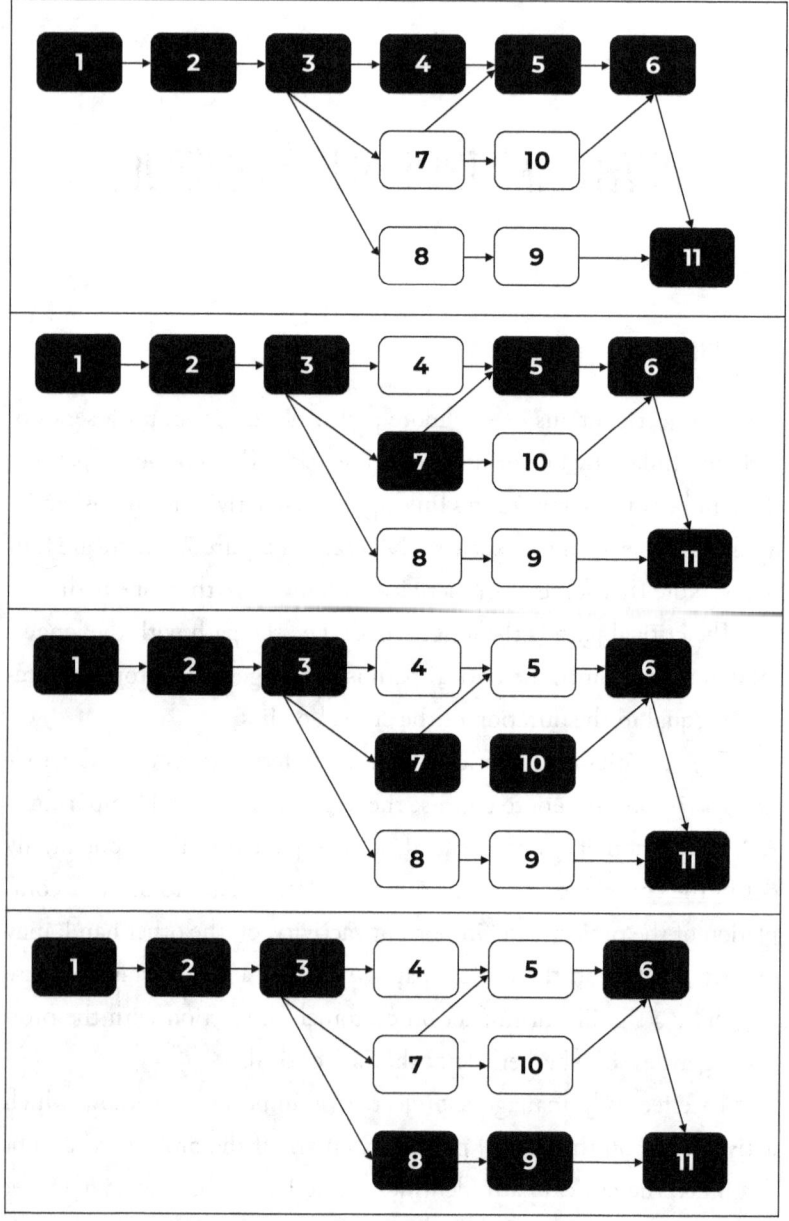

activity has "slipped," the slippage must be made up by shortening the amount of time it takes to complete the remaining activities on the critical path. Otherwise, the project will not finish on time.

Calculating the critical path is an easy, though sometimes tedious, activity. It is simply a matter of identifying the paths and summing their durations. Most project management software programs will automatically identify the critical path, displaying it in red. It is colored black in the Gantt chart in Figure 7.2.

Every project has at least one critical path, although, on rare occasions, there may be more than one. Projects with multiple critical paths are generally difficult to manage because of the large number of critical activities. There is simply more opportunity for slippage.

The critical path may change at any time during the project's implementation. A shift in the critical path is particularly likely to happen when two or more paths are of approximately equal length. As some activities finish ahead of schedule, and others finish late, the critical path can often shift.

Figure 7.3 | Number of Critical Activities

Every critical activity is an opportunity to delay the completion of the project. The more critical activities, the more likely it is that the project completion date will be delayed. So how many critical activities are too many? Obviously, that will depend on a number of factors including the project driver but many project managers feel that more than 30% is too many.

Slack

The critical path makes it possible to identify slack in a project. The difference in the duration of the critical path and the non-critical paths is referred to as "float" or "slack." Slack is important because it

Figure 7.2 | Critical Path

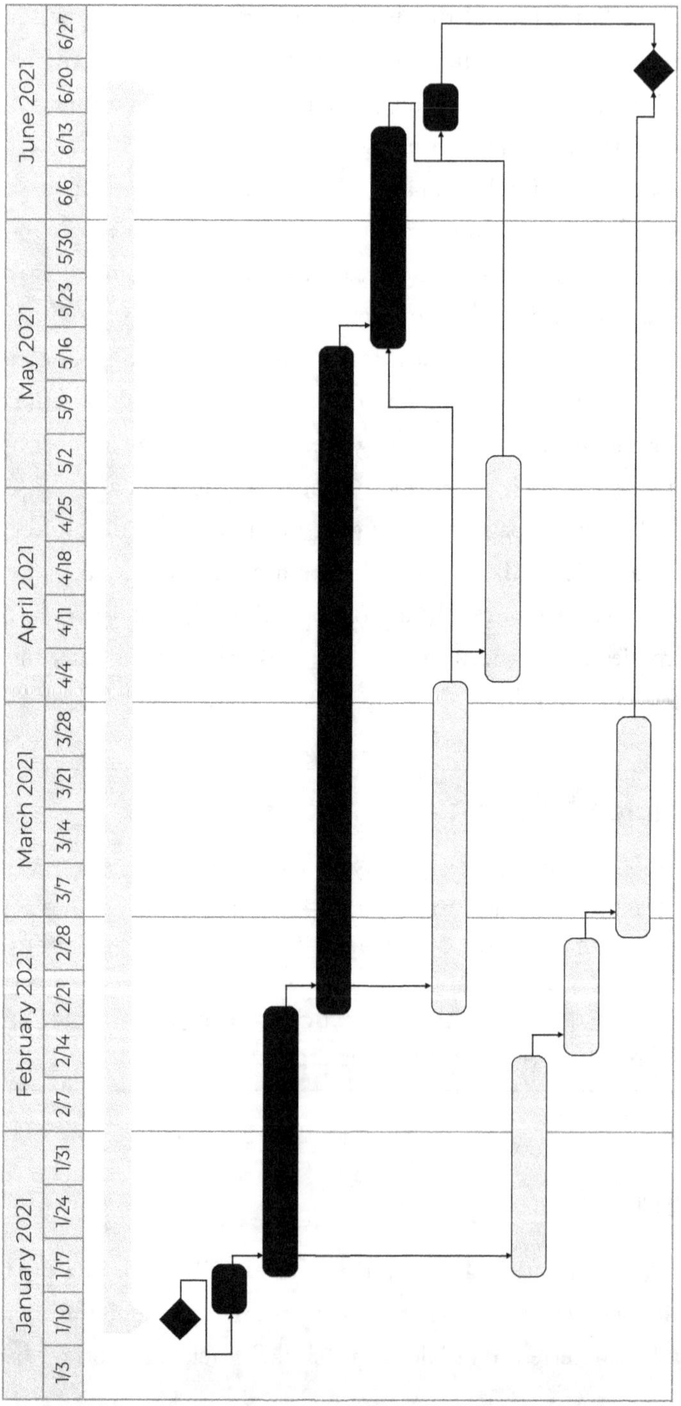

gives the project manager some latitude in resourcing and scheduling project work.

The following dates are used to calculate slack:

- Earliest start date (ES)
  The earliest possible date that an activity can begin given the constraints imposed by predecessor activities.
- Latest start date (LS)
  The latest possible date that an activity can finish without delaying the completion of the project.
- Earliest finish date (EF)
  The earliest possible date on which the activity can be completed. It is equal to the earliest start date plus the duration of the activity.
- Latest finish date (LF)
  The last possible date on which the activity can be completed without delaying the completion of the project.

These dates are used to calculate the amount of slack for each activity and on each path. It is sometimes useful to distinguish between free slack and total slack. *Free slack* is the amount of time an activity can slip before it delays a successor activity. It is the difference between the earliest start date and the latest start date (ES-LS).

Total slack is the amount of time a non-critical activity can slip before it delays the project completion date. While free slack is specific to each activity, total slack is specific to each path. Total slack is always equal to or greater than the amount of free slack for any given activity.

The earliest start date and the latest start date are generally the same for the activities on the critical path. They are the same because critical activities have no free slack. Any delay on the critical path can delay the completion of the project and increases slack on non-critical paths.

Constraints

The third element of activity relationships is the time constraint. In addition to dependencies, lags, and leads, the project manager can modify the schedule using constraints. While dependencies describe the relationship between activities, constraints have more to do with the scheduling of activities. Constraints are used together with dependencies to control activity start and finish dates.

Figure 7.4 lists the most common constraints together with a short description. ASAP (As Soon As Possible) is the default constraint. Unless there is a compelling reason to do otherwise, ASAP should be used, as it results in the shortest project duration and minimizes scheduling risk by preserving slack. There are times, however, when other constraints might be useful, providing the project manager with some options and, when used creatively, giving him or her additional flexibility in scheduling.

For example, in the software development project described earlier in this chapter, the project manager might decide to develop the marketing materials "as late as possible" (ALAP) to include the most up-to-date product information. Changing the constraint to ALAP schedules the activity to begin on the late start date, the last possible date on which the activity can start without delaying the completion of the project.

There might be good business reasons for doing this, but there is also a downside. While ALAP does not affect the total slack, it does impact free slack. The ALAP constraint moves the activity's free slack up front. Since the slack precedes the activity, it has been used before the activity starts. Removing this slack means that it is now a critical activity. If the activity's completion date should slip, there is no longer any slack to absorb the delay, as all of the slack was used before work on the activity began. (See Figure 7.5 for an example of this.) The top Gantt chart shows "Create Advertising" with an ASAP constraint. The Gantt chart below shows it with an ALAP constraint.

Figure 7.4 | Activity Scheduling Constraints

Constraints	Flexibility	Description
As Soon as Possible (ASAP)	Flexible	The activity must start as soon as its predecessors have been completed.
As Late as Possible (ALAP)	Flexible	The activity must start on the last date possible to complete the activity without delaying the project end date.
Start No Earlier Than (SNET)	Moderate	The activity must begin on or sometime after the specified date.
Start No Later Than (SNLT)	Moderate	The activity must start on or sometime time before the specified date.
Finish No Earlier Than (FNET)	Moderate	The activity must finish on or sometime after the specified date.
Finish No Later Than (FNLT)	Moderate	The activity must finish on or sometime before the specified date.
Must Start On (MSO)	Inflexible	The activity must start on the specified date.
Must Finish On (MFO)	Inflexible	The activity must finish on the specified date.

The "Start No Earlier Than," "Finish No Earlier Than," "Start No Later Than," and "Finish No Later Than" constraints (SNET, SNLT, FNET, FNLT) provide an intermediate level of flexibility. You should only use these when other constraints provide too much or too little flexibility. For example, if we are using PowerPoint slides for a briefing,

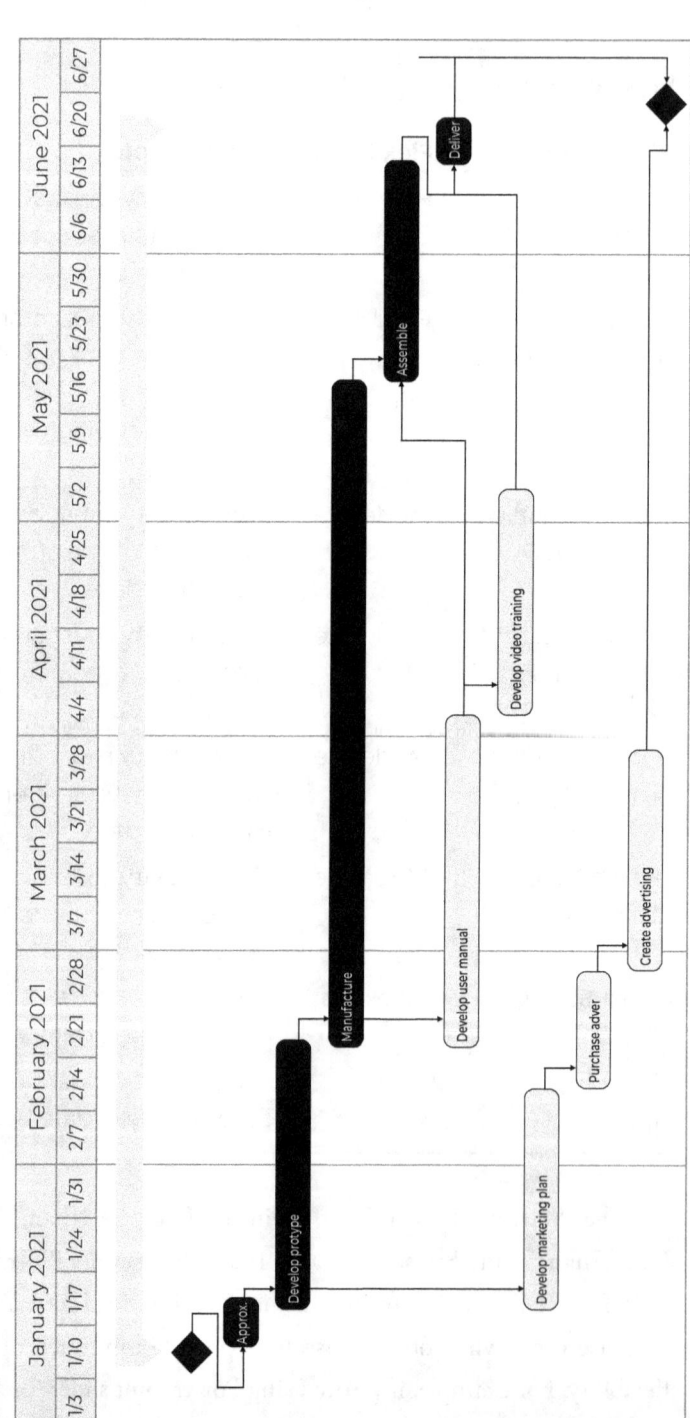

Figure 7.5 | Effects of Constraints on Scheduling As Soon as Possible (top) and As Late as Possible (bottom)

DEVELOPING THE PROJECT SCHEDULE

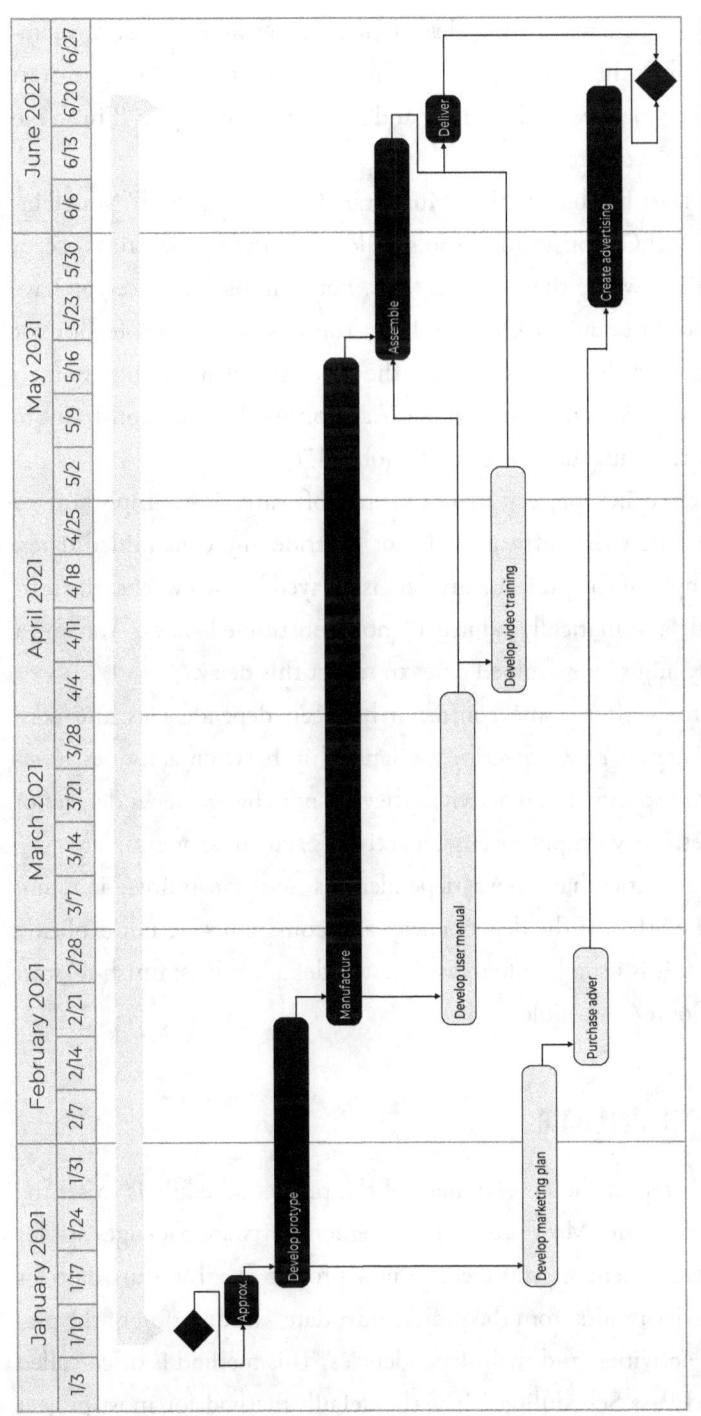

we may not care when the slides are prepared as long as they are completed before the meeting. To do this, we would set a finish-to-start dependency between this activity and its predecessor with a "Finish No Later Than" constraint.

The least flexible are the "Must Start On" (MSO) and "Must Finish On" (MFO) constraints. You should avoid these constraints except in situations where they are necessary. For example, suppose you have scheduled an event for October 17th. You have reserved a facility for that date and flyers printed with the time and date of the event. It would not make sense to assign an "As Soon As Possible" constraint to this event. It must take place on October 17th.

When using project management software, it is important to remember that the software will not override any constrained dates. For example, if the project start date is delayed by two weeks, the software will automatically adjust all non-constrained dates. You must manually adjust constrained dates to reflect this delay.

There is often some confusion between dependencies and constraints. *Dependencies* describe a relationship between activities. *Constraints* are specific to an activity. They do not change dependencies or sequences. They simply specify an activity's start date or end date

All activities have both dependencies and constraints; it is not one or the other. If the dependencies and constraints are not explicitly expressed, it is usually safe to assume the default values: finish-to-start and As Soon As Possible.

The Project Start Date

The final step in the development of the project schedule is to set the project start date. Most project management software packages ask for a start date whenever you create a new project file. The start date for each activity results from the project start date, the duration of the predecessor activities, and their dependencies. This method is often called "Forward Pass Scheduling." It is the default method for most project management software programs and you should not change it unless there is a specific reason for doing so.

When the project has to be completed by a specific date, some project managers like to start with that date and work backward to determine when the project has to start in order to finish on time. This method is called the *backward pass method*. It is discussed later in this chapter.

Sometimes neither the start date nor the end date is known. Perhaps the start date is dependent on a decision to be made by the customer or project sponsor. You can develop a preliminary schedule using an estimated start date. When the actual start date is known, you can update the planned start date to reflect the change.

Keep in mind that work schedules are based on estimated durations, i.e., the period within which the work takes place. The assumption is that the work will be evenly distributed within the duration of each activity. This issue was discussed in the previous chapter on resource planning (See the discussion of work contours on page 109). More precise scheduling will take place during the implementation stage as the scheduled activity start dates draw nearer.

Analyzing the Schedule

Once you have determined the durations, sequences, and start date, the initial project baseline schedule is complete. There is no guarantee at this point, however, that the schedule is a workable one. As we noted in the last chapter, the first draft of a project schedule is rarely, if ever, satisfactory. This situation is not necessarily the result of bad planning. It simply reflects the iterative nature of project staffing and scheduling.

There are several things project managers need to look for when reviewing the initial baseline schedule, including unrealistic durations, over/under-allocations, resource conflicts, staffing patterns, and project completion dates. Chapter 5 addressed over-allocations, resource conflicts, and staffing issues. But what if the project simply takes too long?

The project manager has three options: extending the completion date, changing the project start date, and shortening the critical path. Figure 7.6 graphically displays these options.

Extending the Completion Date

When the initial schedule shows a completion date beyond the deadline, the simplest solution is to extend the completion date. It will probably not be possible to do this in most instances, but it is usually worth a try. If you can extend the completion date, this may be the only change needed to complete the baseline schedule.

Figure 7.6 | When the Project Takes too Long

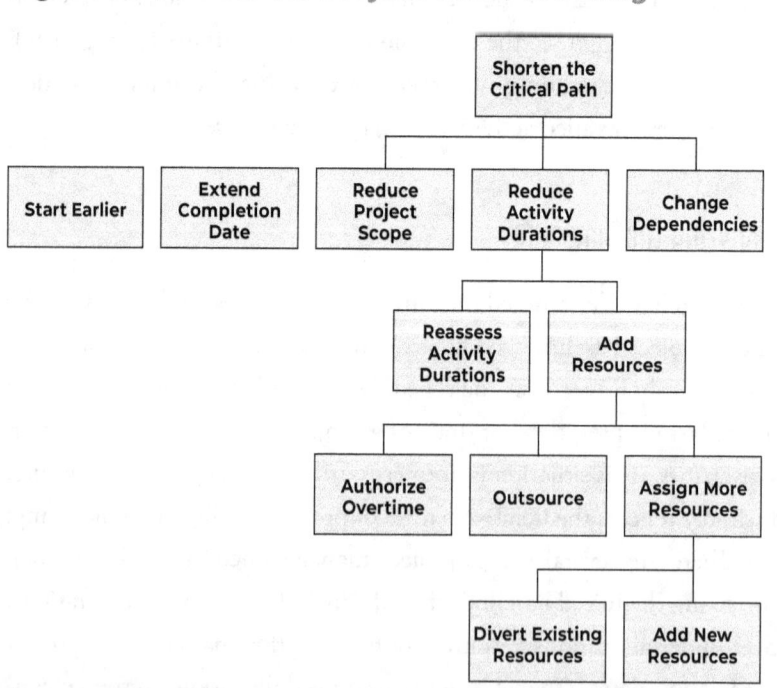

Starting Earlier

Another simple solution is to start earlier. If the plan projects a finish date two weeks after the approved completion date, begin work on the project two weeks earlier. Beginning earlier is often the best solution because it preserves the original deadline with the fewest scheduling changes.

There may, however, be reasons why an earlier start date is not feasible—for example, the resources may not be available, or some dates may be constrained. In this case, it would be necessary to find an alternative solution. All other solutions involve shortening the critical path.

Shortening the Critical Path

There are many ways to compress the critical path. These include:

1. *Deleting one or more critical activities from the project.* Deleting a critical activity reduces the scope of the project. It will also shorten the critical path by an amount of time equal to the duration of the deleted activity; however, this is often a risky strategy. There is a reason why every activity is included in the WBS. Arbitrarily deleting activities may get the project back on track, but it may also cause the project to fail to meet project goals and objectives. It is advisable to consult with the sponsor and major stakeholders before deleting any activities. This action should be considered only as a last resort.
2. *Shortening the duration of one or more critical activities.* Shortening the duration of a critical activity shortens the length of the project by the duration of that activity; however, this method also involves a certain amount of risk. Unless you have padded an activity, it may not be possible to reduce its duration without adding additional resources.

3. *Changing one or more dependencies on the critical path.* Most dependencies in most projects are finish-to-start. Serial activities take longer than activities that overlap. Changing the dependencies of critical activities from finish-to-start to start-to-start or finish-to-finish can reduce the critical path length by scheduling serial work to be done simultaneously.

   Simultaneous activities usually require a greater commitment of resources, since most resources are only available for use on one activity at a time. Overlapping activities usually involve changing dependencies from serial to simultaneous, which may increase the project's cost. On the other hand, delaying the project may also increase the project's cost by tying up resources beyond the planned completion date. A cost-benefit analysis may be needed to determine whether or not to change dependencies.

   Of course, you cannot perform all activities in parallel, so this solution will not work in every situation.

4. *Changing activity constraints for one or more critical activities.* Many constrained activities are not on the critical path. Changing constraints on non-critical paths only increases the amount of slack on these paths. When critical activities are constrained, removing these constraints will shorten the critical path. Since critical activities should not be constrained unless necessary, it is unlikely that this solution will always work.

5. *Breaking critical activities into smaller activities that can be worked simultaneously by different resources.* It is often possible to break activities into smaller activities, which is nothing more than a continuation of the decomposition process. It may be possible to overlap some of these smaller activities, reducing the length of the critical path. Of course, breaking

activities into smaller activities only works if the activity is on the critical path.

6. *Scheduling overtime.* This has the advantage of utilizing existing resources. You do not need to bring team members up to speed on the project. They do not need additional training, and they do not have to relocate.

    The downside is that team members may become "burned out" when required to work extensive overtime. If using non-exempt employees, overtime drives up project costs. If the cost of failing to meet the project deadline is great, this may be an acceptable short-term solution. It is not a good long-term solution.

7. *Assigning additional resources to work on critical activities.* To decrease the duration, we can add additional resources to the activity, which often include team members diverted from non-critical activities. Team members' skill sets and the amount of slack on the non-critical paths determine the extent to which this is possible.

    Activities with free slack give the project manager some flexibility in scheduling resources, making it possible to divert resources from non-critical to critical activities. Adding resources usually decreases duration, which almost always reduces the critical path length, shortening the time it takes to complete the project.

Forward Pass vs. Backward Pass

Project schedules are based on the start date, the sequence of activities, and their durations. You can schedule activities using either a forward pass or a backward pass. Most project management software programs are capable of doing both.

Forward Pass

In a forward pass schedule, activities are scheduled "As Soon As Possible" (ASAP). In other words, each activity is scheduled on its early start date.

The forward pass method is the more commonly used of the two methods. While most computer software programs are capable of doing both, the forward pass method is the default.

Backward Pass

In cases where the project completion date is given, some project managers like to start with the completion date and work backward to determine when the project has to start to meet the deadline. This is called a "backward pass." It starts with the last activity in the project and each preceding activity is scheduled on its ALAP date. ALAP activities are scheduled to begin on their late start date.

Forward or Backward Pass?

While it might seem reasonable to assume that both methods would yield the same result, this is not necessarily the case. A forward pass will schedule all activities on their earliest possible start date (ASAP), while a backward pass schedules activities on the latest possible start date (ALAP). ALAP does not affect the scheduling of critical activities whose early and late start dates are identical. It does, however, impact non-critical activities with free slack, i.e., activities whose completion date does not affect the project completion date.

Since the backward pass assumes ALAP constraints, activities are scheduled after their free slack, if there are any. As a result, schedules based on a backward pass usually contain no free slack.

This will have no impact on critical activities because they have no free slack. The early start date and the late start date are the same. It will, however, impact non-critical activities because the early start date and the late start date are not the same.

Most experts advise against the use of the backward pass method for "backing into the schedule." Eliminating most, if not all, slack increases schedule risk.

If it is critical to meet the project deadline, a better approach is to develop the schedule using a forward pass using specified or given activity durations. If the end date is not satisfactory, then shorten the critical path using the schedule compression techniques described previously until a satisfactory completion date has results. However, it is still possible that you will not meet the deadline without additional resources or a reduction in scope. We can, of course, always force the project to meet a specific completion date, but that does not always result in a workable schedule.

Estimating the Project End Date

The discussion thus far has assumed that schedules are developed based on best estimates of activity durations. As such, the critical path is the best estimate of the project completion date. However, we know from experience that the critical path will probably change more than once during the implementation of the project. A better way to forecast the project completion date is to calculate a range within which the project is likely to finish.

One way to do this is to calculate alternate schedules based on the optimistic and pessimistic estimates for activity durations. Using these estimates provides a range within which the project is likely to be completed.

Finalizing the Schedule

The last step in the planning process is to submit the plan or plans to key stakeholders for final review. This step is not always necessary, particularly for smaller projects, but it is mandatory for most larger projects, providing the stakeholders one last opportunity to raise whatever objections they might have to the project plan. Once approved, key stakeholders are on record supporting the project and the project scope as defined by the project charter and subsequent work plans.

Two things will be of particular concern as we evaluate the project schedule. The first is the triple constraints. Is the planned completion date on or before the project completion date approved in the project charter? Is the project's estimated cost equal to or less than the amount approved in the project charter? Will the execution of the plan result in the successful completion of the work necessary to achieve project goals and objectives?

If the analysis of the project plan finds that one or more of the project constraints are not met, it will be necessary to make some adjustments to the plan. For example, what if the project takes too long? If the project charter specifies a completion date before the planned completion date, it may be necessary to revise the plan to result in an on-time finish. It is not good practice to finish a project behind schedule. It is even less acceptable to plan to finish a project behind schedule!

Milestones

In addition to the activities identified in the WBS, the project manager may want to add some milestones. Milestones, sometimes called checkpoints or events, are like the mile markers on the highways and are used to gauge progress toward the completion of the project. The number and frequency of these milestones will depend on the duration of the project and the rate of project activity. Projects with a large number of activities will have more milestones than those with fewer activities.

The use of milestones is at the discretion of the project manager. There are occasions, however, when the project sponsor or the customer may require specific milestones. In these situations, the milestones

DEVELOPING THE PROJECT SCHEDULE

usually mark the expected completion date of key deliverables and interim payments for project work.

Computer programs use various symbols to represent milestones, often a circle or a diamond. If you are not sure whether a symbol represents an activity or a milestone, check the duration. If the duration is zero, then it is a milestone. Milestones have no duration and no resources.

Tying Up Loose Ends

Another problem that often occurs in project scheduling is that the first draft of the plan includes some activities without predecessors or successors. The only activity that does not have a predecessor is the first activity, often a "Start Project" milestone. The only activity that does not have a successor is the last activity, often a "Project Complete" milestone. The lack of a successor activity is usually more serious. An activity with no successor can never actually delay the project no matter how long the "delay" might be, since no activities are dependent on its completion.

Figure 7.7 | External Dependencies

While it is generally not good practice to have activities without predecessors, there are situations where it is necessary and appropriate to have an activity with no predecessor. This happens when an activity is dependent on some action or activity that is external to the project.

For example, the start of an activity might depend on approval from an external customer. Or, an activity might depend on the completion of an activity in another project.

In such cases, the activity will not appear to have a predecessor since the predecessor is external to the project and therefore not represented in the Gantt chart.

Some project managers like to make a list of activities that lack predecessors and successors. The "Start Project" milestone is the predecessor for those activities lacking a predecessor. Likewise, they create a dependency between those activities without a successor and the "Project Complete" milestone.

It is important to remember that the project manager schedules durations in the planning stage, not work. The work will, of course, start sometime within the scheduled duration, but the initial project work plan does not establish the exact times and dates. As the scheduled dates approach, the project manager will have a better idea of who is available and what needs to be done. About a week or two out, he or she will schedule actual work times.

Summary

The development of the project schedule depends not only on the activity durations but also on the project start date and the relationship of the activities. The start date needs little explanation; it is simply the date upon which the first activity is scheduled to begin. The start date ties the schedule to a specific time frame.

The relationship between activities is a little more complex. Activity relationships consist of two parts: sequence and dependencies. The sequence is determined by the nature of the activities themselves, though there may be some latitude in the order.

When the baseline schedule is complete, you can display it as a Gantt chart, graphically displaying the schedule together with the critical path and the slack on each non-critical path. The critical path is the longest path and therefore determines how long the project will take to complete. The slack on each path is calculated by subtracting its duration from the duration of the critical path. The critical path generally has no slack. Non-critical paths always have some slack.

Project managers must pay careful attention to the activities on the critical path, because any slippage on the critical path potentially delays the completion of the project. When slippage does occur, you must make it up, or the project completion date slips as well.

It is essential to review the initial baseline schedule before finalizing it. Because it is an iterative process, the first draft will rarely, if ever, prove to be workable. Initial project schedules almost always contain resource over- or under-commitments and/or scheduling conflicts.

Slack can be very helpful in dealing with these issues, permitting some flexibility in scheduling. This flexibility makes it possible to adjust the schedule to resolve resource conflicts and overcommitments. It also makes it possible to divert resources from non-critical to critical activities to get the work done more quickly. Reassigning resources is particularly helpful when the project is behind schedule or needs to finish ahead of schedule.

You can use the processes described in this chapter to facilitate the development of a workable schedule that will produce the best results, based on the work identified in the WBS. Unfortunately, there is always the unplanned additional work that inevitably crops up during the implementation of the project. This unexpected work is addressed in Chapter 9, which deals with issues, risks, and changes

COMMUNICATIONS PLANNING

Introduction

The free flow of information is critical to project success; poor communications are at the root of most project failures. Given the importance of project communications, it is surprising how little attention is given to this vital topic.

Figure 8.1 | Number of Communications Channels

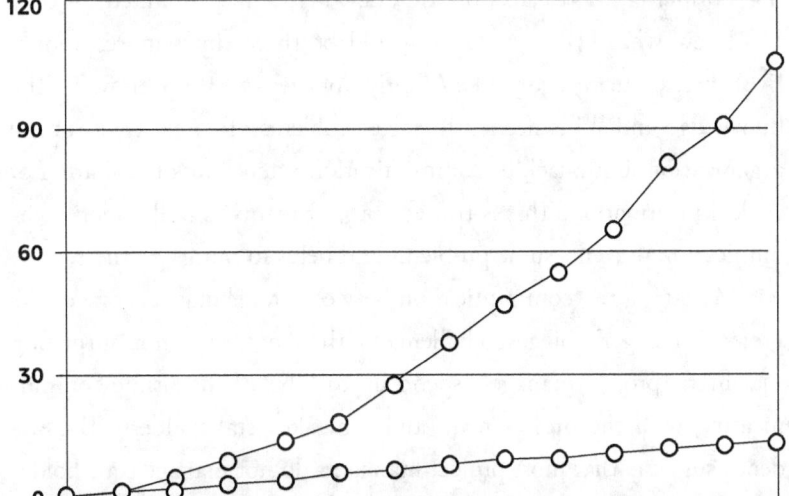

When we talk about project communications, we usually think about the communications between the project manager and his or her team, or between the project manager and the sponsor/customer. Project communication planning must, of course, address how these key stakeholders will communicate with each other, but communication planning must have a much broader focus: it must address communications between all key stakeholders.

There are $n(n-1)/2$ communication channels within a project where n is the number of stakeholders. For example, in a project with 12 key stakeholders (a sponsor, project manager, eight team members, and two other key stakeholders), there are 66 channels of communication.

Figure 8.1 shows the relationship between the number of stakeholders and the number of communication channels. Increases in the number of channels are small when there are few stakeholders, but when the number of stakeholders reaches eight or nine, the number of communication channels increases sharply. Doubling the number of stakeholders from seven to 14, for example, increases the number of communication channels by four times.

As organizations grow, communication becomes more challenging. Former Hewlett Packard CEO, Lew Platt, once remarked, "If only HP knew what HP knows, we would be three times more productive" (https://lucidea.com/blog/if-only-hp-knew-what-hp-knows/). The knowledge and skills needed to solve problems often exist within the organization, but a lack of communication often limits the sharing of critical information. This is true for project teams as well. Good communication prevents some problems and helps to mitigate others.

Managing the communication between stakeholders is one of the project manager's biggest challenges. Therefore, it is not surprising that many project managers spend up to 90% of their time communicating with the project team and other key stakeholders. The evidence suggests that most project managers do not manage stakeholder

COMMUNICATIONS PLANNING

communications very well. In their book, *Project Management Communications Bible*, Dow and Taylor list what they consider the primary reasons for project failure. (See Figure 8.2) These numbers are obviously exaggerated to make a point: good communication between stakeholders is critical to successful project management.

Figure 8.2 | Reasons for Project Failure

Poor requirements definition	2%
Inadequate risk management	1%
Poor scope control	1%
Lack of qualified resources	1%
Communication problems	90%
Other	2%

Dow and Taylor, p. xxix.

Most problems encountered are in one way or another related to a failure to communicate or communicate clearly. Project work is, by definition, collaborative, and there is no collaboration without communication.

The graphic in Figure 8.3 appeared in a newsletter published by the University of London Computer Centre in March 1973. It has been floating around the internet for many years and clearly illustrates the miscommunications that can and often do take place between project stakeholders.

A good project communication plan can help to improve the flow of information between stakeholders and avoid many of the problems associated with miscommunication, helping to ensure that the right people get the right information at the right time. It does not guarantee good communication, but it is an excellent first step.

Figure 8.3 | Miscommunication

The Communication Plan

The communication plan deals with the information and communication needs of the key project stakeholders. The plan should include the following information:

- what information is to be communicated, including format, content, and level of detail
- who will be responsible for communicating the information and who will receive it
- what methods will be used to communicate the information
- the frequency of the communication

What information is to be communication? This depends on the information needs of each stakeholder. The project manager generally determines these needs in his or her discussions with the key stakeholders as a part of the communications planning process. Typically, information requirements include:

- Status/Progress
- Risks
- Issues
- Assumptions
- Benefits
- Any other important information that impacts the project

Status/Progress

Stakeholders will want to know the current status of the project and how it is progressing. Project managers will keep stakeholders updated on the project's status through periodic review meetings and project performance reports.

There are two types of performance reports: status reports and progress reports. Some people make a distinction between the two; it is a distinction without much of a difference. In theory, the status report focuses on the project's current state while the progress report focuses more on recent activity.

Figure 8.4 | Don't Assume All Team Members Understand Things in the Same Way

One reason the armed services have trouble operating jointly is that they don't speak the same language. For example, if you told Navy personnel to "secure a building," they would turn off the lights and lock the doors. Army personnel would occupy the building so no one could enter. Marines would assault the building, capture it, and defend it with suppressive fire and close combat. The Air Force, on the other hand, would take out a three-year lease with an option to buy.

Source: Unknown

In practice, most project managers are interested in what has happened (progress), the current state of the project (status), and the future status of the project (projections). As a result, most performance reports include some or all of this information in a report called the status report or the project report.

There is no standard format for this report. Every organization has its own form based on its own information requirements.

Typically, the information in this report should answer the following questions:

- Is the project on schedule? Is it likely to meet upcoming deadlines?
- Is it within budget?
- How much effort has been used to date?
- Do the deliverables meet customer requirements?
- What risks are likely to affect the project?
- Are there any issues impacting the project? If so, what are they?

The information in the status/progress report should be accurate, current, and clearly presented. It should not include information not relevant to recipients. Brevity is a virtue. At the same time, it should include all the information stakeholders need to know about the project.

Risks

Risks come and go throughout the life of the project. The project manager should include information about current and potential risks on an ongoing basis. Communicating information about risks may help to avoid some risk events.

Issues

Since issues may require immediate attention, it is important to communicate relevant information quickly. The communication plan needs to specify how this will happen. Typically, issues are reported to the project manager and other appropriate stakeholders as soon as they are discovered. The project manager then enters them into the issues log, and takes the appropriate actions. See the discussion on issues in Chapter 16.

Assumptions

Assumptions are first addressed in the project charter, but assumptions, like all other aspects of the project, are subject to change throughout the project. Therefore, the project manager should review the assumptions log periodically, and communicate any changes to key stakeholders. Reviewing the assumptions helps to ensure that everyone continues to share the same understanding of the project and what it is intended to do.

Benefits

It is, of course, essential to keep stakeholders informed on the status of the project, but project communication is about more than just the status: it is also about communicating the value of the project to key stakeholders. This involves a wide range of activities designed to influence their perceptions of the project.

Every project competes with every other project for resources. High-profile, high-priority projects are the most likely to be fully resourced. These projects are also less likely to lose resources when cuts have to be made. It is therefore important for project managers to communicate to senior executives the value of their projects and the benefits the company derives from them. The communication plan should address this issue where appropriate.

Responsibility for Project Communications

Project information is communicated both formally and informally. As the project owner, the project manager is responsible for developing the project plan and any ancillary plans, such as the communication plan.

One of the issues the plan must address is who is responsible for communicating what information to whom, when, and how. As noted previously, this information is often gathered as part of the stakeholder analysis conducted in the project's initiation phase. If no stakeholder analysis has been conducted, it needs to be done as a part of the planning process.

The project manager is responsible for communicating status/progress reports to senior managers, sponsors, customers, and other stakeholders identified in the communications or stakeholder management plan. The project manager may also be responsible for communicating project information to these stakeholders using other formal communications channels such as reports, presentations, and meetings.

These reports usually consist of information provided by team members and other stakeholders involved in planning the project and implementing the project plan. For this reason, the project communication plan should also specify what information needs to be communicated and to whom.

Much of the communication that takes place during the project is informal. Informal project communications arise out of the social relationships and interactions between the people involved in the project. These communications consist primarily of discussions around the water cooler, in the break room, or in the hallway rather than the more formal kinds of communications that take place in meetings or through reports.

COMMUNICATIONS PLANNING

Often these discussions are impromptu events that result from unplanned and unexpected meetings. For example, the serendipitous meeting of the software engineer with the marketing analyst in the lunchroom may provide the project engineer with an opportunity to get clarification on end-user requirements.

Informal communications often help to speed the flow of information by circumventing formal lines of communication. As a Boeing engineer once told me, "Many of our problems are solved on the back of a napkin over lunch at a local convenience store." If the resolution of these problems depended solely on formal channels of communication, they would often take much longer to resolve.

The downside, however, is that information passed through such channels is sometimes incorrect and often difficult, if not impossible, to track back to the source. This lack of accountability makes it a prime source of rumors and speculation. Informal channels become much more significant in the absence of formal project communications.

Methods of Communication

There are more different ways for people to communicate today than ever before. The list seems to grow each year as Internet 2.0 social networking tools such as LinkedIn, Facebook, Instagram, X (formerly known as Twitter), and others become more widely used. While they provide new opportunities for communication between stakeholders, they also complicate the choice of communication methods. Figure 8.5 lists the options available to most project teams categorized by time and format. There are two things we know for sure. Every stakeholder has their preferred method for sending and receiving information, and each method has its strengths and weaknesses.

Figure 8.5 | Communication Methods

	Text	Audio	Audio/Visual
Real-time	Twitter Texting	Telephone VOIP	Face-to-face Meetings Audio/video Conferences
Not real-time	E-mail Online Sites Memos/ Reports Social Networking Sites	Podcasts	Presentations

X (Twitter)/Yammer

Twitter is a method for communicating information in real-time to a large number of people. Twitter was originally designed as a social networking tool but has more recently evolved into an information-sharing service that enables users to send and receive messages known as tweets. Tweets are text-based messages of up to 140 characters expanded to 280 characters in the fall of 2017. That number was again expanded in 2023 to 400 for paid users.

X has grown rapidly since its creation in 2006. By the beginning of 2023, the number of active users was estimated to be around 397 million, though its growth seems to have slowed considerably since 2017.

Some project managers have set up X accounts with privacy controls for project communications. X forces users to be concise since there is a limit on the length of tweets. It is also possible to search tweets by keyword, link to websites, and track users.

COMMUNICATIONS PLANNING

A Google search for "project management" and "Twitter" brings up a surprisingly large number of entries. A review of these posts suggests that project managers use X more for professional networking than for managing projects.

Yammer is a popular alternative to X. Eighty-five percent (85%) of the Fortune 500 companies are using Yammer to facilitate communication between project stakeholders. Like Twitter, it allows users to post short updates of their activities and subscribe to other users' postings. In 2012, Microsoft purchased Yammer and has recently integrated it into Microsoft Teams. Additional information can be obtained at the Yammer website.

Tumblr and Plurk are additional alternatives to X.

Texting

Texting has many of the same characteristics as e-mail but is better suited to real-time communication.

Telephone

The telephone is another commonly used method for communicating project information. It is real-time and interactive, which has both advantages and disadvantages.

Telephone conversations and teleconferences make it possible to disseminate, clarify, and supplement project information and obtain immediate feedback. The sender can determine if the recipient has received the message and, with some degree of certainty, understood it. If the receiver did not clearly understand the message, the sender can clarify the communication until it is understood.

The real-time, interactive nature of the telephone to communicate project information also facilitates project decision-making. As a result, a one-hour phone call or teleconference may be able to accomplish what it might take two weeks to do using other forms of communication.

Like other methods of communication, the telephone (or online voice transmission methods such as iChat or Skype) has its limitations. First, all parties to the conversation must be on the phone at the same time. This is sometimes difficult, particularly for a large team, a team with a heavy workload, or a team dispersed across multiple time zones.

While you can record teleconferences, recorded sessions are not interactive, removing one of the primary advantages of this technology.

Another limitation is that traditional telephones can only transmit audio information. Although recipients can discern underlying meanings by voice tone and pitch, there are no visual cues to aid this process. Body language cannot be transmitted over phone lines.

Moreover, some kinds of project information do not lend themselves to non-visual methods of communication. For example, many technical subjects require the shared use of spreadsheets, diagrams, or graphs. While you can e-mail them to teleconference participants in advance, there is no guarantee that all participants will have them available during the call or that participants will use them to follow the discussion.

Face-to-Face Meetings

A meeting is a form of communication that involves participants who are at the same place at the same time. Communication is both real time and, in most cases, interactive.

Much of the discussion on telephonic communications applies to meetings. Its strengths include the ability to transmit, clarify, expand, and obtain immediate feedback. It is also well-suited to resolving disputes, solving problems, and making decisions.

Meetings have the added advantage of being able to transmit visual information. This includes technical data such as graphs, charts, and spreadsheets and "soft" information such as facial expressions, posture, gestures, and other types of body language that often reflect an underlying message.

Because those who attend meetings interact with each other face-to-face, meetings facilitate the team development process. Face-to-face interactions increase trust and foster commitment to the team.

Of course, meetings have their limitations. The most obvious is that scheduling meetings (real or virtual) is often very challenging. Trying to accommodate multiple schedules, or stakeholders who do not work in proximity to each other can be very difficult, if not impossible. Unless the meeting is a high priority, scheduling may require a lead time of several weeks. For these reasons, meetings are not a good vehicle for quickly disseminating important information.

For additional information on project meetings, see the section on project review meetings in Chapter 14 on page 294.

Video Conference

Video conference technology includes video chats, interactive television, web conferences, and any other means of video interaction. These technologies are commonly used to create virtual meetings (i.e., a meeting where all participants are electronically, though not physically, in the same place at the same time).

There are many technologies available for conducting virtual meetings, and these technologies are constantly changing. Zoom, GoToMeeting, RingCentral, FreeConferenceCall.com, Skype, MS Teams, and Flock are just a few of the video conferencing options available as of this writing.

These methods share many of the same strengths and weaknesses as face-to-face meetings. The most obvious advantage is that virtual meetings allow people working remotely to attend meetings, which is particularly important for virtual teams, i.e., teams whose members work at different locations. Video conferencing helps to ensure all team members can participate.

As real-time, interactive methods of communication capable of transmitting both audio and visual information, video conferences are well suited to communicating both technical information and the underlying messages contained in the tone of voice, facial expressions, and body language.

Another advantage is that video conferencing generally eliminates travel time. Getting to and from meetings often takes as long as the meetings themselves. Eliminating or significantly reducing travel time makes it possible for teams to get more done in less time.

While video conferencing is in most respects superior to those methods that rely solely on written or audio messaging, it is not an entirely satisfactory substitute for face-to-face meetings. Video conferencing does not permit side discussions between participants or informal one-on-one exchanges during breaks. This often inhibits candor and limits the scope of communications.

Video conferencing has traditionally been very expensive, but new technologies have made it possible to do video conferencing on desktop computers, tablets, and smartphones, at a very reasonable price. As a result, video conferencing has become an essential and widely used communication tool for project managers.

E-mail

In recent years, e-mail has become one of the most common methods of communication among project stakeholders. It is easy, quick, and inexpensive. For this reason, it has become the default method of communicating project information for most projects.

There are, however, some real downsides to the reliance on e-mail as a method of project communication. First, most people are inundated with e-mails. Some project managers report receiving hundreds of e-mails a week. With such a large volume of e-mails, it is not unusual for important e-mails to be overlooked, ignored, accidentally trashed, or routed to a spam folder.

E-mails are also subject to a greater level of miscommunication than some other methods of communication. Many stakeholders do not have good writing skills and cannot articulate their thoughts clearly in written form, causing senders and recipients to miscommunicate. This failure to communicate clearly is a common source of problems on projects.

E-mail is generally not considered a secure medium of information transmission. While this is not likely to be a problem for most projects, it may be critical to others. Using a VPN or an encrypted server mitigates this problem.

Lastly, e-mail is not a content-rich form of communication. By that, I mean that it does not always communicate the entire message. Messages have both a cognitive and an emotional component. Research by Mehrabian in the 1960s (Mehrabian and Wiener, 1967, Mehrabian and Ferris, 1967) examined the communication of messages that had some emotional content. He found that:

- 7% of a message is in the words that are spoken.
- 38% of a message is paralinguistic (the way that the words are said).
- 55% of a message is in facial expression.

This research suggests that communication using e-mail may transmit only a tiny fraction of the message. When you add to that the fact that so many people have less-than-ideal writing skills, it is no wonder there are so many communication problems among project stakeholders.

Of course, the implication is that e-mail works best for messages that have little emotional content. It is also good to include critical information in the header to make it more visible to the recipient.

Online Services

Projects teams increasingly use online sites to share information, particularly for medium- to long-term projects. They serve as a centralized repository for project information. They can take many forms but, regardless of the form, they have one primary function: to make project information accessible to stakeholders at any time from almost any place.

There are many different types of online platforms currently in use by project teams. These include websites, ftp sites, SharePoint servers, Dropbox, wikis, and Google Waves. Each has its particular strengths and weaknesses. Project managers are limited to the technology supported by the IT department within their organizations. This is a significant improvement over the fragmented project record-keeping and information dissemination practices that were common just a few years ago.

Written Memos/Reports

Once the staple of project communications, hard-copy memos, and reports are no longer as widely used as before the widespread availability of computer networks. Many organizations are working toward paperless communication and documentation. The shift to digital technologies has created a reliance on electronic communications. Today most hard-copy documents are printouts of documents generated electronically.

LinkedIn

LinkedIn, launched in May 2003, is the largest social networking service for business professionals. As of October 2009, LinkedIn had more than 50 million registered users in more than 200 countries. By March

2011, it had grown to more than 100 million and in early 2023 exceeded 770 million with an average of more than 300 million monthly users.

Some project managers have used LinkedIn for communications within the team (such as status updates, project discussions), document sharing (requirements specs, schedules, PowerPoint presentations), and communicating with project stakeholders. It is particularly useful for dispersed teams and teams separated from other key stakeholders.

Most project managers feel that while LinkedIn has some value, there are better options for communicating project information to team members and other stakeholders.

Facebook

A Google search for project management and Facebook turns up a few links, not very many but more than you might think.

In a recent blog post, "Twitter and Facebook as Project Management Tools?" on the Project Management Tips website, the author concludes that Facebook ". . . has no useful project management value" (http://pmtips.net/twitter-facebook-project-management-tools/). While it may have some marketing and communications uses, it does not do anything to facilitate project communications that traditional methods of communication cannot do better. There were many replies to this post. Most agreed with the author's conclusion.

Some organizations, however, have used Facebook Groups to effectively facilitate team building. Facebook Groups can be particularly effective for virtual teams whose members have not previously worked together and may never have met.

In October 2016, Facebook launched a new platform called Workplace. It is an enterprise connectivity platform that includes groups, instant messaging, and a news feed. It was designed to give organizations the ability to create an internal social network focused on work-related content limited to designated users. Facebook launched

Workplace for Good in June 2018 to provide a free version of Workplace for registered non-profits and staff of educational institutions.

These platforms are competing with Salesforce, Slack, and Basecamp, among others.

Podcasts/Audio Recordings

Podcasts are audio documents recorded in MP3 format and played back on a computer or an MP3 player such as the iPod, iPad, or smartphone. The content is primarily audio though some podcasts include video content.

Since podcasts are downloaded and played back at the user's convenience, podcasts do not lend themselves to time-sensitive communication. Stakeholders may or may not choose to download them, and even if downloaded, they may or may not immediately listen to them.

Some project managers, however, have found podcasts helpful in communicating certain types of project information. For example, stakeholders can download and listen to status reports, discussions of project risk, or other project issues that interest them. Listening to these podcasts can help to keep them current with the project.

Some project managers have recorded project team meetings so that team members not able to attend can listen to them later. This also makes it possible for stakeholders who often do not attend meetings to listen to them if they so choose. For many, this is a better solution than pouring over the minutes of previous team meetings.

You can also use podcasts to facilitate the training of project team members. Experienced team members can communicate their knowledge and expertise by talking about their experiences with particular types of project activities. These podcasts can be used as a form of just-in-time training.

Presentations

The project manager is often called on to give presentations about the status of the project or some other project-related topic. These presentations are often formal. They frequently involve PowerPoint or Keynote, and the audience may include customers, vendors, senior managers, community groups, or others.

This form of communication is usually one way, though the presenter may respond to questions. While often designed to be informational, the project manager may have a personal agenda that includes generating support for the project.

Presentations are not always delivered to a live audience. Often, they are video recorded and uploaded to an internal server or a video service such as YouTube or Vimeo for later viewing.

These methods are most effective when integrated into an overall project communications strategy.

Frequency of Communication

Frequency has to do with how often project information is disseminated. Since good decision-making depends on the free flow of project information, all project stakeholders must have timely access to the information necessary to make informed decisions. It is the communication plan that outlines how this will happen.

Stakeholders decide what, how much, and how often information they want to receive project communications. The frequency, of course, depends on the type of information and the needs of the recipient. Typically, this will be once a week but may be more or less frequent depending on the pace of the project and the type of activity.

Regardless of the frequency, information must be timely. If the project manager does not keep stakeholders informed, they may be surprised and often upset when unexpected changes occur. Stakeholders need to be briefed in advance of a potential issue and updated as the issue is addressed. The status report should contain no surprises. Stakeholders do not want to learn about problems when it is too late to give input or help resolve them.

While the project communication plan is developed in the initiation and planning stages of the project and finalized in the planning stage, it is subject to continuous review and revision like all other planning documents. It is essential to review the communication plan whenever there is a change in stakeholder composition, status, etc., including events that may impact stakeholders.

Does every project require a communication plan? The answer is "Yes," but that does not mean the communications plan is always a formal written document. For smaller projects, much of what would go into a traditional communication plan can be discussed informally as a part of the stakeholder analysis and at initial meetings with team members. Effective project managers can balance the need for good project discipline with the need to respond quickly to changing project needs.

Summary

Managing the communication between stakeholders is one of the most critical aspects of the project manager's job. As a result, project managers spend up to 90% of their time communicating with the project team and other key stakeholders.

Successful project communication is getting the right information to the right people at the right time. This does not happen by chance; it is the result of careful project communications planning, starting with the communication plan.

The plan should include at a minimum what information is to be communicated, including format, content, level of detail, who will be responsible for communicating the information and who will receive the information, what methods will be used to communicate the information and the frequency of the communication.

COMMUNICATIONS PLANNING

Project managers have numerous options for communicating with team members and other stakeholders. These options can be categorized as text, audio, or audio/visual and realtime or non-realtime. Every method has its strengths and weaknesses. Meetings and phone calls are among the most frequently used real-time methods for communicating with stakeholders and e-mail is the most common of the non-real-time methods. The choice, of course, will depend on the stakeholder, the type of information, and the urgency of the situation.

9

RISK MANAGEMENT PLANNING

Introduction

Projects never go exactly as they are planned. Things happen. Goals and objectives are revised, resources are cut, new technologies are developed, and any number of other things—all potentially impacting the time, cost, and scope constraints of the project. We call these things "risk events." Managing risk is an essential part of the project manager's job. How well he or she addresses risk can greatly affect the project outcome and the customer's level of satisfaction with the result.

Risk planning is first formally addressed in the project charter, where high-level project risks are documented. Undertaking a project without understanding these risks is not a good business practice.

Note that this chapter is about risk management, not about minimizing or eliminating risk. Risk management is a comprehensive approach to utilizing project resources based on the project constraints and the risks associated with these constraints. Risk management makes it possible for the project manager to manage the project proactively, increasing the likelihood that the project will successfully achieve its goals and objectives.

What Is Risk?

The *PMBOK* (7th ed., p. 248) defines risk as "an uncertain event or condition that, if it occurs, has a positive or negative effect on one or more project objectives." There are two key concepts embedded in this definition. The first is the notion of uncertainty. Risk is about what might happen, not what will or will not happen.

The second is impact. If the risk event occurs, it will affect project goals and objectives. Not all uncertainties are risks. For example, the value of the yen may decline relative to the dollar, but it is not a risk unless it impacts project goals or objectives. Risk is about uncertainties that matter. If it does not matter, it is not a risk.

It is also important to note that risks are not just events but may also be situations or conditions that affect project goals and objectives. For example, a high level of inflation might impact a long-term project adversely. Inflation is a condition, not an event.

While it is true that most risks are negative, i.e., threats, some risks are positive; these are more aptly called "opportunities." For example, the launch of a new product may generate sales that exceed the company's ability to deliver. This is a good problem to have, but this situation is still a risk because it is an uncertain event that impacts the project. Effective project management requires that we manage both the positive and the negative risks. (For a good discussion of positive risks, see Bisson, August 2014.)

Risks are often confused with problems or issues. Although related, the two are distinctly different. Risks involve uncertainty. Problems are events that have already occurred or are certain to occur in the foreseeable future and, therefore, do not involve any degree of uncertainty. Every risk event is a potential problem, and every problem was at one time a risk, whether anyone recognized it as such or not.

Risk Planning

Good risk planning is an essential prerequisite to effective project management. Most organizations, however, lack an effective process to manage risks. In response to the continued high project failure rates, the International Standards Organization introduced the ISO 31000 Risk Management Guidelines. These guidelines were first published in 2009 and updated in 2018. ISO 31000 provides guidance to organizations on how to implement a risk management system.

A systematic approach to project risk management includes:

- Risk Identification
- Risk Documentation
- Risk Analysis and Prioritization
- Risk Response Planning

We will address each of these in the following sections.

Risk Identification

Risk identification is about identifying which risks may affect the project. There should be a systematic process for doing this, usually involving a review of the project charter, the project scope statement, the WBS, lessons learned from previous projects, and other relevant documents. Subject matter experts and people who have worked on similar projects can provide valuable information about risks the team might not otherwise have anticipated.

It is also important for all stakeholders to be involved in the risk-identification process. This process should include not only the sponsor but other stakeholders such as customers, end-users, and other relevant stakeholders. Working collaboratively, they are likely to produce a more comprehensive list than any of them could working individually.

All projects are subject to risk, and the number of potential risks is very large. The purpose of risk identification is to develop a list of important risk events or conditions. The identification process is not intended to identify every possible risk event, but the number of risks identified should be sufficiently large to include those of greatest importance.

When identifying project risks, it is sometimes helpful to focus on the types of risk to which projects are subject. Figure 11-4 of the *PMBOK* (6th ed., p. 406) lists four risk categories. These are:

1. Technical, Quality, and Performance Risk
These risks have to do with the technical aspects of project deliverables and the technologies used to produce them. Projects utilizing cutting-edge technologies are generally riskier than projects that use older, proven technologies. Is the technology capable of meeting project requirements? Is the technology capable of achieving the project's goals and objectives? Server crashes and software vulnerabilities are common technical risks.

2. Project Management Risk
These risks have to do with the management of the project. Project management risks include risks such as the failure to clearly define the goals and objectives of the project, the failure to communicate them to the stakeholders, the failure to appropriately staff the project team, and the failure to develop an effective implementation plan.

3. Organizational Risk
Organizational risks are those risks that are internal to the organization itself. For example, does the organization have a systematic process for managing projects? Do those assigned to the project have sufficient training and experience to accomplish their assigned work? Does the organization select projects that have a high probability of success? Does the organization adequately fund projects?

4. External Risk

External risks are those risks external to the organization. These include risks like weather, the regulatory environment, the marketplace, subcontractors, and suppliers. These are risks over which the project team generally has little if any control.

Risk Impacts

Another way to classify risks is by their impact (negative or positive) on the project constraints. From this perspective, risks could be classified as those that impact the scope, the schedule, the resources, and the quality of project deliverables.

Scope Risks

Scope risk events impact the scope of the project. Scope risks arise out of changes in scope, gaps between the project plan and customer requirements, and defects. The possibility that a customer may request an additional feature in a software project would be an example of a scope risk.

Schedule Risks

Risks that delay or accelerate the project schedule fall into this category. Schedule risks consist of delays, inaccurate estimates, and delays caused by dependence on other projects.

Delays constitute a significant schedule risk for many projects and are most likely to occur on the critical path because there is generally no slack to absorb late finishes. Delays are also common occurrences in convergence activities. If a convergence activity has three predecessors, it will start late unless all three finish on time.

Optimistic estimates of duration are another example of schedule risk.

Resource Risks

As the name implies, resource risks are those risks that impact the resources assigned to the project. Resource risk includes people, equipment, and supplies, as well as money. Common cost risks include rework, an increase in the cost of materials, and poor cost estimates, along with risks related to project staffing and personnel. The loss of project personnel is a common resource risk example.

Quality Risks

These are the risks that impact customer requirements. A deliverable that fails to meet the customers' requirements is likely to lead to customer dissatisfaction. Project management processes are also a source of risk, as is the lack of systematic procedures to accomplish project work.

Generating the Risk List

The easiest and most effective way to develop a list of project risks is to brainstorm with the project team members and other important stakeholders. Experience suggests, however, that most people who work on projects are not very good at brainstorming. Much of what passes for brainstorming is just discussion and analysis. For this reason, it may be helpful to review the rules of brainstorming with the stakeholders at the beginning of the session. For a good discussion of brainstorming and a list of brainstorming rules and guidelines, see *The Team Handbook* (Scholtes, Joiner and Streibel, 2018).

RISK MANAGEMENT PLANNING

Unfortunately, many teams have difficulty identifying more than a few risk events. The first few risks are easy because they are the most obvious. After these first few, it becomes increasingly difficult. It often helps to employ a technique called "Structured Brainstorming." Rather than trying to brainstorm a list of all risks, team members brainstorm risks within risk categories. For example, the team could brainstorm risks within the categories listed above, starting on page 190: technical, project management, organizational, and external. Alternatively, they could brainstorm by risk impact, i.e., scope, schedule, resources, and quality.

By brainstorming separately within each category, team members will generate a more comprehensive listing of project risk events than using a less-structured method. Using risk categories also helps the team focus their attention on potential issues they may not otherwise have thought about. It helps to avoid glaring omissions, though no process guarantees the team will identify every important risk.

Some risks may impact the entire project or a significant part of it. Structured brainstorming, as described above, should generate a significant number of project risks, but the use of this approach may miss some risks specific to individual work activities. A more granular approach is to review each work package in the WBS and ask, "What could go wrong here?" Using the WBS to guide the brainstorming session will generate a list of specific risk events. Unfortunately, this approach does not work so well for large projects in which the number of work packages may be in the thousands.

Brainstorming, when done right, can be a very effective tool for generating risk events. It has, however, one significant drawback: team members must be at the same place at the same time. Virtual teams, or teams that cannot physically meet, for whatever reason, cannot brainstorm in the traditional sense. They must use alternative methods.

One alternative is to use an online platform like Zoom. While it is not quite as effective as in-person brainstorming, some virtual teams have made it work for them.

Another alternative is the Delphi or Wideband Delphi technique discussed in Chapter 3. You can use this method for a variety of issues, including the development of the WBS, the estimation of activity durations, and the generation of risks. In this section, we will discuss this method in the context of risk event generation.

To begin the Delphi process, team members individually develop a list of risks and conditions. The project manager collects the list from each team member and combines them into a single list, eliminating duplicates. The project manager sends out the revised list to team members. The revised list does not indicate which risks came from which team members or stakeholders. It is entirely anonymous. Anonymity helps team members to judge the risk events on their merit, uninfluenced by who suggested them.

Each member reviews the first composite list and adds or subtracts from it. A second revised list is developed from these responses. The process is repeated until there is a consensus on the list of risk events. This generation process may take only two or three iterations, though it may take more for large, complex projects.

Organizations that have recurring projects often develop a risk profile for their projects. This profile is simply a list of appropriate questions you can use in the risk-identification process. These questions are usually grouped by risk type. Scope questions may include questions like, "Are the customer requirements clearly expressed?" Or, "Is there a consensus on what these requirements are?" The use of risk profiles speeds up the risk-identification process and helps ensure the team does not overlook common events or conditions.

So, how many risks constitute a sufficient listing? As a rough rule of thumb, it should contain no fewer than 20. In large, complex projects, it will probably be many more. Those ultimately deemed to pose the greatest threat to the project are often not among the first 10 to 20 risks on the list. Stopping the process with fewer than 20 risk events may therefore cause the team to fail to identify one or more risks that must be addressed if the project is to succeed.

Common Risk Identification Problems

Risks need to be specific. All too often, project teams generate risks that are too general. Weather, for example, might be a risk for many construction projects, but the appropriate response will depend on whether it is excessive heat, wind, rain, tornadoes, floods, or hurricanes. An effective mitigation response for rain would probably not be an effective strategy for a tornado. If it is difficult to determine an appropriate response plan of action, the risk might be too vague. Be more specific.

Another common mistake is to focus on symptoms rather than causes. For example, the team might identify scope creep as a project risk. To effectively address this problem, it is necessary to understand the cause. Is it unclear requirements? Is it constantly changing requirements? Is it a lack of consensus among key stakeholders? Whatever action the team takes, it must address the underlying causes, not the outward symptoms.

There are several tools available to help discover the underlying risks or root causes. One is the Ishikawa Method (sometimes called a fishbone diagram) and the 5 Whys Method. An online search will yield many websites with detailed information about these methods and how to use them.

Risk Documentation

Documentation is the next step in the development of the risk management plan. Risks are usually documented using what is called a risk register. The risk register is where the risks, the risk analysis, and risk response information are documented. A spreadsheet often serves as the register. The register is easy to set up in a spreadsheet program like Excel, and all of the calculations are done automatically using formulas. Data in a spreadsheet can be searched and sorted, making it easier to analyze and prioritize risks.

Some project managers use project management software programs to document project risks. Like most other project documents, it needs to be continuously reviewed and updated throughout the project.

The risk register should include the name of the risk, the risk's probability of occurrence, and the impact of the risk on the activity or the project as a whole. Figure 9.1 also contains the RPN (to be discussed shortly), schedule, and cost risk exposure (also to be discussed shortly), as well as the recommended course of action. The register sometimes includes the name of the person responsible for the activity associated with the risk.

Risk Analysis and Prioritization

Once you have completed the identification and documentation processes, it is necessary to analyze the risks and prioritize them. Organizations have limited time and resources, and the number of risks to which projects are subject is very large. For this reason, it is not possible to take action on all risks. It is important to analyze and prioritize them so the project team can focus its efforts on those risks expected to have the greatest impact on the project's success.

To successfully prioritize risk events, it is necessary to understand the three principal components of risk. These are:

- The event
- The probability that the event will occur
- The impact the event will have on the activity/project

The degree of risk is a function of the last two bullet points: the event's probability of occurrence and its impact on the project. Risk increases as probability and impact increase. High-risk events are those likely to occur and have the potential to significantly impact the goals and objectives of the project. Low-risk events are unlikely to occur and will have little or no impact on the project, even if they should occur.

Figure 9.1 | Risk Register

#	Risk Event	P	I	RPN	Cost Increase	CRE	Delay (Days)	SRE	Action	Cost	Residual
1											
2											
3											
4											
5											
6											
7											
8											
9											
10											
11											
12											
13											
14											
15											
16											
17											
18											
19											
20											
21											
22											
23											
24											
25											
26											
27											
28											
29											
30											
	Total					0.00		0.0			

Estimates of likelihood and impact must be made for each of the risks listed in the risk register. Determining risk probabilities and impact is often challenging. To develop accurate estimates, it is often helpful to review historical data, visit with subject matter experts, and consult whatever other relevant sources of information are available.

Techniques designed to assess risk fall into two categories: qualitative or quantitative risk analysis, examined more thoroughly below.

Qualitative Risk Analysis

Most qualitative risk assessment matrices use scales with three categories: "low," "medium," and "high," though some project managers prefer scales with five or more categories. Figure 9.2 is an example of a qualitative risk assessment chart. Every risk in the risk register is assigned a likelihood and an impact value.

Figure 9.2 | Qualitative Risk Analysis

	Impact			
		High	Medium	Low
Likelihood	High	■		
	Medium			
	Low			

The result is a rank ordering of project risks. Risks that fall into the High-High cell (shaded black) are the most significant risks and are the highest priority. These are the most significant highest priority risks—the ones most likely to occur and which would cause the most damage to the project. The project team must pay particular attention to these risks.

RISK MANAGEMENT PLANNING

The cells that are shaded gray include the medium-risk events. The project team will have to decide what, if anything, they are going to do to address these risks. Risks that fall into the un-shaded cells are a low priority and will probably not need to be addressed. They should, however, be put on a watch list and reviewed periodically. During the implementation of the project, some of these risks may become a greater threat, and the team will need to address them.

In addition to dividing risks into high, medium, and low categories, we can further divide them by risk category. It is clear from Figure 9.3 that there are more schedule risks than scope, cost, resources, or quality risks. If time is the driver for this project, schedule risk will have the highest priority. It has the largest number of high-risk threats and the largest number of overall threats. Risks to the project scope are second. Together they make up almost half of all the risks identified.

Figure 9.3 | Qualitative Risk Analysis Using Risk Categories

Category	High	Medium	Low	Total
Scope	3	7	12	22
Schedule	6	10	18	35
Cost	2	4	9	15
Resources	1	4	8	13
Quality	1	6	10	17
Total	13	31	57	101

Terms like "High," "Medium," and "Low" are rather subjective. To reduce subjectivity, you can assign a probability to each risk event based on its impact on the project constraints. Figure 9.4 is an example taken from the *PMBOK* (5th Ed., p. 318).

Qualitative risk analysis is relatively quick and easy. It provides a rank ordering of the project risks resulting in a prioritized list of threats to the project goals and objectives. It is best suited to smaller projects in which there are relatively few significant risks. Larger and more complex projects usually involve the use of quantitative risk analysis.

Quantitative Risk Analysis

A qualitative risk analysis produces an ordered list of project risks. Quantitative risk analysis goes a step or two beyond that. It assesses the impact of risk events or conditions on the goals and objectives of the project on a numeric scale.

A register like the one shown in Figure 9.1 serves as the basis for the analysis. The first step is to estimate the likelihood and the impact of each risk on a numeric scale, usually 1 to 99 (or 1 to 9 for likelihood and 1 to 10 for impact; it doesn't make much difference). Likelihood scores of 0 and 100 are not used since they indicate complete certainty and, therefore, no risk. Likelihood and impact estimates are multiplied together to get the RPN (Risk Probability Number). By sorting the risk events from high to low on the RPN column, risks will appear from highest to lowest.

Risk Triggers

An important part of risk management involves the identification of risk triggers. A trigger is something that indicates a risk event may be imminent. For example, if a vendor experiences sudden and severe financial difficulties or a sudden increase in employee turnover, it may foreshadow an inability to meet scheduled delivery deadlines. Not all risks or conditions will have triggers. Some risks can occur without warning, but a trigger will precede others. The risk management plan should include triggers for any high-risk events, if possible.

Figure 9.4 | Qualitative Risk Analysis Scales

Relative or Numerical Scales

Project Objective	Very Low .05	Low .10	Moderate .20	High .40	Very High .80
Cost	Insignificant cost increase	<10% cost increase	10-20% cost increase	20-40% cost increase	>40% cost increase
Schedule	Insignificant time increase	<5% time increase	5-10% time increase	10-20% time increase	>20% time increase
Scope	Scope increase barely noticeable	Minor areas of scope affected	Major areas of scope affected	Scope reduction unacceptable to sponsor	Project end item is effectively useless
Quality	Quality degradation barely noticeable	Only very demanding applications are affected	Quality reduction requires sponsor approval	Quality reduction unacceptable to sponsor	Project end item is effectively useless

Risk Exposure

Risk events are, by definition, uncertain. Some of the risk events or conditions documented in the risk register will occur, and others will not. The problem is that we do not know in advance which will occur and which will not. Risk exposure has to do with the expected cumulative impact of these risks on the project time and cost constraints. It is defined by the mathematical equations:

Cost risk exposure (CRE) = cost overrun x probability
Schedule risk exposure (SRE) = delay x probability

To calculate the cost risk exposure (CRE) for a risk event, multiply the probability that the event or condition will occur by the impact on the project. For example, if a server failure has a 20% probability of occurrence, and the cost of a server failure is $20,000, then the cost risk exposure would be $4,000 ($20,000 x 20%). The total-cost risk exposure for the project is calculated by summing the cost risk exposure estimate for each risk event in the register. The total estimated cost of the entire project is equal to the estimated cost of the work identified in the WBS plus the cost risk exposure (i.e., the cost of the work not identified in the WBS).

To cover the project's cost, the project budget should include the cost of the work identified in the WBS, plus a contingency fund equal to the cost risk exposure.

The schedule risk exposure is calculated just like the cost risk exposure. The delay in the project schedule caused by the risk event is multiplied by the probability of occurrence. If there is a 20% chance that the server will fail, and the failure will delay the project for five days, then the schedule risk exposure for this risk would be one day (5 days x 20%). The schedule risk exposure is the sum of the schedule risk for all of the risks listed in the register.

The total estimated duration of the project is equal to the time it takes to complete the scheduled work (i.e., the estimated duration of the work identified in the WBS) plus the schedule risk exposure (i.e., the estimated duration of the work not identified in the WBS).

Although many projects fail to finish on time because of poor estimates of activity durations, a more significant reason is that project managers do not include the schedule risk exposure in their timelines. They do a moderately good job of estimating the duration of the planned work but fail to include the unplanned work.

We noted earlier in our discussion of padding (see page 129) that one solution to the schedule estimation problem is to add a buffer at the end of the project. The general rule of thumb is that the size of the buffer should be equal to 10 to 15 percent of the duration of the project. Schedule risk exposure provides a more accurate estimate of the size of the buffer necessary to protect the project schedule from unexpected events that inevitably cause them to miss their planned completion dates. The buffer should be equal to or greater than the schedule risk exposure. This is the best approach to creating a buffer because the buffer size is tied to the degree of risk: the riskier the project, the larger the buffer.

Risk Response Planning

One of the questions most frequently asked in discussions of project risk management has to do with how to respond to the risks identified in the risk analysis. Unfortunately, there is no simple answer. The reason is that different organizations have different levels of risk tolerance. Some organizations are willing to accept considerable risk, while others are much more risk averse.

Risk response planning enables the project manager to manage projects proactively by preparing for risk events in one of the following ways. Negative risks can be avoided, mitigated, transferred, or accepted. Positive risks, also called opportunities, can be exploited, shared, enhanced, or accepted. Let's look at each of these: mitigation, transference, and acceptance.

Mitigation

Mitigation refers to actions taken to reduce the probability of risk events and their impact on project goals and objectives. In a complex IT project, for example, working with a new vendor may increase project risk. This risk might impact the cost, schedule, or quality of the project deliverable. To mitigate this risk, the organization might contract with an experienced vendor who has performed well on previous projects of a similar nature. Working with an experienced vendor, however, might increase the cost of the project. Together with the sponsor or the customer, the project manager will have to decide if the decrease in risk is worth the additional cost.

Figure 9.5 | Risk Response Categories

Negative Risks (Threats)	Positive Risks (Opportunities)
Mitigate	Exploit
Avoid	Enhance
Transfer	Share
Accept	Accept

One of the most common schedule risk-mitigation strategies is to pad the project by adding time and resources. Padding is supposed to protect the schedule from risks that threaten to cause delays in the project. As we saw earlier, this is not an effective mitigation strategy because it does not increase the likelihood of completing the work on time.

While many project managers tend to favor mitigation, David Hillson points out that ". . . there's a relationship between risk and reward. If we mitigate all the risk out of the project, we're certain to remove some of the potential benefits." (*PM Network*, July 2004, p.

37) Therefore, proposed mitigation efforts should be subjected to cost-benefit analysis before a decision is made to proceed.

There is, however, a limit to the number of risks that you can mitigate. Mitigation expenses add to the project's cost, and with limited resources, organizations can generally only develop plans to address the most serious risks.

Avoidance

Risk avoidance strategies involve actions designed to avoid the risk, eliminate the cause of the risk, or revise the plan so the risk event is no longer a threat to the project.

Using proven technologies, standard designs, and methodologies, contracting out highly specialized work, and upgrading old and outdated equipment are a few examples of risk avoidance strategies.

Avoidance can be a good strategy because it completely removes the threat to the project. In some cases, it may not be feasible. Some other forms of risk response, such as mitigation or transference, must be considered in such instances.

Transference

Transference is a risk-management strategy that transfers the risk and its consequences to a third party. Insurance is the most common example of risk transference, where the insurer is paid to assume the risk. The organization trades a smaller known cost for a higher uncertain cost.

Charitable organizations, for example, often sponsor golf tournaments to raise funds to support their work. To attract players, many of them offer a significant cash prize for hitting a hole-in-one. In most cases, the value of the prize is greater than the organization's ability to pay. One solution is to transfer the risk by purchasing insurance. Yes, there are companies that specialize in hole-in-one insurance! One such company advertises on its website that it has provided coverage for over 300,000 hole-in-one events, putting contests, shootout competitions, and other prize promotions paying out over $40,000,000 in cash and prizes.

Contracting is another form of transference. Organizations often subcontract very specialized work to an organization with experience and expertise in the field.

Other examples of risk transference include guarantees and warranties. It is important to remember that transference, like mitigation, comes at a price, and that price must be built into the project's total cost.

Some risks cannot be transferred. Many construction projects, for example, are inherently dangerous. While construction companies are usually well insured, insurance does not replace the need to take appropriate safety precautions in the workplace or absolve them from ultimate responsibility for workplace accidents.

Acceptance

Based on a thorough analysis of project risks, the project manager or the project sponsor may decide to accept the risk, i.e., not to take any action to mitigate, transfer, or avoid the risk event. Acceptance happens most often when both the probability and the impact of the risk event are low. A project manager in Kansas, for example, is probably willing to accept the risk of a hurricane and would therefore not take any action to mitigate, transfer, or avoid the risk of such an event.

Pretending that a risk does not exist is not the same as accepting it. Acceptance is a conscious decision on the part of the project manager and key stakeholders based on an analysis of project risk factors. On the other hand, ignoring risk is a conscious or unconscious decision to do nothing without analyzing the risk's probability of occurrence or its impact on the project. Accepting risk is often the best course of action. Ignoring risk is rarely the best course of action.

Opportunity Response Strategies

Exploit

This action helps to ensure the organization can capitalize on the opportunity. It could include expanding the project's scope, increasing the project budget, or any number of other actions that would increase the likelihood of realizing the opportunity. In a sense, it is the opposite of avoidance. Organizations generally seek to avoid negative risks and exploit positive ones.

Share

These are actions taken to share the benefits of the project. For example, contracts with vendors often contain incentives to share the benefits of improved performance.

Enhance

Mitigation is an action taken to minimize the impact of negative risks. Enhance responses are actions taken to maximize the impact of a positive risk event. From this perspective, enhance is the opposite of mitigate. Speeding up construction during a period of good weather would be an example of enhancement.

Accept

Like risk acceptance, the organization accepts the project's benefits but takes no action to exploit, share or enhance it.

Selecting a Risk Response Action

Do we mitigate, avoid, transfer, or accept a negative risk event? There is no simple answer to this question. It depends on several factors. First, how many significant risks are there? With limited time and resources, most organizations can only mitigate, avoid, or transfer a small number of risks and must therefore accept many, if not most, risks.

Probably the most important factor is the project budget. Mitigation, avoidance, and transference are not free. Since project budgets tend to be very lean these days, there are usually little or no funds available to cover the costs of mitigation, avoidance, or transference.

The last factor is the organization's risk appetite. How much risk is the organization willing to accept? The willingness to accept risk is called "risk appetite." The *PMBOK* (7th ed., p. 248) defines risk appetite as "the degree of uncertainty an organization or individual is willing to accept in anticipation of a reward." Some organizations, non profits, and government agencies, for example, generally have a low appetite for risk, while businesses, and start-ups, in particular, have a much greater risk appetite. Organizations with a low-risk appetite will mitigate, avoid, or transfer much more risk than those with a higher-risk appetite.

Inherent Risk vs. Residual Risk

The discussion of risk up to this point has focused on what is called "inherent risk." Inherent risk is the risk identified using the methods described in the previous sections of this chapter. It is sometimes referred to as raw risk.

Residual risk is the risk that is left over after actions, if any, have been taken to address the risk (mitigation, avoidance, or transference). The residual risk plus the cost of addressing the risk should be less than the inherent risk.

RISK MANAGEMENT PLANNING

Risk of the Project as Opposed to the Project Risks

Activities identified as high risk should be scheduled early in the project if at all possible. While this may seem counterintuitive, it makes good sense. High-risk activities have a high probability of failure. When failures occur early in the project, there are more resources available to deal with them. Scheduling risky activities late in the project when there is little time left, and few remaining resources, increases the probability of project failure.

Risk management does not end with the risk management plan; it is ongoing throughout the life of the project. During the implementation of the project plan, some risks will fail to materialize, and new risks will undoubtedly emerge. The point is that risk management starts with the project's initiation and continues throughout the life of the project.

Most organizations, perhaps as many as 90% or more, do little or no project risk planning. The problem is that addressing risk takes time and costs money. Since projects tend to have short deadlines, there is little time to do more than is absolutely necessary. For many organizations, risk management consists of nothing more than going through the motions of documenting risks. Many organizations don't even make a pretense of risk management.

Virtually all project plans should include a risk-management component. In small, short-term projects, risk planning will be minimal, but in larger, longer-term projects, a more detailed risk management plan is essential.

The level of risk varies throughout the life of the project. Risk is highest in the initiation and planning stages and lowest in the later stages. As the project progresses, there are simply fewer activities left to go wrong.

Figure 9.6 | Workarounds

The PMBOK (6th ed.) defines a workaround as a response to a threat that has occurred, for which a prior response had not been planned or was not effective.

The impact of risk events also varies with the life of the project. The impact, however, is greatest in the later stages of the project when most of the project resources have been consumed, and there is less time left to make adjustments. According to an old saying, "The sooner you get behind, the more time you have to catch up." Unfortunately, it also means more time to get further behind.

In the absence of risk planning, the project team must depend on workarounds when risk events occur. For example, when a machine breaks down unexpectedly, you must repair it as quickly as possible. If this work has not been planned and no resources have been set aside to ensure that it gets done, the team must find a workaround. Diverting resources from other projects or activities may well delay other work.

Summary

All projects are subject to some risk. Successful project management, therefore, requires some degree of risk management. The concept of risk was first addressed in the initiation stage. High-level risk identification takes place in the development of the project charter. More detailed risk planning, if warranted, takes place in the planning stage of the project.

Risk is about uncertainty and deals with events that, if they were to occur, would impact the project. The project manager must be particularly concerned with those risks that could significantly negatively impact the project.

RISK MANAGEMENT PLANNING

Managing risk involves identifying, documenting, analyzing, and prioritizing risks. Risks are generally identified by the project team, who brainstorm a list of potential risks. These risks are recorded in the risk register, usually an Excel spreadsheet.

The risks that have been identified are then analyzed using qualitative or quantitative methods of analysis. Qualitative methods are more commonly used in smaller projects, while quantitative methods are used predominantly in larger projects.

The project team must then develop a response strategy for each risk event. Strategies could include mitigation, avoidance, transference, or acceptance. For most risk events, acceptance is the most cost-effective strategy.

Most organizations do little or no risk-management planning. They simply develop workarounds when things go wrong.

While risk is first addressed in the early stages of the project, project managers must be concerned about risk throughout the project life cycle.

CHANGE MANAGEMENT PLANNING

Introduction

No project ever goes exactly as planned. Therefore, the project manager and the team members must be alert to changes and the need to adapt to change.

Dealing with project change is one of the biggest challenges project managers face. It is an ongoing challenge since change happens constantly throughout the life of the project. Despite this, many, if not most, project managers tend to resist change, as change represents uncertainty, risk, and potential failure. By signing the project charter, the project manager has committed to producing a set of deliverables within a given time frame. Project managers often consider change an obstacle to fulfilling this obligation and, therefore, an obstacle to successfully completing the project. Many project managers spend much of their time and energy protecting the plan against attempts to change it.

Resisting changes is not a productive approach to project management. First, change is inevitable, and second, changes to the project scope, timeline, and resources are often necessary to ensure a desirable outcome. Not only do events often necessitate changes, but there are, throughout the life of the project, constant political pressures to expand the scope of the project and decrease the resources assigned to the project. Even with a well-designed change-management process, dealing with change can be difficult.

However, a systematic change management process can make it a little easier to deal with change. One of the most important advantages of a formal change management process is that it helps to protect the project from unnecessary changes. By ensuring that proposed changes are considered systematically, proposed changes are more likely to be carefully considered and more likely to be accepted by stakeholders as necessary.

No project is planned and executed in a vacuum; each is carried out at a specific time in a specific place. The characteristics of this environment impact the project, how it is planned, and how it is managed. The project environment is not static, however. Because the environment is continuously changing, the project team must be ready to adapt, i.e., make the necessary changes in the project to ensure its success.

For this reason, it is important to develop a plan describing how change is initiated, who is authorized to approve changes, what processes will be used to accept or reject changes, and how approved changes will be implemented and communicated. This plan is a component of the overall project plan.

In many organizations, the change management process is not specific to the project but is a part of their project management protocols. The flowchart in Figure 10.1 shows a typical change management process. There are four steps to this process:

- Identifying environmental changes that impact or have the potential to impact the project
- Identifying and evaluating proposed project changes
- Approving and implementing project changes
- Communicating project changes

Identifying Environmental Changes

Projects are designed to achieve a goal or set of goals within a specific time and place. The characteristics of this environment impact the design and implementation of the project, including many environmental factors that potentially affect a project. These include political, legal, cultural, technological, economic and financial, external environmental, institutional, infrastructure, and internal factors.

Political Factors

The political environment is shaped by government policies and the effect of those policies on the marketplace. Political instability and shifting government policies make managing projects more difficult. For example, a change in zoning laws could greatly affect a project that is designed to develop a property for commercial use.

Legal Factors

The legal environment consists of employment, health and safety laws, and government rules and regulations. For example, the construction industry has to deal with planning and environmental regulations, safety regulations, licensing, insurance, and taxation laws. These are generally well-defined, making it possible to predict their impact with a reasonable degree of accuracy. Problems may arise, however, when laws change during the life of a project.

Cultural Factors

Cultural norms differ by age, gender, race, and ethnicity, and can all impact a project in various ways. Cultural differences can make project management challenging. Crime and corruption may also have a significant impact on projects and how they are managed. Other factors may include:

- Cultural norms and expectations
- Population demographics (e.g., age, gender, mobility, etc.)
- Population's general attitude towards certain issues (e.g., health, environment, etc.)

Technological Factors

Changes in technology can and do have an impact on the management of projects. New technologies that replace existing technologies may impact the project's execution and render the project irrelevant or unnecessary. For example, a new technology could reduce the need for resources and the time needed to complete the project.

Economic and Financial Factors

There are a large number of economic and financial factors that can impact projects. These include:

- Wages
- Taxes
- Interest rates
- State of the economy
- Funding for the project

For long-term and international projects, additional factors must be considered. These include:

- Import and export taxes
- Inflation rate
- Exchange rate
- Supply chain

External Environmental Factors

These include factors such as weather, climate, geographical location, and natural disasters—all posing special challenges to projects, construction projects in particular.

Institutional Factors

Successful project management also depends on understanding and addressing institutional factors such as organizational expertise, staffing levels, and established project management protocols.

Infrastructure Factors

The physical environment within which the project is carried out plays an important role in the decisions made about the design and execution of the project. The geographical location, ground conditions, and weather patterns are the most common examples of physical influences. Some types of projects are more impacted by infrastructure factors than others.

Internal Factors

Not all environmental factors that impact the project are external to the project. Some internal factors are:

- Time, cost, and scope estimates
- Problems or opportunities that arise during the project
- Customer or sponsor requests
- Sponsor/customer priorities
- The project team
- End-user requirements

Projects are designed and implemented in the context of these environmental factors. Changes in any of these factors may impact the project positively or negatively. For this reason, the project team must be alert to these factors and how they might affect the project, as well as how to adapt the project to ensure they can successfully complete the project.

Potential risks should be a standing item on the agenda of all project team meetings.

Identifying and Evaluating Proposed Project Changes

If the project manager does not believe an environmental change constitutes a threat to the project, no further action is required, though the team might want to monitor it to ensure it does not become a threat.

Suppose the team determines that an environmental change might threaten the project, in which case, it must be added to the risk register, analyzed, and prioritized using a process like the one depicted in Figure 10.1. A formal change-management process like this involves a thorough investigation and analysis of change impacts. This includes discussing the implications of the change for the project scope, resources, timeline, and cost.

After completing its analysis, the team must decide what action to take. If they decide to accept the risk, no further action is needed. Otherwise, the team must develop a response to the threat or opportunity. If the response does not impact the Triple Constraints, many organizations will allow the project team to implement the response without submitting a change request. Otherwise, they must submit a change order request to the approving authority.

Figure 10.1 | Responding to Environmental Changes

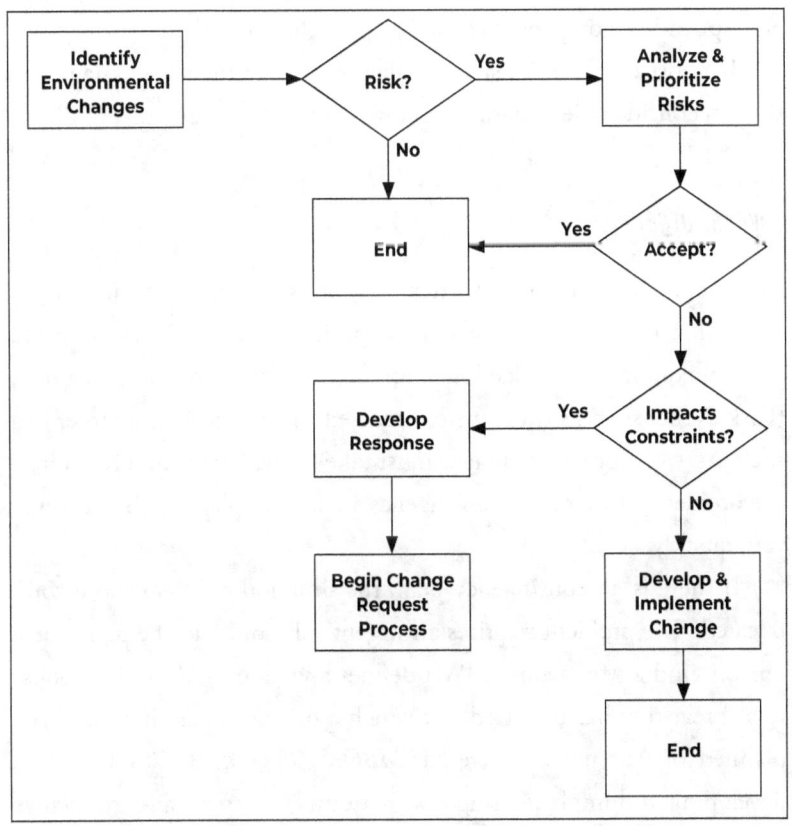

In project management, change orders are also called variations or variation orders. Any modification or change to work specified in the contract, charter, or WBS is treated as a variation. These modifications fall into three main categories:

1. Addition to the work specified in the agreement
2. Omission to work specified in the agreement
3. Substitution or alteration to work specified in the agreement

Change orders are routine, particularly for large, long-term projects. The change order request form provides the information necessary for the approving authorities to make a reasoned decision on the proposed change. It describes the proposed change and why it is necessary. See Appendix F on page 447 for a sample change-order form.

In most organizations, any stakeholder may request changes, but there is considerable variation in how these requests are processed.

Level of Urgency

In the course of the project, there may be situations in which events occur that immediately threaten the project's success. For example, a piece of equipment breaks down, forcing the project to come to a halt. (Risk events such as these were discussed in the previous chapter.) In such cases, the project manager must take immediate action to address the problem. If there is a contingency plan, that plan can be executed very quickly.

If there is no contingency plan, the situation becomes more complicated. The problem requires an urgent solution, and the team must quickly find a workaround. PMI defines a workaround as "A response to a threat that has occurred, for which a prior response had not been planned or was not effective." (*PMBOK*, 5th ed., p 576) However, developing and implementing a workaround, using a standard change management process, would be too slow and cumbersome. For this reason, many organizations have an emergency change order process, making it possible to approve project changes quickly when the situation requires it.

Verifying the Availability of Funds

Project changes almost always add to the cost of the project. If the organization has a detailed risk-management plan, there should be a contingency fund to cover the expected risks. Otherwise, these costs have probably not been factored into the project budget. For this reason, many organizations require the initiator to determine the cost of the change and whether there is a contingency fund sufficient to cover it.

Approving and Implementing Change

Before the team can implement a change, it must be approved by those charged with approving project changes. Generally, the project sponsor or the PMO is the approving authority. For external projects, it is usually an authorized representative of the client's organization.

Some organizations have a change control board (CCB) that controls project changes, generally made up of subject-matter experts within the organization, though occasionally it will include others. Including a customer representative on the CCB, for example, may help to ensure that proposed changes do not negatively impact project acceptance.

Analyze the Impact

A typical change-order approval process is shown in Figure 10.2. This is a high-level schematic of a typical change-approval process. The first step in the authorization process is to analyze the impact of the proposed change or changes to the project. The initiator of the change request must also ensure that these changes are understood and accepted by the key stakeholders.

This analysis should focus on how the proposed changes will affect the Triple Constraints: time, cost, and scope. If none of these constraints are affected, the approving authorities can often make a decision without further delay. If, on the other hand, the proposed change affects one or more of the Triple Constraints, the approving authorities must weigh the benefits of the changes against the cost of not making them. The approving authority will use this information to determine the ultimate disposition of the change request.

Accept or Reject Proposed Changes

Approving authorities have several options. These include

- Approve
- Conditionally approve
- Approve with delay
- Reject

The first option is to accept the change. At this point, the project manager is authorized to begin the implementation of the proposed change. It then serves to modify the work agreement and is considered an integral part of the project plan. This information is then communicated to key stakeholders.

A second option is to accept the proposed change subject to specified modifications. The approving authority may require certain modifications to the proposed change as a condition of approval. These are spelled out in the change-order request and sent back to the initiator. Presumably, the request will be approved when the team has made the necessary modifications.

A third option is to accept the proposed change subject to a delay in the implementation. For example, the approving authority might approve the change subject to the availability of funds.

Lastly, the approving authority can reject the proposed change. In such cases, the initiator can look for an alternative course of action or continue with the planned work activities as scheduled. In either case, the proposed change is no longer under consideration.

All change-order requests must be entered into the change control log, regardless of their ultimate disposition. Entering them into the log helps maintain a clear and accurate record of proposed changes and the actions taken, if any, to address them. The failure to maintain an accurate change log can lead to confusion, making project execution more difficult. The change log also helps ensure that proposed changes are understood by the key stakeholders and communicated clearly to them.

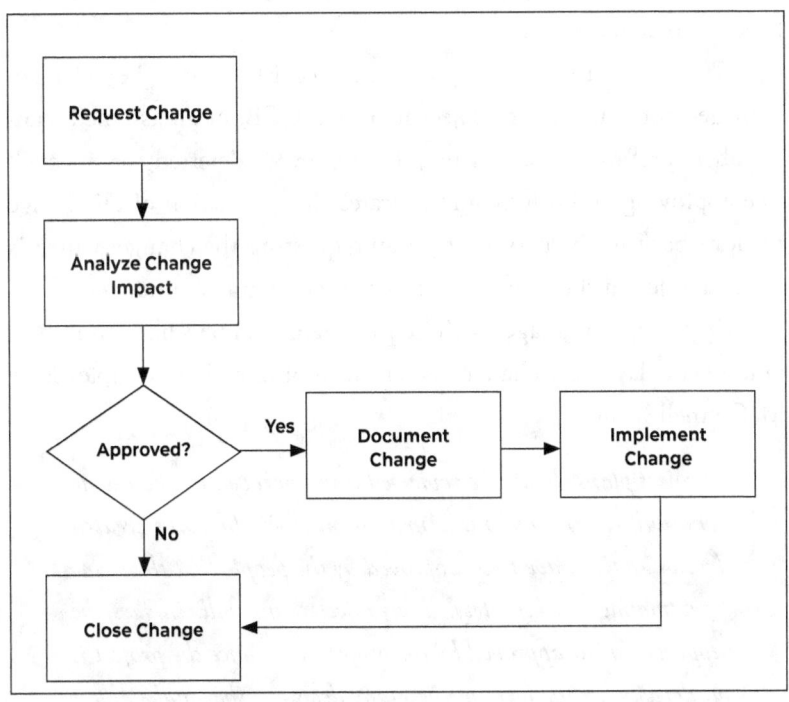

Figure 10.2 | Change Order Approval Process

Another advantage of a formal process is that it helps to control change. There is an old saying in the project management community that "If project content is allowed to change freely, the rate of change will exceed the rate of progress." A formal process will facilitate necessary changes while minimizing unnecessary changes.

A formal change-management process also helps to increase buy-in by involving all project stakeholders in the change process. While stakeholders will not agree with all proposed changes, they are more likely to accept and support proposed changes when they are involved in the approval process.

The analysis of the proposed change and its impact on the project should help determine if the proposed change needs to be made. Many change orders are routinely approved. The approving authority reviews the change order. They may ask for more detail or clarifications before taking action on the request. Many are straightforward and require little or no deliberation.

Change requests are processed according to the change-management plan by the project manager, CCB, or an assigned team member. Proposed changes may be approved, deferred, or rejected. The approving authority communicates the disposition of all change requests back to the person or group requesting the change, which is then recorded in the change log as a project-document update.

Most project managers believe that team members have an important role to play in the change management process. For example, Steve McConnell wrote:

> *"Project plans should be reviewed and approved by the people who will carry them out. Am I serious that the plans created by a manager have to be approved by the people that the manager manages? Absolutely. The project plans will, in fact, be approved or disapproved by the project team once the project is underway, in the form of the many decisions they make about how to follow the plans and whether to follow them. If the project team doesn't approve of the project plans, the plans will not in fact be followed." (McConnell, 1998, p. 91)*

Unfortunately, not all organizations involve project team members in the change process to the extent that best practices suggest they should.

Document Approved Changes

When a project change is approved, the project manager must ensure that the change log is updated to reflect the change, or that it was approved as amended and the request closed. Then all project plans must be updated to reflect the approved change. There have been many examples of project teams executing outdated plans. It seldom turns out well.

Increasingly, project managers are using computers, tablets, and smartphones in place of hard copy logs. Online databases are also replacing hard copy logs for issues, risks, and assumptions as well as change orders.

Implement Approved Changes

The approval of the change order authorizes the team to make the approved changes in the project plan and other related documents. If the change-order request petitions the approving authority to implement an existing contingency plan, the implementation is usually rather straightforward.

If, on the other hand, there is no contingency plan, the team must develop a plan to resolve the issue. That plan serves as the basis for the change request. If the issue needs immediate attention, the team must develop a workaround.

Communicating Project Changes

Complex, long-term projects are often subject to frequent changes; for these types of projects, a good change-management plan is particularly important. Perhaps the biggest challenge is to keep everyone on the same page. To do this, the plan should mandate that all significant changes are communicated promptly to all appropriate stakeholders using agreed-upon communications channels. These issues are first addressed in the stakeholder analysis and formalized in the communications plan.

It should be clear what aspects of the project are being changed. For example, when changing the schedule, new timelines should be sent out to all appropriate stakeholders. It is also a good idea to highlight the changes. It may not be readily apparent what activity deadlines have changed or what resource assignments have been revised. The project manager should specifically communicate the changes to ensure that team members and other stakeholders do not overlook them.

Changing Goals and Objectives

While the change-management process helps manage changes to the work plan, project goals and objectives should also be subject to the same change control procedures. It is difficult to manage a project when the goals and objectives are constantly shifting.

Constant changes in goals and objectives are most likely to occur in projects with multiple stakeholders with divergent views. The project manager needs to make sure stakeholders understand the impact that changing goals and objectives have on the project time, cost, and scope. Stakeholders are much more likely to suggest changes when they do not understand how they impact the project.

Summary

No project is ever completed exactly as planned. Change is inevitable. Changes to the project are inevitable. Many changes are also desirable since they help keep the project relevant. Changes result from the fact that projects are carried out in an environment that is constantly in flux; projects must adapt to these changes or risk failure. A change-management process aims to make necessary changes as easy as possible and unnecessary changes as difficult as possible.

A typical change-management protocol includes identifying environmental changes and evaluating their potential impact on the

CHANGE MANAGEMENT PLANNING

project. The project manager working with key stakeholders needs to evaluate those changes that have been identified as possible risks. If he or she decides to mitigate, avoid, or transfer the risk, a change order must be developed and submitted to the approving authority. Information about approved changes must be entered into the change log and disseminated to the project stakeholders.

QUALITY MANAGEMENT PLANNING

Introduction

There are number of reasons why projects fail, a major one being, as noted earlier, that they fail to satisfy the customer. Perhaps they did not finish on time, they went over budget, or they did not accomplish the required scope of work. Whatever the details, failure to satisfy the customer is a *quality* issue.

Because quality is so important, some project managers consider it to be a fourth constraint. In other words, the project is constrained not only by the Triple Constraints, i.e., time, cost, and scope, but also by quality. Whether you consider it a universal constraint like time, cost, and scope, it is an important constraint.

The Concept of Quality

Quality is a concept that many project managers do not understand very well. Many project stakeholders do not understand this concept very well either. To be fair, the term "quality" has been used in so many different ways that it is hard to know exactly what it means in any given context.

In recent years, two definitions of quality have predominated. One is "freedom from deficiencies," and the other is "fitness for use." The first gained prominence in the late seventies in Philip Crosby's book *Quality Is Free* (Crosby, 1979), in which he outlined his "zero defects" approach to quality.

The zero defects approach views quality as the absence of defects. Every product or service (project deliverable) has a set of specifications presumably based on customer requirements. Quality is the result of meeting those specifications; failing to meet them results in a defect. Quality is, therefore, a matter of producing products and services that conform to specifications, i.e., that are defect-free. The *PMBOK* appears to take this approach to quality. It defines quality as "the degree to which a set of inherent characteristics fulfills the requirements." (*PMBOK*, 7th ed., p. 47)

J.M. Juran, one of the major "quality" figures of the 20th century, had an alternate perspective on quality. Juran defined quality in terms of fitness for use (Juran, 1989). In other words, quality is measured by how well a product or service fulfills its intended use. From this perspective, a small sports car would not be a high-quality car for a soccer mom with four children, even if it were defect-free.

These two perspectives are not as different as they would at first appear. While Crosby focused on eliminating defects and Juran focused on user requirements, quality depends on meeting specifications (zero defects) based on user requirements (fitness for use).

Quality, regardless of how you define it, is critical to project success. A project that fails to meet customer requirements or does not fulfill its intended purpose is unlikely to satisfy the customer. Customer satisfaction is important because it is the primary determinant of project success, as we noted earlier. Customer satisfaction, however, does not happen by accident. It requires a good quality management plan supported by a disciplined effort by the project manager, the project team, and other key stakeholders.

The Quality Management Plan

The quality management plan is a component of the project management plan. It helps to ensure that the project deliverables meet the customer's requirements as described in the project charter and any other documents used to define the project's scope. In other words, it is about the customer's specifications and how the project team will ensure that the project deliverables meet them. Managing the project to meet customer specifications requires three processes:

- quality planning
- quality assurance
- quality control activities.

Quality planning is addressed in the following section. Quality assurance and quality control are addressed in Chapter 13.

Quality Planning

Juran identified five components of quality planning in his book *Juran on Leadership for Quality* (Juran, 1989). These are:

1. Determine who the customers are.
2. Determine the needs of the customer.
3. Develop product features that respond to the needs of the customers.
4. Develop processes that can produce those product features.
5. Transfer the resulting plans to the operating forces. (Juran, 1989, p. 20)

Each of these is discussed in the following sections.

1. **Who are the customers?**
   The first step in project quality planning is to identify the project customers. The *PMBOK* does not define the term

"customer," but, according to one dictionary, a customer is "a person or organization that buys goods or services from a store or business." In short, without customers, there are no projects. While this definition may be satisfactory for some purposes, it is too limiting for discussions of project quality.

First, a transaction does not have to involve an exchange of money to have customers. While projects designed to produce deliverables for external customers usually involve an exchange of money or other things of value, projects for internal customers often do not. For example, an IT department may develop software for the human resources department. The project is a budgeted expense, so there is no direct exchange between the IT department and the customer, i.e., the Human Resources department.

Second, some customers never receive the project deliverable(s). For example, a marketing director may purchase software for use by the analysts within his or her department. In this situation, the marketing manager purchased the software, but it is the analysts who are the actual recipients of the product. In these situations, it is customary to distinguish between the customer and the end user though both are, in fact, customers.

The Baldrige Criteria provides a more useful definition. The 2023-2024 Baldrige Criteria for Performance Excellence defines the customer as the ". . . actual and potential users of your organization's products, programs, or services . . . Customers include the end users of your products, as well as others who might be their immediate purchasers or users. These others might include distributors, agents, or organizations that further process your product as a component of their product." (NIST, p. 45)

For our purposes, a customer is a person or group of persons for whom the project has been undertaken. This definition

QUALITY MANAGEMENT PLANNING

includes purchasers as well as end users. It is also important to recognize that, just as projects may, and often do, have multiple stakeholders, they often have multiple customers as well.

Because projects can and often do have multiple customers, it is important to prioritize customers and customer groups, which is important because not all customers are equal.

Normally we differentiate between key customers and other customers. The project impacts all customers, but key customers often have the power to impact the project. They play a major role in its success or failure.

2. **Determine the Needs of the Customer**

   The project management team must translate the customers' needs into project requirements. Failure to satisfy project requirements means the project may not meet the customer's needs, causing the project to fail.

   Customer and other stakeholder requirements are normally determined in the early stages of the project as a part of the stakeholder analysis. (The stakeholder analysis is discussed in some detail in Chapter 2.) The "Must Do" and "Must Not Do" columns of the stakeholder register in Figure 2.6 on page 38 constitute the most critical stakeholders' requirements.

   In theory, identifying customer requirements is relatively easy. In practice, it sometimes turns out to be quite difficult. The problem is that stakeholders often do not have a clear conception of what they want the project to accomplish. Ambiguous expectations must be clarified. Without clear objectives, it is difficult to produce deliverables that meet customer requirements and impossible to measure the success of the project.

   It is also common to find that stakeholders have conflicting requirements. The project team must reconcile these conflicting requirements; failure to do so often leads to conflict over the project's scope contributing to delays and cost overruns.

Unfortunately, clarifying goals and resolving conflicts between stakeholder requirements are not the only obstacles the project manager may have to deal with. For example, the cost of meeting customer requirements may exceed the project budget. Or, the time it takes to meet the requirements may stretch the project timeline beyond its required completion date. In such cases, the project manager must prioritize requirements and decide which can be met and which cannot. This will undoubtedly involve a renegotiation of the project requirements with relevant stakeholders.

3. **Develop product features that respond to the needs of the customers.**

    Another problem is that customer requirements often reflect what the customer *wants* rather than what the customer *needs*. Most projects are created to solve a problem. It is not uncommon for the customer to request a solution without understanding the nature of that problem. This creates a dilemma for the project manager: do what the customer wants or do what the customer needs.

    The solution usually involves discussing the problem with the customer and negotiating a solution acceptable to all stakeholders. Failure to resolve this issue will almost certainly cause the project to fail.

4. **Develop processes capable of producing the required product features.**

    Knowing customer requirements is important, and creating project deliverables that meet these requirements is critical. The primary purpose of project quality planning is to ensure that the project produces a deliverable(s) that satisfies the customer.

    The WBS is, in fact, the document that lists the activities needed to meet customer requirements. In theory, completing these activities will result in the customer's satisfaction with the project deliverables. This assumes, of course, that the WBS includes all the necessary work with appropriate standards for each activity, and that the work meets the standard. Unfortunately, these assumptions are frequently not met. (The best way to develop a WBS that includes all necessary work is to use the methods discussed in Chapter 4.) While these methods do not ensure a complete enumeration of the work necessary to meet customer requirements, experience has shown that they minimize the likelihood that necessary activities will be overlooked.

The next step is to determine performance standards for each activity. The customer determines these standards, though the team may supplement them with external requirements such as building codes, environmental regulations, and company policies. When the work has been completed to standard, the activity has been successfully completed.

These standards must be specific and measurable. If, for example, we are planning a conference, it would be necessary to secure a venue for the event. The standard for this activity might be a signed contract for a venue with four breakout rooms and a common area capable of seating 75 people. When the contract has been signed with a venue that meets these requirements, the activity has been successfully completed. These standards/requirements make up the project performance metrics.

The project manager must determine how to ensure that all completed activities meet or exceed customer requirements. This process involves an additional set of quality control activities, which might include audits, reviews, and testing. The completed WBS must include these quality control activities. Including them in the WBS helps to ensure they will be incorporated into the project plan.

5. **Transfer the resulting plans to the operating forces.**
   This final step of the quality planning process is to transition the project to an ongoing operation, a process that is beyond

the scope of most projects. The acceptance of the deliverable normally represents the end of the project. For example, when a software program has passed final testing and the customer accepts it as complete, the project is over. Ongoing training, operation, and maintenance are beyond the project's scope unless specifically included in the charter. Project acceptance is discussed in Chapter 17.

Project Quality vs. Quality of the Project Deliverables

Successfully completing all the project work listed in the WBS does not guarantee that the customer will be satisfied with the project deliverable(s). Remember that the purpose of a project is to solve a problem or to meet a need. If the project does neither, it does not matter that all project work was completed to standard or finished on time. The customer will not consider it a successful project.

To satisfy the customer, the project must meet or exceed the key success factors identified in the project charter. However, finishing the work to standard on time and within budget may not be enough.

Little Q

The definitions of quality cited earlier describe quality as a characteristic of the deliverable. The deliverable satisfies its intended use, or it does not. It is defect free, or it is not. In recent years, however, quality experts have begun to define quality more broadly. The most recent editions of the *PMBOK* make it clear that quality now applies not just to the project deliverables but to the processes used to produce them. This view has led to the distinction between "Little Q" and "Big Q." These two perspectives on quality are contrasted in Figure 11.1.

Traditionally project quality has focused solely on the project deliverables ("Little Q"). Therefore, quality management planning has

QUALITY MANAGEMENT PLANNING

focused on the project, its end user(s), and their requirements. It has failed to address "Big Q" issues such as efficiency, cycle time, support services, cost of poor quality, and strategic alignment, among others.

Figure 11.1 | Quality Perspectives

Little Q vs. Big Q		
Topics	**Content of Little Q**	**Content of Big Q**
Products	Manufactured Goods	All products, goods and services, whether for sale or not
Processes	Processes directly related to manufacture of goods	All processes; manufacturing, support, business, etc.
Customers	Clients who buy the product	All who are affected, internal and external
Industries	Manufacturing	All industries; manufacturing, service, government, etc., whether for profit or not
Cost of Poor Quality	Costs associated with deficient manufactured goods	All costs that would disappear if everything were perfect

The 7th edition of the *PMBOK*, the most recent edition, points out that quality management must address both the quality of the deliverables and the management of the project itself. In other words, project quality management and control must address both the "Little Q" and the "Big Q" issues.

Big Q

The Big Q standards are outlined in the *PMBOK*. The *PMBOK* is a de facto project quality standard. It is not the only one. There are others such as ISO 10006, Prince II, and ASQ's Team Excellence Award Criteria, to name just a few, but PMI's *PMBOK* is the most widely accepted and most widely used project quality standard.

Experts estimate that up to 40% of project work is non-value added. In other words, it is work that uses resources but does not contribute to the customer's perception of value. These non-value-added activities include inspections, transportation, delays, storage, and rework. Process analysts refer to these activities as "waste." In lean manufacturing terminology, it is called *muda,* Japanese for waste.

Customers do not care about waste as long as they get a deliverable that meets their requirements in a timely way at the agreed price. The project manager and his or her organization, however, should and usually do care. Inefficiencies erode the bottom line eating into the organization's profits. Despite this fact, few organizations measure non-value-added work. As a result, many, if not most, organizations are unaware of the loss of productivity that results from inefficient project management.

Successful project management involves using quality standards such as *PMBOK* best practices to satisfy "Big Q" goals. Many organizations have developed their own project management protocols that include guidelines for managing projects together with recommended tools and techniques. The use of these best practices helps to minimize the amount of non-value-added work, making it possible to finish projects better, faster, and cheaper.

Unfortunately, many project managers are not as concerned with quality issues as they should be. Many appear to have bought into what some have called "the Microsoft Paradigm" of getting it out the door quickly and then fixing it as the customers report the bugs. This

QUALITY MANAGEMENT PLANNING

approach involves a moderate-to-high level of risk and is not the best way to satisfy customers.

When projects get behind schedule, project teams often compromise on the quality of the deliverable in an effort to get back on schedule. This is usually a misguided effort. As Steve McConnell has pointed out, "My strong impression is that customers do not remember that high-quality software was delivered late or that low-quality software was delivered on time as much as they remember whether they liked using the software." (McConnell, p. 127) Project teams frequently underestimate the importance of quality.

So, what does a quality management plan look like? It will depend on the size and complexity of the project. Typically, it includes information on appropriate standards, performance metrics, how problems will be reported, and how corrective action will be taken. Often these processes are described in the organizational policies and procedures manual and apply to all projects.

A Project Quality Management Plan is a document that outlines the policies, procedures, and processes that will be used to ensure the quality of a project deliverable. Here are some key components that you might find in a typical project quality management plan:

1. Quality objectives: This section outlines the overall objectives of the project in terms of quality, such as meeting customer requirements, adhering to industry standards, and achieving specific performance metrics.
2. Roles and responsibilities: This section describes the roles and responsibilities of the project team members in relation to quality management. It may also include details on how the team will communicate and collaborate to ensure quality.
3. Quality standards: This section defines the quality standards that will be used to measure the success of the project. These may include industry-specific standards, customer requirements, or internal organizational standards.

4. Quality assurance processes: This section outlines the processes that will be used to ensure that the project deliverables meet the defined quality standards. This may include testing, inspections, or reviews.
5. Quality control processes: This section outlines the processes that will be used to monitor and control the quality of the project deliverables throughout the project lifecycle. This may include corrective actions, change management, or process improvement.
6. Quality measurement and reporting: This section outlines the metrics that will be used to measure the success of the project in terms of quality. It may also include reporting requirements for project stakeholders.
7. Quality improvement plan: This section outlines the strategies that will be used to continuously improve the quality of the project deliverables. This may include process improvement initiatives, training programs, or performance feedback mechanisms.

Overall, a project quality management plan should be a comprehensive document that outlines the strategies and processes that will be used to ensure the project deliverables meet the defined quality standards.

Does every project require a quality management plan? The answer is "no," but the project manager is responsible for ensuring that the project deliverables meet customer requirements with or without a formal plan. For smaller projects with clearly defined outcomes, a formal quality management plan is probably not necessary. For larger, more complex projects, quality planning is essential.

Summary

Quality has been defined as "fitness for use" or "conformance to requirements." Either way, it has to do with producing a deliverable that satisfies the project's customer. Failure to satisfy the customer results in project failure.

Quality does not happen by accident. It is the result of good planning and effective execution. It starts with the quality plan, a component of the project management plan. The quality plan describes how the team will ensure that the final deliverable meets the customer's expectations. To do this, the team must determine who its customers are, and what their needs are, develop products that meet those needs, and develop processes to produce those products.

Lastly, quality refers not just to the characteristics of the deliverable but to the process that produces it. "Little Q" refers to the former, and "Big Q" to the latter. Successful project outcomes depend on both.

THE CRITICAL ROLE OF THE PROJECT MANAGER

Introduction

Some project managers talk about initiation and planning as if this is where the work begins. They view these first two stages of a project as something that must be gotten out of the way so that the real work of the project can begin. This misconception is in part responsible for the failure of many project teams to spend the time necessary to adequately define and plan projects.

Project managers in Europe and Asia typically spend more time planning than their counterparts in the United States, often spending as much as 40% of the project life cycle developing the project plan. On the other hand, many American project managers tend to minimize up-front planning, relying instead on the change management process to deal with issues arising from insufficient project planning.

The execution stage also represents a transition point in the project. The first two stages, initiation, and planning, depend heavily on the technical skills of the project manager and his or her team. In the execution stage, success depends increasingly on what is commonly called the "soft" skills or "people" skills.

Successful project managers recognize the important role of people skills in project management. In the end, it all boils down to how well the project team executes the project plan. As one experienced project manager put it, "No project ever failed because the project manager couldn't draw a good Gantt Chart." Many projects fail because the project manager could not develop an effective, high-performing team.

While the project's success depends on *all* the project stakeholders, the efforts of the project manager are critical. The following sections describe the project manager's roles and responsibilities. The roles and responsibilities of other important stakeholders are described in Chapter 13.

Facets of the Project Manager Role

The role of the project manager during the execution stage is to direct and manage the implementation of the project plan. To do this, the project manager has a number of responsibilities, which include:

- coaching and mentoring
- resolving problems and conflicts
- providing resources
- setting goals and priorities
- providing technical advice and guidance

All managers, not just those who manage projects, should take these responsibilities very seriously.

To successfully fulfill these responsibilities, the project manager must possess a rather diverse skill set. The *PMBOK* (5th ed., p. 18) lists the following skills as critical to success as a project manager:

- Leadership skills
- Team-building skills
- Motivation skills
- Communication skills
- Influencing skills
- Decision-making skills
- Political and cultural awareness skills

THE CRITICAL ROLE OF THE PROJECT MANAGER

Figure 12.1 | PM Job Description

Sample Job Description

- Ensure that the project team starts and completes the project
- Plan and execute the project in accordance with the contract quality assurance requirements and procedures.
- Manage and monitor the team's performance to ensure that project tasks are completed within budget, on schedule, and within the planned scope of work.
- Manage change to the approved scope of work.
- Communicate with the customer
- Completion and submittal of contract required deliverables.
- Securing acceptance and approval of deliverables from the customer.
- Preparing status reports, evaluating and reporting project risks, and escalating concerns to senior management that cannot be resolved within the project team.
- Provide status updates to company senior management.
- Notify senior management of safety concerns, and execute stop work authority for an activity that presents a danger to the health and well-being of a person or persons in the work place.

- Negotiation skills
- Trust building skills
- Conflict management skills
- Coaching skills

While these skills do not appear to be in any particular order, there is no doubt that communication should be at the top of the list. The ability to communicate is one of the most important skills in project management, if not *the* most, as it is in so many other human activities. That is why, as we noted in Chapter 8, project managers spend up to 90% of their time communicating with the project team and other key stakeholders.

Figure 12.2 | Technical Skills vs. People Skills

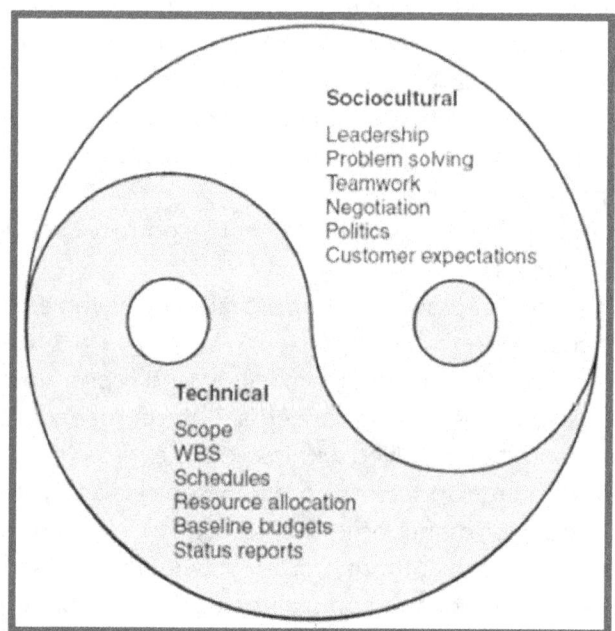

Source: Ali Hadi Jebrin

It is also interesting to note that most of these skills focus primarily on working with other people. While technical competence is important, the ability to work with people is critical to success as a project manager. That is one reason why the concept of emotional intelligence has gained such traction in the project management community in recent years.

Emotional intelligence (EQ) has to do with a person's ability to deal effectively with social situations. Daniel Goleman, a well-known researcher in the field of emotional intelligence, has identified four dimensions of emotional intelligence. These are:

- Self-awareness – the ability to read one's emotions and recognize their impact while using gut feelings to guide decisions
- Self-management – the ability to manage one's emotions and impulses and adapt to changing circumstances
- Social awareness – the ability to sense, understand, and react to others' emotions while comprehending social networks
- Relationship management – the ability to inspire, influence, and develop others while managing conflict (Goleman, 1998)

Project managers with high EQ tend to be more effective than those with a lower EQ. Much project work involves interaction between the project manager, the project team, and other key stakeholders. The ability to manage these interactions effectively is an obvious advantage.

As Andy Barnitz, an experienced project manager for Allstate Insurance, put it, "The greatest setback a project can have isn't resources or funding constraints, unrealistic deadlines or poor project sponsorship; it is the project manager's inability to effectively understand and manage the team." (Malooley, 2015, p. 52)

While many believe this is an inborn trait, research indicates that you can increase your EQ through training and experience. Unfortunately, many project managers, particularly those with a technical background, fail to appreciate the importance of social skills and, therefore, fail to make an effort to improve them.

Project Manager as Coach

If project management were a sport, the project manager would be the coach. This is a good analogy because the project manager is, in many respects, like the coach of a football, basketball, or baseball team. The project manager is responsible for the performance of the project team, just as the coach is responsible for the performance of his or her players.

Figure 12.3 | What Successful Coaches Do

- Inspire or motivate the team
- Develop a game plan
- Ensure the team can execute the game plan

It is not surprising, then, that coaches are judged primarily on the performance of their teams. For better or worse, winning coaches are considered successful, and losing coaches are judged to be failures. I once attended a luncheon to honor a local football coach. Having just completed a very successful season, the coach commented on how much people loved him when they were winning. The president of the university immediately stood up and said, "George, we would love you just as much even if you hadn't won a single game this season. In fact, we would miss you a lot."

Of course, the coach had not scored any touchdowns. He hadn't kicked any field goals, and he hadn't blocked any punts. His success was completely dependent on what the players on the field did. So why are some coaches so successful while others are not?

Many of the most successful coaches have written books on how to succeed in sports and in life. These books are based on the lessons they have learned through years on the field or on the court. Many of these books have made the bestseller list, and some have been quite popular in the business community. The assumption is that the lessons learned in athletic endeavors translate to success in the business world as well as life in general.

The one thing these coaches have in common is that they do three things extremely well. They inspire or motivate the team to perform above and beyond expectations. Secondly, they have a game plan. They have a strategy for victory. They do not expect the players to figure it out as they go. And lastly, successful project managers ensure that the team can execute the strategy. It does not do any good to have a plan if the team cannot execute it. Let's look at each of these in more detail.

Motivating the Team

One of the problems many project managers face is how to work with a project team whose team members report to a functional manager. Because the project manager does not hire or fire team members, does not write their performance reviews, and does not determine their raises or promotions, project managers have little or no control over team members. So how can the project manager encourage team members to work effectively together to make the project successful?

The project manager can always order team members to carry out their assigned activities, but authoritarian approaches are seldom very effective. Team members can and will respond by doing just enough to stay out of trouble. This type of approach does not result in superior performance. Successful projects are staffed by team members committed to the project and willing to do whatever it takes to get the work done. Successful project management is about more than doing just enough to get by.

The first step the successful project manager will undertake in developing an effective project team is to ensure that team members are motivated, i.e., they are committed to the project and are willing to do whatever it takes to successfully complete it. The literature on motivation is lengthy, and a full review of this research is beyond the scope of this discussion. We will, however, review a few recent works that have particular relevance for developing a highly motivated project team.

This research indicates that teams who invest themselves in their work are more likely to complete their projects successfully. Steven Covey has written extensively on this subject. In *The 8th Habit*, he wrote about motivation as a choice that employees (team members) make. How much of themselves do they give to their work? (Covey, 2004, p. 22) This concept is often referred to as "employee engagement."

Covey listed six levels of employee involvement or engagement in their work. These are in ascending order:

- Rebel or quit
- Malicious obedience
- Willing compliance
- Cheerful cooperation
- Heartfelt commitment
- Creative excitement

The purpose of team building in project management is to create an engaged team whose members are characterized by "creative excitement." Creative excitement happens, according to Covey, when employees are "paid fairly, treated kindly, used creatively, and given opportunities to serve human needs in principled ways." (Covey, 2004, p. 24)

Research on this issue indicates that most Americans are not highly engaged in their work, and in fact, a Gallup poll reported in *Leadership in Project Management*, 2007 found that 14% of American workers are "actively disengaged" at work. Their lowered motivation is responsible for $300 billion in lost productivity per year. Subsequent research by Gallup has reaffirmed these findings. In 2021, Gallup found that engagement had only increased by 1% since that 2007 report (https://www.gallup.com/workplace/352949/employee-engagement-holds-steady-first-half-2021.aspx). These results were obtained from a random selection of employees but probably would not have differed much had the surveys been conducted exclusively among people assigned to project teams.

So, how do we motivate employees to become engaged project team members? Some studies point to two factors that contribute significantly to the development of high levels of motivation.

The first is recognition. Studies have found that one of the most significant motivators is recognition for a job well done. People need feedback, positive feedback in particular. People regulate their behavior

THE CRITICAL ROLE OF THE PROJECT MANAGER

based on external feedback. Positive feedback builds confidence and reinforces behavior.

A second important motivator is the feeling of being in on things, and receiving timely and accurate information about workplace issues instead of being dependent on the grapevine for information. Good project management starts with the project manager. It begins at the top.

One trap that many organizations fall into is expecting teamwork while rewarding team members for their individual achievements. Emphasis on individual achievement creates an environment where team members compete over rewards and recognition rather than working together to achieve project goals and objectives. This explains why "Employee of the Month" and similar recognition programs seldom contribute much to the bottom line. People do what they get rewarded for doing. If you want teamwork, you have to reward teamwork.

Developing a Game Plan

Successful coaches develop a game plan for each game. They understand that success is achieved through the coordinated efforts of a dedicated and highly disciplined team focused on doing whatever it takes to win. For this reason, much of the pre-game preparation involves reviewing game films and developing strategies designed to maximize their strengths and capitalize on their opponent's weaknesses.

Likewise, successful project management depends on a good project plan. While motivation is an important factor in the success of the project, motivation by itself is not sufficient. Without a plan of action, even highly motivated teams are largely ineffective. The plan provides the team with the information necessary to successfully complete the project. It establishes the priorities that guide decision-making throughout the project.

Scott Berkun, a former project manager at Microsoft, wrote in *The Art of Project Management* (Berkun, 2005, p. 332) that priorities are what make things happen. Project managers make things happen by establishing clear priorities, effectively communicating those priorities to the project team, and keeping the team focused on those priorities. Without priorities, it is difficult to complete a project within its time, cost, and scope constraints but it is not enough to set priorities. The project manager must also ensure that project priorities guide the team's work throughout the execution of the project. That is sometimes difficult. As Berkun points out, "If you can't say no, you effectively have no priorities." (Berkun 2005, p. 339) Saying "No" is not always easy, but it is essential to keep the team focused on what they need to do to successfully complete the project.

Ensuring the Team Can Execute the Plan

A high level of motivation and a good game plan are necessary, but even in combination, they are insufficient to ensure a high level of performance. To be successful, team members must execute the plan. They cannot do this without the appropriate skills.

Coaches train their players to ensure they can carry out the plan. They review game films and practice the plays they will need to execute during the game. Likewise, project managers must ensure that team members have the skills and ability to implement the project work plan.

The WBS helps to identify the skill sets required to complete the project work. The list of required skills should be used in the team selection process to avoid gaps between the skills required by the project and the skills of the personnel assigned to the project team.

If there is any doubt, the project manager should do a skills audit (See Chapter 4 for a discussion of the skills audit). This audit involves an informal check of project requirements against team members' skills. By conducting an audit, the project manager can identify any gaps between the teams' skills and the task requirements.

Where there are gaps, the project manager must take some action to close them. This action may involve adding a team member,

THE CRITICAL ROLE OF THE PROJECT MANAGER

outsourcing the task, or helping current team members develop the required skills. All of these actions take time. They cannot wait until the last minute. It is important to conduct the audit during the planning stage rather than wait until implementation begins.

Like most analogies, the analogy between sports and project management has its limitations. Project management is not a sport, and some of the techniques used by coaches are not appropriate in the workplace. We can't punch team members like Woody Hays, throw chairs like Bobby Knight, or curse like Rick Pitino.

While it is clear that team members must have the skills necessary to execute the work identified in the project plan, the skills required of the project manager are less clear. For example, does the project manager need to be an expert in the field? There are arguments on both sides of this issue. Some project managers believe that if they have a competent team whose members are committed to the project, they can manage almost any project, even one outside their area of expertise. Even though the project manager plays a key role, project management is a team sport.

Many, if not most, project managers would agree with this position. Unfortunately, not all project teams consist of experts who are committed to the success of the project. In these situations, the project manager who lacks subject matter expertise is at a serious disadvantage in dealing with team members who may have their own agendas. The project's success depends on his or her ability to overcome these obstacles and get the team behind the project.

Regardless of how much expertise the project manager may have, most projects require a broader range of skills than any one person can hope to have. So, to a certain extent, every project manager has to rely on the team's commitment to the project. Good project managers do not simply hope this happens. They work to make it happen. It is part of the team-building process.

Project managers need to understand that their success depends on the success of the team. They cannot succeed if their team fails.

For this reason, the project manager's primary focus should be on doing whatever is necessary to help the team successfully complete its assigned work.

While the project manager is responsible for managing the project, he or she also serves as the project team leader. Successful project management, therefore, depends not just on the project manager's management skills, but on his or her leadership skills as well.

Project Manager as Leader

As a manager, the project manager is responsible for using the organization's resources to achieve the project goals and objectives. This means that effective project managers must have good management skills. But the project manager is also the leader of the team responsible for implementing the project plan. That means the project manager must also have good leadership skills.

While some people do not distinguish between managing and leading, the two are distinct yet complementary activities. The conventional wisdom is that you manage things and lead people. For example, you can lead a team, but you cannot lead a budget. Leadership is about setting goals and objectives and motivating people to do the work necessary to achieve them. Management is about allocating resources to achieve the goals and objectives.

In their book entitled *The Leadership Challenge* (Kouzes and Posner, 2017), Kouzes and Posner wrote that their research identified the traits people admire most in their leaders. Four traits have continuously topped the list. For people to willingly follow someone, they must perceive that person as:

- honest
- forward-looking
- competent, and
- inspiring

Team members are also looking for these same traits in their project team leaders, and people who exemplify them are much more likely to succeed as project managers than those who do not.

But being a successful project manager requires more than just having the right personal traits. It also requires the right actions. So, what makes some leaders more effective than others? Kouzes and Posner argue that effective leaders engage in what they call the Five Practices of Exemplary Leadership. These are:

- Model the way
- Inspire a shared vision
- Challenge the process
- Enable others to act
- Encourage the heart

Model the Way

Successful leaders model the behaviors they expect from others. They do not expect their followers to do anything they would not be willing to do themselves. And, they understand that what they do is more important than what they say. Actions speak louder than words.

Inspire a Shared Vision

Effective leaders develop a compelling vision for their projects. The project vision is often expressed in the form of a vision statement describing what the project will accomplish in terms that will motivate team members to commit to it and stakeholders to support it.

A classic example of a project vision statement is the Special Message to the Congress on Urgent National Needs delivered by President John F. Kennedy before a joint session of Congress on May 25, 1961. In this address, he said,

"First, I believe that this nation should commit itself to achieving the goal, before this decade is out, of landing a man on the moon and returning him safely to the earth. No single space project in this period will be more impressive to mankind, or more important for the long-range exploration of space; and none will be so difficult or expensive to accomplish. We propose to accelerate the development of the appropriate lunar spacecraft. We propose to develop alternate liquid and solid fuel boosters, much larger than any now being developed, until certain which is superior. We propose additional funds for other engine development and for unmanned explorations, explorations which are particularly important for one purpose which this nation will never overlook: the survival of the man who first makes this daring flight. But in a very real sense, it will not be one man going to the moon—if we make this judgment affirmatively, it will be an entire nation. For all of us must work to put him there."

Challenging NASA to do something that had never been done before was certainly inspiring to those charged with making it happen. While it may not be possible to frame all projects in such a challenging way, there are things a project manager can do to make even routine projects more challenging and inspiring.

Challenge the Process

Good leaders do not sit back and wait for opportunities to come to them. They go out and make things happen. More often than not, this involves developing innovative strategies for dealing with the challenges they face as project managers. Innovation, of course, involves a certain amount of risk, but good leaders are willing to take risks and learn from their failures.

Enable Others to Act

Good leaders, like good project managers, understand they cannot do it alone. To succeed, they must enlist the support of others. They must create an environment that empowers team members to act. Good leaders make those around them better. Covey calls this "The Eighth Habit."

Encourage the Heart

Successful leaders show their appreciation for a job well done. They understand the power of recognition and appreciation as forces to motivate team members. Good leaders give credit for success and take the blame for failures.

Project managers who follow the Five Practices of Exemplary Leadership are much better able to develop a team that reaches the highest level of engagement, the level that Covey calls "creative excitement." (See Chapter 17 for a discussion of the importance of recognition.)

While the efforts of the project manager are critical to the success of the project, the project manager cannot do it alone. It takes all of the stakeholders working together to complete the project successfully. The role of the project sponsor, the project champion, the project team, and the project support personnel are discussed in the next chapter.

Summary

Of all the people involved in a project, the project manager plays the most critical role, as the success of the project often depends on how well he or she performs. This role involves several activities, including mentoring, coaching, resolving conflicts, providing resources, setting goals and priorities, and providing technical advice and guidance to the team.

Project managers are like coaches in many respects. To be successful, they must motivate their teams to work together to achieve project goals and objectives. They must focus team efforts on implementing the project plan. They must also ensure that team members have the skills and abilities to successfully carry out the work necessary to complete the project.

The project manager is both a manager and a leader. While the project manager is responsible for managing the project, he or she is also the project team leader. The project manager must not only manage project resources but also provide effective leadership.

According to research, good leaders are role models. They are able, through their words and deeds, to inspire others to act. They act proactively, and they empower others to act. And lastly, they understand and practice the power of recognition. Kouzes and Posner call this the "Five Practices of Exemplary Leadership."

ROLES OF KEY STAKEHOLDERS

Introduction

While the efforts of the project manager are critical, successful project management depends upon the contributions of a large number of people. Each has a role to play, and the success of project depends on their contributions. The key stakeholders include:

- project sponsor
- project champion
- customer
- project manager
- project support personnel
- project team

How this often diverse group of people connects, relates, and works together will, in large part, make or break the project. Understanding the roles of key stakeholders, and the dynamics of effective teams, will enable the project manager to lead the project to a successful outcome.

The Project Sponsor

The project sponsor is the person who has the authority to assign resources and enforce decisions about the project. The sponsor is usually a high-level executive within the organization. While lines of authority may be unclear in some organizations, particularly if there are multiple stakeholders, the project charter helps to fix responsibility for the project. It is generally the project sponsor who approves the project by signing the charter.

The role of the sponsor is usually defined in the initiation stage of the project. While project sponsors may fulfill several roles, the job description generally includes two primary responsibilities:

1. supporting and defending the project
2. serving as a liaison between the project manager and senior management.

Support and Guidance

The project sponsor is usually a key stakeholder whose primary responsibility is to provide support to the project manager and the project team. This may include encouraging them and/or providing advice. It may also include working to obtain additional resources or protecting those resources already allocated to them.

However, there are cases where sponsors are appointed for reasons other than their interest in the project. Project sponsors are sometimes assigned to a project because it falls within their functional domain, or perhaps because there is no one else available to serve as the sponsor. These sponsors are often minimally engaged with the project, increasing the probability that the project will fail.

Active sponsors, on the other hand, have a significant impact on project success rates. Therefore, it is not surprising that many project managers complain about what appears to be an increasingly common phenomenon: the absentee or disappearing sponsor. For whatever reason, the sponsor loses interest in the project (assuming they had any interest to begin with) and fails to live up to his or her responsibilities as the project sponsor. One recent survey listed this among the top 10 obstacles to successful project management.

ROLES OF KEY STAKEHOLDERS

Liaison with Senior Management

Project managers, particularly those in large organizations, may not have easy access to senior managers, the people who control organizational resources. The project sponsor often serves as a liaison between the project manager and upper management. As such, he or she facilitates the flow of information about the project to senior managers and from senior managers back to the project manager.

Fostering Sponsor Engagement

What can a project manager do to engage a project sponsor who lacks interest in the project? An article in *PMNetwork by Diane White* (Engaging Sponsors (2014), 28(11), 18–20) suggests some actions. These include scheduling regular meetings with the sponsor and monitoring the sponsor's attention to the project. These actions enable the project manager to identify problems early and take corrective action quickly.

The lack of support from the sponsor(s) puts the project at risk. In such instances, the project manager may need to reengage the sponsor or find a project champion.

The Project Champion

Project managers are often described as people with much responsibility and little authority. This lack of authority means there is considerable potential for things to happen over which the project manager has no control. For this reason, project success often depends on someone with significant clout within the organization who is willing to defend and support the project. This person is the project champion.

The role of the project champion is usually an informal one. Although champions have a more formal role in Six Sigma process improvement projects and Lean Manufacturing projects, this role tends to be less structured in most other contexts. The most recent editions of the *PMBOK* do not even mention the role of the project champion.

To serve effectively as a project champion, a person must meet two requirements. First, he or she must have a vested interest in the project. Why else would anyone want to serve in this role? A person who has an active interest in the project is more likely to play an active role in the planning and execution of the project. For this reason, the sponsor often serves as both the project sponsor and project champion.

Second, the project champion must be a relatively high-ranking person in the organization. If the project champion is not high enough in the organizational hierarchy, he or she may not be able to successfully defend the project against attempts to divert its resources, increase its scope, or remove obstacles that might delay its completion. A good project champion can also help to keep the project high on the list of organizational priorities.

Sometimes the project champion is highly involved in the project from the very beginning and may be instrumental in getting it approved. The project champions most engaged in the project tend to be those who also serve as the project sponsor. In some cases, there is no obvious project champion, and the project manager must search for someone willing to take on this role.

The Project Customer

The project customer is the person or group of persons for whom the project is undertaken. Customers include those who have authorized the project, those who have paid for it as well as end users. It may also include distributors, agents, or other stakeholders that are, in one way or another, connected with the project deliverable(s).

We noted earlier that projects often have more than one customer. Managing a project with multiple customers becomes challenging when the customers have conflicting expectations for the project. Unfortunately, this is not an unusual situation. It is not atypical for the project sponsor, the project customers, and other key stakeholders to have different interests and expectations for the project. Often these differences are mutually exclusive.

In these situations, the project manager must seek to forge a consensus between them on major project goals and objectives. The project manager's negotiating and influencing skills are very important in these situations. The failure to reconcile these differences will make the project difficult to manage, and the outcome is unlikely to satisfy some key stakeholders.

Under the pressure of tight deadlines, some project managers begin the implementation of the project plan even though there is no consensus on goals or objectives. They mistakenly believe they can work out these differences during the implementation stage of the project. More often than not, they cannot persuade stakeholders to reach an agreement. The project then experiences serious problems, resulting in deliverables that fail to satisfy any of the customers or other important stakeholders.

While conflicting project expectations are a problem, it is not the only one the project manager has to deal with. Another difficult problem is the lack of customer involvement. Many projects require ongoing feedback from the customer. Often customers are responsible for reviews and approvals as well as providing needed information to the project team. Customers not engaged in the project may cause the project to be delayed by not fulfilling their responsibilities on time.

Since firing the customer is generally not an option, the project manager must ensure that customers understand their responsibilities and the consequences of not meeting those responsibilities. The project manager should do this before beginning the implementation stage of the project.

Project Support Personnel

Undoubtedly the most under-appreciated stakeholders are those who serve in support roles. Support personnel are usually not members of the project team but provide products and services without which the project could not be successfully completed. Support personnel include human resource specialists, travel managers, procurement personnel, IT specialists, and anybody else who supports the team's work by providing essential products or services.

Many project managers take support personnel for granted. Often, they go unnoticed except when things go wrong. It is important to understand the critical role they play in the success of the project and to make sure they receive recognition for their contributions.

Good project managers go out of their way to cultivate good relationships with support personnel. They treat them as if the project's success depends on their support because they know it often does. Many project managers have called in favors from support personnel to save a failing project. That is only possible when the project manager has developed a reservoir of goodwill among those whose support is critical to the success of the project.

The Project Team

The project manager is responsible for managing the implementation of the project plan. However, this does not mean the project manager is solely responsible for getting the work done. Implementation is generally a team effort. Successful implementation, as noted earlier, depends on clearly defining the project, developing a good work plan, selecting the right people, and motivating them to get the work done.

Selecting the Project Team

Project teams are constituted in a variety of ways. There is also a great deal of variation in the stage at which project teams are formed and assigned to the project. Table 13.1 below illustrates this diversity.

The *PMBOK* does not address the team selection process other than to note that project team members are usually appointed based on their availability, competency, experience, interest in the project, and/or their cost rate. In practice, it is often a combination of these factors, assuming, of course, the pool is large enough to provide a choice.

In larger organizations, senior leaders or the Project Management Office usually appoint the project manager and the members of the team. In smaller organizations, it is more common for the project manager to select team members. In practice, however, project managers often have to settle for whoever is available, and they often have to negotiate with functional managers to get the people they want.

Team members can be appointed at any time between the conception of the project and the beginning of the implementation. Most experts believe that the team members should be appointed as early in the project as possible. The more involvement they have in the initiation and planning stages of the project, the more likely they are to commit to its successful completion. One additional advantage of appointing team members at the beginning of the project is that it allows them to contribute to the development of the project charter and the ancillary work plans. The ones who do the work are the ones who know best what needs to be done, how long it will take, and what resources will be needed. Their knowledge helps to avoid the all-too-common situation in which senior managers initiate and plan projects that are unrealistic and destined to fail.

Figure 13.1 | Team Selection Issues

Selection Based on	Appointed by	Selection Time Frame
Skills	Project manager	Beginning of the initiation stage
Availability	Sponsor/senior leader	End of the initiation stage
Self-selection	Functional manager	Beginning of the execution stage
PMO Steering Committee	PMO steering committee	

In some organizations, teams are permanently constituted. In such cases, project teams are permanent work units. They are more likely to be engaged in repetitive types of work such as laying carpet, installing computer systems, etc.

Sometimes organizations include members of key stakeholder groups such as external suppliers on the project team. Some include customers and end users. Including suppliers, vendors, and customers on the project team makes it more likely that divergent perspectives are incorporated into the team's work.

Team Size

So, how big should a project team be? It depends, of course, on the type and scope of the project. Research suggests that size does matter. While one might assume that bigger is better, studies suggest otherwise. It appears that larger is not necessarily better. This may, in part, be due to the Ringelmann Effect.

Figure 13.2 | The Ringlemann Effect

Maximilien Ringelmann, a 19th century agricultural engineer conducted a number of social experiments. In these experiments, he noticed that as the size of the group increases, individual members become increasingly less productive. This is because of what Ringelmann called "social loafing", a phenomenon in which group members exert less effort because they feel less responsible for the end result.

Most studies have found that the optimal size is between five and 12 members. Teams with fewer than five members may lack sufficient perspectives, skills, and creativity. Teams with more than 12 members may experience increased conflict, decreased efficiency, and a greater potential for fragmentation into sub-groups.

A recent article on LinkedIn (Studzinski, 2021) summarized the research concluding that the optimal size is 4.6 members. This estimate appears to be an average based on the results of published research. Most organizations will have trouble finding the .6 of a member.

The Team Contract

The team contract is a tool used by some project managers to promote teamwork and clarify team goals and expectations. By signing the contract, team members commit themselves to the project and formally acknowledge their roles and responsibilities.

Some project managers have reservations about using such a formal process. Nevertheless, it does not hurt to have team members discuss and adopt a set of ground rules to govern their interactions with each other and with other stakeholders. Commitment to the project and team members' responsibilities to each other might be some of the issues addressed in such an exercise.

Stages of Team Development

We frequently talk about appointing members to project teams but in most cases, we are appointing them to groups. Teams must be developed. The process by which we get a group of people to work together as a team is called "team building." Team building is one of the project manager's primary responsibilities.

Figure 13.3 | The Tuckman Model of Team Development

	Forming	Storming	Norming	Performing
Performance level	Collection of individuals	Group	Team	High-performing team
High				x
Good			x	
Medium		x		
Low	x			

In *The Wisdom of Teams* (Katzenbach and Smith, 2006, p. 45), Katzenbach and Smith define a team as ". . . a small number of people with complementary skills who are committed to a common purpose, performance goals, and approach for which they are mutually accountable."

Groups go through a series of stages on their way to becoming high-performing teams. This process is often called the Tuckman Model. Bruce Tuckman identified four stages of team development. These are "Forming," "Storming," "Norming," and "Performing." Later a fifth stage was added, called "Adjourning."

Forming

This stage begins when the team first comes together. Team members tend to be cautious at first, particularly if they do not know each other well. They tend to talk about "safe" topics and engage in "safe" behaviors. In this stage, the team members begin to feel each other out, learning each other's likes and dislikes.

The project manager sets the tone during this stage. Members look to him or her for guidance. It is not easy to develop a team culture that facilitates high performance; it is even harder to change an established culture. Because changing culture is so difficult, it is important to develop a culture that demands the best from each team member right from the very beginning.

Storming

As team members get to know each other, they begin to feel more comfortable and let down their guard. Team members no longer give careful consideration to every utterance. They begin to express their feelings with less concern for how they will be perceived. As a result, conflict between team members begins to emerge.

Norming

The team reaches this stage when its members begin to understand what they can say or do. Team norms begin to develop, creating a more harmonious team environment that facilitates trust, an essential prerequisite to high performance. Team members also begin to accept their roles on the team and their responsibilities to each other.

Performing

Performing is the stage at which the team "gels." Team members have fully accepted their roles and responsibilities. Team members have bonded, and they have set aside their personal agendas in favor of shared project goals and objectives.

Adjourning

Later, the Adjourning stage was added after subsequent research identified a new set of behaviors associated with the team's dissolution. This research found that there is a bereavement period at the end of the project. At this point, team members begin to realize that their work together has come to an end. They may no longer work together or perhaps even see each other again anytime soon.

Not all teams make it to the Performing stage. Some teams never progress beyond the Storming stage. Some teams reach the Performing stage and then fall back to the Storming stage. In short, there is no guarantee of forward progress, and backsliding in response to conflicts or changes in team composition is not uncommon.

The purpose of team building is to develop a high-performing team. Effective project managers can move groups through the first three stages relatively quickly. It is not always easy. It often requires significant effort on the part of the project manager as well as the individual team members. Propelling the team to the high-performance level is a real test of the project manager's team-building skills, and many teams never make it all the way.

Many organizations underestimate the importance of team building. In many cases, managers and supervisors consider team-building activities an unnecessary use of resources in a time of tight budgets. Experience shows, however, that teamwork has a significant impact on the ability of teams to complete their work successfully. McConnell, for example, argues that team chemistry may be as important, if not more so, than technical competence. (McConnell, 1998, p. 103)

Team Quality

We know that some teams, irrespective of size, are more effective than others. Research has found a number of factors that distinguish high-performing teams from those that do not perform so well. The characteristics of a high-performing team include (Buchholz and Roth, p. 14):

- Participative leadership
- Shared responsibility
- Align on purpose
- High communication
- Future-focused
- Focused on task
- Creative talents
- Rapid response

However, not all teams exhibit the characteristics of a high-performing team. Some will attain these attributes through appropriate team-building activities. Most will fail to overcome the obstacles that prevent them from becoming a high-performing team. Patrick Lencioni identified what he has called the "Five Dysfunctions of a Team" in his book by the same name (Lencioni, 2002). These include:

- Lack of trust
- Fear of conflict
- Lack of commitment
- Avoidance of accountability
- Inattention to detail

Most of these obstacles manifest themselves during the early stages of the project. Failure to overcome these obstacles prevents teams from reaching their full potential. Effective project managers will seek out and implement appropriate resources, tools, and exercises to help strengthen their teams and encourage growth where needed.

Team-Building Exercises

There are many tools and techniques that project managers can use to facilitate team development. These range from five-minute team warm-up exercises to activities that may take hours or even days. The *Team Handbook* (Scholtes, Joiner, and Streibel, 2018) contains a wide variety of team-building exercises and activities.

The Myers-Briggs Type Indicator (MBTI) is a tool that has been used with great success by many project managers to facilitate team development. The MBTI is a psychological test designed to identify individual preferences with respect to basic psychological predispositions.

So, what implications does this have for project management? Myers-Briggs helps team members better understand how and why they make the choices they do, but it is also a very helpful team-building exercise. It facilitates team building by helping team members understand and appreciate how different people approach situations differently. It demonstrates that there is no one right way to do things and that effective teams consist of individuals who complement each other.

Another popular team-building exercise is the "Lost on the Moon" exercise. This exercise demonstrates the importance of teamwork and the value of diverse perspectives. (See Appendix D for information on this exercise.)

Virtual Teams

In recent years, the use of virtual teams has become increasingly common. A virtual team consists of members, usually not co-located, who work together with little or no face-to-face contact. Team members interact with each other primarily through e-mail, teleconferences, webinars, and video conferences.

The biggest problem with virtual teams is that they are virtual. They do not have the benefit of face-to-face interaction in real-time. If team members are well acquainted, this may not be a significant issue, but if many of the team members have not worked together before, building a cohesive team will probably be more difficult. A face-to-face kickoff meeting and periodic face-to-face meetings can help to establish and maintain a sense of camaraderie among virtual team members, but it may be difficult to get the team together for such meetings.

However, the fact that a team is virtual can also be a strength. Unlike traditional teams, they are not limited by geography. Virtual teams can draw from a much larger pool of potential team members. The project manager can recruit the best possible people to work on the project without regard for where they live or work. This larger pool includes people who ordinarily work at home, those who have a disability that would otherwise prevent them from active team participation, and those who are physically located at a distant location.

There is some evidence to suggest that it may be easier to recruit people to work on virtual teams. For example, a recent survey conducted by Staples found that 71% of telecommuters say the ability to work remotely is an important benefit when considering a new job. (*PMNetwork*, April 2015, p. 17). Likewise, many people consider the opportunity to work on virtual teams as a benefit.

Of course, not all projects lend themselves to virtual teams. Virtual teams work best when team members can divide the work into smaller activities they can accomplish working individually. For example, software companies often use virtual teams to develop their products. On the other hand, virtual teams, because of the nature of the work, rarely work on construction or other types of projects that require a physical presence.

PMI recently reported that as many as half of all project teams work virtually. Some of that may result from an increasingly larger number of projects that lend themselves to virtual teams. There is anecdotal evidence to suggest that the COVID-19 pandemic also accelerated the use of virtual teams.

Time Management

Time is a major challenge for project managers and their team members, as it is a commodity in short supply. Everybody wants everything done yesterday. For this reason, team members need to manage their time effectively. It seems surprising that so few people have a systematic way of prioritizing their work in order for the most important things to be accomplished first. This makes time management a crucial skill for project managers as well as their teams.

There are two widely-used approaches to time management. One is the approach described by Covey in *The Seven Habits of Highly Effective People* (Covey, 1989). The other approach, often referred to as GTD, was developed by David Allen and is described in his book *Getting Things Done*. (Allen, 2001)

The Covey Approach

The Covey Approach, sometimes called the Eisenhower Method, can be summarized with the phrase "organize and execute around priorities." Covey argued that good time management requires prioritizing tasks based on their importance and their urgency (Covey, 1989, p. 146-182). Those items on our to-do list that are urgent and important should have the highest priority, followed by those that are important but not urgent.

One method designed to facilitate execution based on priorities is the Pomodoro Technique. This technique was developed in the early 1990s by Francesco Cirillo (Cirillo, 2009). He suggests that you divide your workday into 25-minute periods of uninterrupted work that he calls *pomodoros*. Each *pomodoro* is followed by a three- to five-minute break. As to-do items are completed, they are checked off the list. You can download Cirillo's book and supporting materials from www.pomodorotechnique.com.

Figure 13.4 | The Eisenhower Method

The use of this name stems from a quote attributed to Dwight D. Eisenhower, World War II General and U.S. President. He once said "I have two kinds of problems, the urgent and the important. The urgent are not important, and the important are never urgent."

Approaches like this can be very effective, but they require a great deal of discipline. Not everyone has that much discipline.

The Allen Approach—Getting Things Done

Allen takes a slightly different approach to time management. He argues that approaches based solely on priorities are inefficient because they ignore the importance of context. He points out that it makes more sense to group like to-dos together. For example, group phone calls together rather than doing them based strictly on priority. Grouping them is more efficient than alternating between phone calls, e-mails, and meetings.

The GTD method has five steps: collect, process, organize, review, and do.

1. **Collect**
   Collect all to-dos together in a single place.

2. **Process**
   Determines what needs to be done.

3. **Organize**

   Assign to-dos into "contexts," for example, meetings, e-mails, phone calls, etc.

4. **Review**

   Place these organized lists back into your brain, at least enough so you have the lists you need when you need them.

5. **Do**

   Do the things on the list.

Allen has developed an almost cult-like following in recent years. Many websites have sprung up to provide a forum for people using or interested in his approach to time management (for example, www.43folders.com). Several software packages are also available to help people automate this approach.

The Problem of Multitasking

Multitasking has become one of the biggest impediments to good time management. Twenty or 30 years ago, projects were an additional duty. People did their jobs, and, in whatever time they had left, they worked on a project or two. Today most people work primarily on projects, almost always more than one or two, and their work is what they do when they can fit it in. This increase in workload makes good time management skills essential. In today's environment, project managers must know how to juggle projects effectively. Good multitasking skills are the key to success in project management.

Although multitasking is an unavoidable part of project management, it is important to keep in mind that it is an inefficient way to work. In a recent article in a PMI software publication, the author stated that multitasking is the single most important cause of lost worker productivity. It costs the U.S. economy billions of dollars every year.

According to DeMarco in his book entitled *Slack* (DeMarco, 2001), ". . . multitasking causes at least a 15% decline in productivity. It is much higher for tasks (such as troubleshooting or design, for instance) that require complete immersion before the resource can make progress."

The inefficiencies stem from two sources. First, you have to shift gears each time you move from one task (or project), and there is "down" time associated with each transition. Second is the "ramp up" time needed each time you start a new task (or project).

Figure 13.5 illustrates the scheduling implications of multitasking. On the top path, each task finishes before the next one starts, i.e., no multitasking. In the bottom path, when Task A is half complete, resources are shifted to Task B.—i.e., multitasking. When Task B is half complete, resources are shifted to Task C, then back to A, B, and C until all tasks are completed.

Figure 13.5 | Multitasking

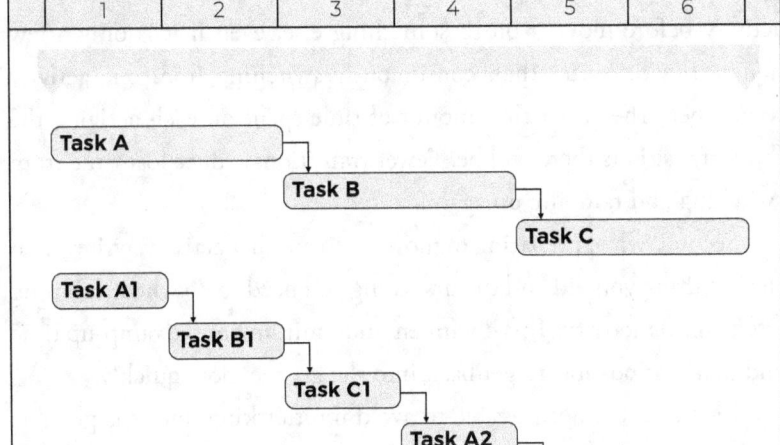

When resources are focused on Task A, as in the top path, it finishes at the end of the second week and Task B at the end of the fourth week. When multitasking, however, Task A does not finish until the end of the fourth week, and Task B finishes at the end of the fifth week. As a result, Task A takes two weeks longer to complete, and Task B takes one week longer for a total delay of three weeks.

It appears that Task C finishes at the same time in both scenarios but this is not entirely correct. The Gantt chart does not include the transition time between tasks. If we include these transitions in the schedule, it would show that multitasking delays the completion of all three tasks.

Multitasking does not make sense from an economic standpoint either, frequently resulting in shifting work from high-priority activities to lower-priority activities. Multitasking, therefore, violates the principle of executing around priorities if we define priorities in economic terms.

While we cannot eliminate multitasking, there are two things we can do to minimize the inefficiencies it causes. First, focus on one activity at a time. Try to carve out as much time as possible to work on each activity before moving on to something else, even if it is only a few hours. That is better than continuously switching from one activity to another. The larger the amount of time spent on each activity, the fewer transitions there will be. Fewer transitions reduce lost time from switching and ramping up again.

Second, when preparing to move on to another activity, write down the last thing you did and the first thing you need to do when resuming work on this activity. This documentation minimizes the ramp-up time and makes it possible to get back into the groove more quickly.

In short, it is not possible to avoid multitasking, but it is possible to reduce the lost productivity by minimizing the amount of multitasking and making the transitions between activities or projects more efficient.

The Kick-off Meeting

It is important to get the project off to a good start for all stakeholders. For this reason, the first project team meeting is extremely important. This meeting is often called the "kick-off meeting." Many project managers take this opportunity to begin the team-building process, often holding these meetings off-site and in a casual atmosphere. The agenda tends to be a mix of business and social activity designed to give team members a chance to get to know each other in a neutral environment.

For projects that involve more than one organization, the kick-off meeting often takes the form of what is called a "partnering meeting." This is the meeting in which the partnering organizations can meet with each other to discuss the project and how they are going to work together to complete it.

For many project teams, this meeting may be the most important meeting of the entire project. Virtual teams, for example, may not have another chance to meet during the course of the project. This meeting may be their only face-to-face opportunity to get to know each other, define their roles, and begin the team-building process.

Summary

Successful project management depends upon the efforts of a large number of people; project managers cannot do it alone. Projects are more likely to succeed when the sponsor plays an active role. Project champions can also increase the likelihood of project success. Selecting the right team is also very important. Selections are based on many factors, including skills, abilities, availability, interest in the project, and the project budget.

There is great variability in how and when project team members are appointed. It is common for senior managers to initiate and plan projects. The project is then handed off to a project manager and his or her team for implementation. Experience indicates, however, that projects are usually most successful when the project manager and the team are involved earlier in the project life cycle.

Assigning people to a team does not make them a team. Teams must be built. Team building is the process by which team members learn to work together effectively. Team building generally requires a great deal of time and effort on the part of the project manager and the project team.

Research by Tuckman found that team development takes place in stages known as Forming, Storming, Norming, Performing, and adjourning. It is the project manager's responsibility to move the team through these stages as quickly as possible. The goal is to reach the Performing stage, the stage at which the team operates at maximum effectiveness.

Research on team size finds that small teams may lack sufficient skills and diversity of perspective while larger teams often suffer from increased conflict, decreased efficiency, and a greater potential for fragmentation into sub-groups. Analyzing a number of published studies, Witolf Studzinski concluded that ideal team size was 4.6.

Time management is always an issue by the very nature of the environment in which projects are carried out. Stephen Covey developed the most widely used approach to time management. He believed that people effectively manage their time when they execute around priorities. He summarized this with the phrase, "Put first things first."

One of the biggest challenges to effective time management is multitasking. The transition between tasks represents a significant loss of productivity. Multitasking also tends to undermine priorities because it diverts resources from higher-priority activities to lower-priority activities. While you can never eliminate multitasking, you can minimize it. The best way to do this is to minimize the number of transitions and make the transitions quickly and smoothly.

TRACKING PROJECT PERFORMANCE

Introduction

We live and work in an incredibly complex, constantly changing environment, where it is impossible to anticipate all the possible events that might affect the execution of the project. No wonder no project ever goes exactly as planned! "Bad planning" is not necessarily the culprit behind a project gone awry.

We noted earlier that project control is exercised by comparing planned results with actual results. When the plan is unclear or lacking detail, it will be impossible to make meaningful comparisons. Without such comparisons, it is difficult to exercise control over the project. This is why so many projects appear to fail during the execution stage when the failure actually occurred in the initiation or planning stages.

One of the project manager's primary responsibilities is to ensure the project remains within the constraints documented and agreed to in the project charter. To do this, it is necessary to monitor the implementation closely. Research indicates that if a project begins to exceed time or cost parameters by the time it is 15% complete, it has an extremely high probability of failure. Because most projects have tight budgets, there are no additional resources available to accelerate progress to the extent necessary to get the project back on track. For this reason, it is essential to closely track the project's vital signs, especially early on in the project, while there is still some hope of recovery.

Failure to monitor closely may also result in cost overruns, or inability to meet project requirements, putting the project in jeopardy. For this reason, it is imperative to know what to track, how often, and to what level of detail.

The project manager must make these decisions before implementation begins. Tracking activities uses resources, and must therefore be planned like any other project activity. Unfortunately, teams often get caught up in planning the work and overlook the project management activities necessary to ensure the project work gets done.

Most organizations have a standard process for tracking project performance. This process usually includes all the steps necessary to determine progress, how progress will be measured, and how often it will be measured.

What to Track

Since there is not enough time or resources to track everything, the team must focus their efforts on those activities and indicators most critical to the successful completion of the project. Items most commonly tracked include:

>   schedule
>   budget
>   scope of the project

Failure to complete the project within these constraints (time, cost, and scope) usually has negative consequences. The attention paid to each item tracked will, of course, vary from phase to phase and project to project.

In addition, the team should also regularly review assumptions, risks, and issues. Each of these is discussed in the following sections.

TRACKING PROJECT PERFORMANCE

Project Schedule

Projects get behind schedule one day at a time. That being said, it is not unusual for large, long-term projects to finish months or even years behind schedule. Denver International Airport and the "Big Dig" in Boston are notorious examples. While these projects suffered for a variety of reasons, the point is that it is important to take prompt corrective action. This is not possible unless you closely monitor the project work.

On-time completion is almost always important, particularly when the schedule is driving the project. Three dates are used to track progress on scheduled activities:

- **The planned start and finish dates**
  The initial baseline start and finish dates
- **The expected start and finish dates**
  The scheduled start and finish dates revised to reflect the early and late finish dates of predecessor activities
- **The actual start and finish dates**
  The dates the work was actually started and finished

One of the most popular types of project charts used to track project progress is the Gantt chart. Developed by Harvey Gantt in 1910, the Gantt chart has become the standard for tracking and reporting project progress. Gantt charts, sometimes called "timelines," graphically display project activities on a calendar. Many people find it easier to see progress when displayed graphically, as shown in Figure 14.1.

If an activity starts on time and finishes on time, then the planned start date, the expected start date, and the actual start date will be the same. Unfortunately, that is not the world in which we live. Things always happen, and, as a result, these dates often vary considerably.

In the Gantt chart in Figure 14.1, Requirements is 100% complete. It had a planned start date of March 28th and a planned end

Figure 14.1 | Planned, Expected, and Actual Dates

#	Title	Q1 / 2023	Q2 / 2023		Q3 / 2023
		March	April	May	June	July
0	**Software Project**					
1	Start					
2	Requirements					
3	Design					
4	Code					
5	Test/Approve					
6	Package					
7	Ship					
8	User manual					
9	Training materials					
10	Marketing materials					
11	Finish					

date of April 17th. It started on time but, unfortunately, was not completed until April 24th, one week after its planned completion date. The planned start date for the next activity was April 18th but because work on Requirements took a week longer than planned, the design work was delayed one week. It now has an expected start date of April 25th. Note that all activities have two bars: a planned and expected date. The Gantt chart shows the impact of this delay on all subsequent work on the project.

Once an activity starts, the expected start date is irrelevant. The expected start date becomes the actual start date regardless of when the activity was initially scheduled to begin and end. The planned date remains the same regardless of changes in the expected dates unless the baseline schedule is revised. In some projects, the schedule is revised so often that it no longer makes sense to compare the current schedule with the original baseline schedule. In these instances, a new baseline schedule must be developed against which future work can be compared.

Gantt charts have the added advantage of showing dependencies and highlighting the critical path. All project management software packages are capable of creating Gantt charts. The ease of creating them is one of the primary reasons why many project managers choose to use project management software to track progress. This type of software not only makes it easy to generate Gantt charts but, perhaps more importantly, easy to update them.

There are several good freeware programs available for project managers who would like to generate Gantt charts and do not need the power of MS Project, Merlin, or any of the many other project management software packages available. While I have seen project managers develop Gantt charts using Excel, I do not recommend it. They are time-consuming to develop and update. Spreadsheets are much better suited to tracking project cost control than developing Gantt charts.

Project Budget

Just as the project must be monitored to ensure it stays on schedule, the project manager must also monitor the project expenditures to ensure project costs remain within budget. The most commonly used tool for tracking project expenditures, particularly for small to medium-sized projects, is the control chart. The spreadsheet in Figure 14.2 is an example of a project cost control chart.

The metrics used to track project expenditures are analogous to those used for tracking the schedule, with a planned and actual value for each expenditure. The planned cost is the baseline cost estimate. The actual cost is the amount actually paid to complete the work.

Tracking expenditures is a reasonably straightforward process. In effect, each work package becomes a line item in the project budget. Project expenditures are tracked by work package, and records are regularly updated—the more detailed the WBS, the more detailed the project budget. In large projects, work package costs are rolled up to obtain subproject costs. For example, the planned cost of the Requirements subproject (2.0) is equal to the planned cost of 2.1, 2.2, and 2.3.

Some project managers use a combination of spreadsheets and project management software to track projects. Project management software makes it easy to print network diagrams and Gantt charts while tracking project performance. The activity list in Figure 14.2 was initially developed using MS Project and exported to Excel.

While this might seem like extra work, there are several reasons why project managers do this. First, Excel is much easier to work with than MS Project. While MS Project is a very powerful program, that power comes at a price. The learning curve is very steep, and many project managers do not use it often enough to become proficient. On the other hand, Excel is straightforward to use, and most project managers have a relatively high level of proficiency with it.

Second, it is easier to share project data using Excel. In most organizations, virtually everyone who works on projects has Excel or some other similar spreadsheet program, while MS Project licenses are usually more limited. Thus, if the project data are stored in a spreadsheet, you can share them with stakeholders without regard for what software they might have or their proficiency level.

Project Scope

The third constraint is scope, the work that must be performed to achieve project goals and objectives. The scope of the project is first formally defined in the project charter, which outlines what needs to be done to solve the problem or capitalize on the opportunity and includes a high-level description of the scope. The project scope statement contains a more detailed description of the scope. The work packages identified in the WBS constitute the most detailed description of the project scope.

The project manager must closely monitor project activity to ensure that planned work is carried out and non-planned work is not. Of course, things always happen during the life of the project that make it necessary for the team to perform work not originally planned and therefore not included in the WBS. However, it is incumbent on the project manager to ensure that any necessary additional work gets done and that the WBS and other relevant documents are revised to reflect the change.

One of the biggest obstacles to the successful completion of the project is scope creep. The term "scope creep" refers to the expansion of the project scope to include activities not necessary to achieve project goals and objectives. In most cases, this expansion occurs in small increments and is not accompanied by commensurate increases in time or cost. For this reason, scope creep puts the project at risk.

Quality Control

Monitoring activities should focus not just on the Triple Constraints—time, cost, and scope—but should also ensure that all work meets

Figure 14.2 | Project Cost Control Chart

WBS Code	WBS	Planned	Actual	Planned–Actual	% Difference
0	BS Web Project	$32,250	$25,800	$6,450	20%
1	Start project				
2	Requirements	1250	$1,350	–$100	–8%
2.1	Review charter	$500	$550	–$50	–10%
2.2	Verify requirements	$250	$300	–$50	–20%
2.3	Develop SOW	$500	$500	$0	0%
3	Contents	$12,850	$11,550	$1,300	10%
3.1	Identify required content	$2,100	$1,800	$300	14%
3.2	Acquire/develop content	$10,500	$9,500	$1,000	10%
3.3	Transfer content to vendor	$250	$250	$0	0%
4	Vendor	$3,700			
4.1	Bidding	$1,700			
4.1.1	Develop bidding list	$300			
4.1.2	Develop RFP	$1,200			

TRACKING PROJECT PERFORMANCE

4.1.3	Send RFP	$200
4.2	Selection	$2,000
4.2.1	Develop selection criteria	$750
4.2.2	Review bids	$1,000
4.2.3	Select winning bid	$250
5	Development	$6,500
5.1	Create Design	$2,000
5.2	Develop prototype	$3,500
5.3	Review prototype	$750
5.4	Approve design	$250
6	Implementation	$7,950
6.1	Select host	$150
6.2	Obtain Domain	$300
6.3	Setup website	$2,500
6.4	Test website	$2,000
6.5	Train users	$3,000
7	End project	

customer requirements. The quality control activities, usually described in the quality management plan, are designed to serve this purpose. The primary quality control tools are:

- inspections
- audits
- testing

Inspections

Inspections involve direct observation of the work, often by a third party, to ensure the work is done correctly and that project outputs meet customer requirements. For some types of projects, inspections are essential. On construction projects, for example, all work is inspected to ensure the right materials are used and that no shortcuts are taken with respect to construction methods. However, for other types of projects, software development projects, for example, inspections serve no useful purpose.

Inspections, which are designed to detect discrepancies between what the customer wants and what the project has produced. are a reactive approach to ensuring quality work, and do not actually prevent such discrepancies. If an inspection reveals that the work does not meet customer specifications, it usually has to be redone, which adds to the cost of the project and may delay the completion of subsequent work.

A more proactive approach is to develop a process that maximizes the likelihood the project deliverables are done right and that they meet customer requirements. See the discussion of quality management planning beginning on page 229.

Audits

In project management, most audits—of which there are many kinds—focus on finances or performance. Usually conducted after the project has been completed, financial audits are designed to verify that the money went where it was supposed to go. Sometimes audits are conducted by an internal auditor; other times, a third-party organization is contracted to perform the audit.

Financial audits are generally reserved for projects with large budgets where misuse of funds is more likely to involve large amounts of money. There might also be other reasons for conducting an audit, such as evidence of financial irregularities. Some public and non-profit sector customers may also require financial audits.

Performance audits are used to verify the work in the WBS was performed and that it met project specifications. Again, performance audits are more common among long-term, high-budget projects or when required by law or contract. Like financial audits, they are usually a part of the project wrap-up.

Testing

Testing is a common validation method designed to verify that the output of the project or project components meets customer requirements and that it serves its intended function. Software development is a good example. Because software is so complex, you cannot assume it will perform exactly as intended. Therefore, project acceptance plans often include a final test as a condition of acceptance.

It is important to remember that inspections, audits, and tests, while often necessary, are non-value-added activities. They add nothing to the project deliverables that have value to the customer. They do, however, represent a cost and should, therefore, be avoided unless there is a specific reason to do them.

Assumptions

The project charter identifies the major assumptions upon which the success of the project depends. The sponsor's approval of the project charter is an implicit acceptance of these assumptions. (See the discussion on page 52. Therefore, the team must monitor the assumptions throughout the execution and controlling stages of the project. Remember that the success of the project depends on the validity of the project assumptions. If, at any point, it turns out that one or more of these assumptions are no longer valid, it will be necessary to reassess the project.

For example, a few years ago, I worked on a project that included a relatively large number of assumptions. One of the most critical assumptions was that team members would be available for the entire duration of the project. The sponsor refused to sign the charter because he believed this assumption was unrealistic, given the organization's current workload. As a result, the project manager had to increase the size of the team so the success of the project was no longer dependent on this assumption.

A review of the assumptions log should be a regular agenda item at all project review meetings. When it appears the validity of any of the project's assumptions has become questionable, the team should analyze the assumption(s) to determine if they are still valid. If not, they should take appropriate action.

Risks

Like assumptions, risks are first addressed in the project charter; identifying the threats most likely to impact the project is an important initiation activity. In the planning stage, the project team may develop a formal risk management plan identifying the ongoing risk-management activities they need to carry out. Risk management does not end until the project has been completed.

The team must monitor the risks identified in the planning stage and the risk triggers, i.e., those events that serve as an early warning for the impending occurrence of a risk event. The discussion should include how the team would respond should these risks materialize. The team should also discuss the likelihood, impact on the project, and potential response strategies (mitigation, avoidance, transference, or acceptance) of emerging threats.

In addition to looking for risk triggers, the project manager, project team, and other key stakeholders should continuously look for new risks. While some risks may pre-date the beginning of the project, many others will arise during the project. Therefore, a review of project risks, both existing and emerging, should be a standing item on the team meeting agenda.

Issues

While the concept of risk has to do with potential problems or opportunities, issues are events that have already occurred—e.g., problems that affect the schedule, budget, scope, or some other important aspect of the project. The project team must monitor project work closely so they can detect issues as they arise. Adverse impacts grow exponentially with time, so delays in addressing them become increasingly expensive to resolve.

When issues arise, it is important to document them. Most project managers maintain an issue log specifically for this purpose. They enter a description of the problem into the log and any information that might be of value in resolving it. Typically, this information includes:

- A description of the issue
- Date reported
- Reported by
- Assigned to
- What needs to be done to resolve the issue
- The priority of the issue
- The date by which the issue needs to be resolved
- Expected cost
- Any other information important to the resolution of the issue

The issue log needs to be reviewed at each project review meeting to ensure all outstanding issues are being addressed. Problems that have been resolved need to be documented, including information about how each case was resolved so it can be included in the "lessons learned" discussions.

The process for addressing issues was described in Chapter 12. See Appendix F for a sample issue log.

Project Review Meetings

One of the primary sources of information about the project is the periodic project review meeting. There are at least four types of project review meetings. These include:

- Project team review meetings
- Executive management review meetings
- Customer project review meetings
- Team review meetings

Few people feel they do not have enough meetings to attend. However, most of us feel burdened by what we perceive as an excessive number of meetings we *must* attend. Doyle and Strauss (1976) reported that employees spend on average between seven and 15 percent of their work time in meetings—which adds up to more than 9,000 hours or approximately 365 days during an employee's work career!

When we ask people about the last meeting they attended, most report that it was a waste of time. Many wondered why they were even asked (or required) to attend. Rather than contributing to their work, many viewed it as a work interruption.

Figure 14.3 | 20 Rules for Effective Meetings

- Develop healthy meeting habits
- Effective meetings serve a purpose
- Choose the right people, place and time
- Prepare to succeed
- What's your agenda?
- Help your team focus
- Cultivate open communications
- Start right... Start on time
- Keep your mind on the goal
- Learn to lead objectively
- Bring out the best in everyone
- Be quiet and listen
- Encourage diverse points of view
- Keep debates friendly
- Know when to say when
- Anticipate the next steps
- Report your results
- End on time... Or ahead of schedule
- Follow up, follow up, follow up
- Strive for improvement

Source: Ron Fry, 1999

Unnecessary and unproductive meetings are not just a waste of time; they also waste limited project resources. Meetings are expensive. For example, a one-hour meeting of eight to 10 mid-level employees may cost as much as $1,500 to $2,000 or more. In a study reported by the *Harvard Business Review* (https://hbr.org/2016/01/estimate-the-cost-of-a-meeting-with-this-calculator), Bain & Company found that a single weekly meeting of mid-level managers cost one organization $15M a year!

Many organizations fail to recognize the high cost of wasteful meetings. While they often impose strict spending limits on their employees, they waste thousands of dollars on unnecessary or unproductive meetings. Watching the budget does not help because few organizations budget for meetings. Can you imagine a meeting canceled or postponed because the budget for meetings had been exceeded? It would never happen.

Do not misunderstand; meetings are an essential part of effective project management. The solution is simply to hold meetings only when necessary and, when they are necessary, conduct them efficiently. While this may be difficult to do, it is far from impossible.

In the book *Why Work Sucks and How to Fix It* (Ressler and Thompson, 2008), the authors suggest several remedies, including making all meetings optional. Would meetings be more productive if you had to give people a reason to attend? Imagine having to convince people the meeting would be a more productive use of their time than whatever else they had planned to do at that particular time.

So, what would you have to say or do to convince people that attending the meeting is the best use of their time? Or, in other words, what can you accomplish in a meeting that you could not accomplish better by some other means? Generally speaking, meetings are most effective when they involve decision-making, problem-solving, or team-building activities.

When you do have meetings, it is important to run them efficiently. Fortunately, there are some proven methods for getting the most out of your meetings, including project review meetings. (See Doyle and Strauss, 1976) They suggest the following:

Start on Time, End on Time

Effective time management requires that people have some predictability in their schedules. An important step in making schedules more predictable is to start meetings on time and end them on time. It can be done, but it requires some discipline.

In most organizations, people do not arrive on time for meetings. Instead, they trickle in one by one. As a result, it is not uncommon for many team members to be 10 to 15 or more minutes late for the meeting. Good meeting management requires that this behavior change; the most effective way to do this is to start meetings on time. Do not wait for stragglers. When people know the meeting starts on time, they are more likely to be on time.

When participants arrive late for the meeting, do not try to catch them up by reviewing the information already covered. Reviewing missed information reduces the incentive to arrive on time and wastes the time of those who were punctual. Instead, offer to review the information they missed at the end of the meeting.

Remember that arriving late is not a problem if the latecomer does not miss anything. It only works when the meeting addresses issues important to participants. If I can arrive at a meeting 15 minutes late and not miss anything, I will come 20 minutes late for the next meeting!

Finishing the meeting on time is also essential. It forces participants to focus on what is critical. As a result, they are less likely to engage in tangents. It also provides predictability. Participants know they can schedule another meeting or get back to their work at a specific time.

Use an Agenda for All Project Review Meetings

Everyone should know what to expect before coming to the project meeting. That means there must be an agenda, and it should be sent out in advance. Receiving the agenda in advance of the meeting does two things. First, it allows participants to prepare for the meeting. And second, it will enable them to add items to the agenda if necessary. This last point may seem insignificant, particularly if team members seldom contribute additional items. Still, it helps to reinforce the notion that the project is a collaborative effort for which all team members are responsible.

Ideally, each agenda item should have a fixed amount of time allotted to it. This makes it easier to finish on time because participants know in advance how much time each item has been allotted. Attaching a time limit on each agenda item is based on the principle that deadlines create urgency. Without time frames for each item, there is no urgency to bring the discussion to a close until the time for adjournment approaches.

The amount of time assigned to each item is, at best, an educated guess. Sometimes the discussion takes less time, and sometimes it takes more. It usually takes more. The timekeeper must monitor the clock and keep the project manager or facilitator aware of the amount of time remaining.

If it appears the team cannot complete the discussion within the allotted time, the timekeeper should ask the project manager what he or she would like to do. There are three options: extend the time allotted to the issue, assign one or more team members to discuss the issue offline and report back at the next meeting, or table the discussion until the next meeting. If the discussion extends beyond its allotted time, you should subtract the additional time from subsequent agenda items. The meeting ends on time, even if one or more items take longer than allotted.

Assign Meeting Roles

Meetings are more efficient when members are assigned to specific roles, the most common of which are facilitator, scribe, and timekeeper. These roles should be assigned in advance of the meeting and rotated after each meeting so that no team member is burdened with the same task at every meeting. In addition, rotating roles reinforces the collegial nature of the relationship between team members.

Distribute a Copy of the Minutes

You should distribute the minutes to all team members shortly after the completion of the meeting. Shortly is a relative term. Generally speaking, the minutes should go out within 24 hours of the end of the meeting, which is essential when action items have been assigned. These items should be highlighted so recipients do not overlook them.

The distribution list should include all team members and all key stakeholders unless they have specifically asked not to receive them. Copies should also be kept and archived with other project records after the project's completion.

Project Team Review Meetings

A project review meeting is a meeting of key stakeholders to review progress, discuss issues, and make decisions on how to move forward, in order to ensure the project stays on track and achieves its goals. The meeting starts with a presentation of the project status, including updates on timelines, budgets, and deliverables. Next, the group discusses any issues or challenges that have arisen and identifies the root causes before developing strategies for addressing them.

Once the issues have been discussed, the group makes decisions on how to move forward, which may involve revising timelines or budgets, changing project scope, or reassigning resources. The meeting concludes with a summary of the decisions made and any action items.

Executive Management Review Meetings

In addition to regular status reports, some project management protocols require the project manager to meet with senior leaders regularly to discuss the project. The project manager usually gives a high-level overview of the project's progress and expected future performance in these meetings. He or she may also request guidance and, if necessary, assistance in resolving issues.

The frequency, content, and format of these meetings are determined in the planning stage, though any of these may require change during the implementation of the project for various reasons.

Few project managers look forward to executive review meetings, particularly when the project is not going well. There are, however, a few things the project manager can do to make these meetings go more smoothly. The first, and probably most important, is to be prepared.

At a minimum, senior managers will want to know the status of the schedule and the budget. Project managers must be prepared to brief this information. For example, if the project is behind schedule or over budget, they need to explain how it happened and what they plan to do to get the project back on track.

Be honest and candid—project managers who appear evasive or less than entirely truthful invite additional scrutiny. Senior managers are more likely to question a project if they feel the project manager is holding back relevant information or is putting an overly optimistic spin on the situation.

It is also important to be brief. Get to the point quickly. Senior executives are busy and do not have time for long explanations or details that ultimately have no bearing on the decisions they have to make. Therefore, project managers who can communicate clearly and succinctly and stay focused on critical issues have a distinct advantage over those who cannot.

Executive project review meetings are also an opportunity to share project successes. Remember that every project competes with every other project for resources. When resources run short, the projects with the lowest priority are the ones that get cut back. Executive review meetings are an opportunity for the project manager to keep the project visible and remind senior leaders of the importance of the project.

Customer Review Meetings

Most, if not all, customers want periodic updates on the status of their projects. In addition to regular status reports, many customers also want occasional face-to-face meetings. Larger projects are likely to require more face-to-face meetings because the stakes for these projects are high. Like executive review meetings, the frequency, content, and format of these meetings should be decided before the implementation begins.

Some projects are internal, i.e., the customer is an employee or department within the organization. An IT upgrade, developing a new performance appraisal system, and developing a new public relations campaign are examples of an internal project. Meetings with internal customers are very much like executive review meetings and should be handled similarly.

Review meetings with external customers, on the other hand, are often quite different. First, the project manager may be less likely to have an established working relationship with an external customer. Second, they have different chains of command and often have different goals and objectives.

Project managers may share sensitive information with internal customers but tend not to share it with external customers. For example, they are more likely to downplay risk when meeting with external customers. These differences will also impact the nature of review meetings.

While projects for internal customers are often mandated, projects for external customers are frequently the result of a competitive bidding process. A legal contract governs the planning and execution of the project, and the project manager is expected to manage the project in such a way as to maximize the likelihood of future business from the customer.

This has important implications for managing the project and how the project manager conducts customer review meetings. However, it is easy to exaggerate the differences, particularly when the customer is a valued partner. The project manager should work to achieve a win-win outcome, which should guide the conduct of customer review meetings.

Virtual Meetings

More and more, teams are made up of individuals who do not work at the same location or at the same time. Virtual project review meetings have become increasingly common with the rise of remote work and online collaboration tools. Fortunately, there are many technology-based alternatives—most frequently conference calls and video conferences. These meetings can be conducted through video conferencing software, which allows participants to see each other and share documents and presentations in real time. It's important to ensure the technology is reliable and that everyone knows how to use it.

The structure of a virtual project review meeting is similar to an in-person meeting but with the added challenges of remote communication and coordination. Participants may join from different locations and time zones, making it important to ensure everyone has access to the necessary technology and communication channels.

One advantage of virtual meetings is that they can be recorded for future reference, allowing participants to review the discussion and decisions made. This can be particularly helpful for team members who were unable to attend the meeting in real time.

Overall, virtual project review meetings can be almost as effective as in-person meetings when conducted properly. By using reliable technology, establishing clear communication protocols, and ensuring that everyone has a chance to participate, virtual meetings can help keep projects on track and ensure that everyone stays informed and engaged.

Meeting Evaluations

A study by Gerschel and Polsky (2015) found a correlation between efficient meetings, team productivity, and morale. To improve the efficiency of meetings, it is important to conduct periodic meeting evaluations. There are many evaluation surveys on the internet, all more or less including the same topics, such as:

- Agenda
- Objectives
- Information shared
- Meeting location
- How decisions were made
- Handouts
- Opportunities for participation
- Assignment of follow-up tasks

Some evaluation instruments also include open-ended questions, along the lines of:

- Was this meeting worth your time?
- What went well in this meeting?
- What could have gone better?

The project manager should use the evaluation results to improve meeting performance. A note of caution: don't administer evaluations unless you intend to use the results to make improvements.

An example of a project meeting effectiveness survey can be found in Appendix C.

Summary

One of the important administrative decisions made during the planning stage has to do with what information needs to be tracked during the execution of the project work plan. Some are obvious. Time, cost, and scope—the Triple Constraints—virtually always need to be tracked. It is also important to monitor all work to ensure that it meets customer requirements. Failure to meet these requirements often leads to customer dissatisfaction.

There are often other aspects of the project that need to be tracked. The selection of performance measures depends largely on the nature of the project and the needs of key stakeholders. Other commonly tracked items include assumptions, risks, and issues.

Tracking the cost and scope involves comparing planned performance values with actual performance values. The most common tools used for this purpose are the control chart and the Gantt chart. The control chart is a simple spreadsheet containing planned and actual cost and schedule measures. The Gantt chart, or "timeline" as it is sometimes called, is used primarily to display the work on a project calendar. Gantt charts make it easy to see where activities have started late or failed to finish on time.

Inspections, audits, and testing are common methods used to ensure that project work conforms to customer requirements. However, since these are non-value-added activities, you should only use them where necessary.

Meetings are an important part of the monitoring process. They are a primary source of information about project activity and one of the most important means of decision-making, problem-solving, and team-building.

The most common types of project meetings are project review (team) meetings, executive review meetings, and customer meetings. Project team meetings include the project manager, the team, and occasionally others such as ad hoc team members, subject matter experts, and key stakeholders.

While meetings are essential to effective project management, most organizations have too many meetings, and most meetings are less productive than they could and should be. The solution is to hold meetings only when necessary and to conduct them following best meeting practices.

The number of virtual teams has increased in recent years resulting in an increase in virtual meetings. With the increased sophistication of modern video conferencing, virtual meetings have become a viable alternative to in-person meetings.

PROJECT REPORTING

Introduction

Performance and progress reporting play an important role in the management of project. After all, while project meetings are important, they take time, and finding a date and time when all the stakeholders are available is often impossible. Moreover, some stakeholders may choose not to attend project meetings but would still like regular updates. Hence the need for reports.

The project manager working with key stakeholders determines the number, type, and frequency of performance reports and the distribution list for these reports, documenting this information in the stakeholder analysis, the communications plan (if there is one), and the project charter. There are three basic types of project reports:

1. status reports
2. progress reports
3. future status/forecasting reports

Sometimes elements of one or more of these reports are combined into a single report. These reports should be short (one page or less if possible) and sent out on a predetermined schedule to the stakeholder distribution list.

Status Reports

As the name suggests, a status report is a snapshot of the project at a given point, focusing on current cost and schedule performance. A typical status report might include some or all of the following:

Schedule Information

- Activities scheduled to start but that have not yet begun
- Activities scheduled to begin within the next week, two weeks, etc.
- Activities in progress
- Completed activities
- Activities that have begun but are behind schedule
- Milestones reached
- Earned Value (SPI) or percent complete

Cost Information

- Cash flow
- Budget status
- Activities that are over budget
- Resources that have exceeded budget
- Earned value (CPI)

Miscellaneous Information

- Assumptions
- Risks
- Issues

Most project management software programs can generate reports that contain many, if not all, of the items listed above. Most of these items are widely used and well-understood. However, two require some explanation: Percent Complete and Earned Value.

Percent Complete

Although there are many approaches for reporting project status and progress, "Percent Complete"— an estimate of the percentage of work on an activity that has been completed—is the most frequently used method. For example, if half of the work on an activity has been completed, the "percent complete" for that activity is 50%. Many, if not most, organizations require project managers to report Percent Complete, and virtually all project management software packages can record, track, and report it.

While "Percent Complete" would appear to be a simple way to measure progress, estimates are problematic for various reasons. First, such estimates are often inaccurate and unreliable. Second, it is often difficult to estimate what percentage of the work has been completed with any degree of accuracy.

Many estimates of Percent Complete are based on the amount of time that has been spent on the activity. For example, team members have worked for one week on an activity with a planned duration of four weeks, so the work must be about 25% complete. This estimate assumes that work will progress uniformly throughout the duration of the activity and that work will not be affected by any unforeseen delays. These are unrealistic assumptions.

Another problem with percent complete as a measure of progress is that it often results in biased estimates. If it were an unbiased measure, one would expect estimates to be randomly distributed around the true value for the percentage of work completed. That is not the case, however. Instead, estimates are skewed toward the short side. Project managers frequently overestimate progress because team members tend to report optimistic estimates. Overestimates of progress are largely due to a desire to keep the project manager happy and an unwarranted belief that the work will proceed smoothly.

For these reasons, some organizations report activities as zero percent complete or 100 percent complete. There is no in-between. Before work on an activity has started, we can be 100 percent certain that it is zero percent complete. After it has been completed, we can be reasonably certain that it is 100 percent complete. Anything in-between is guesswork.

In this approach, progress is measured using milestones. The project is on schedule if milestones are reached on time. The project is behind schedule if milestones are not reached when scheduled.

Some project managers object to this approach, arguing that estimates of Percent Complete are needed to measure progress adequately between milestones. The implication is that the milestones are too far apart. The response to this objection is simple: add more milestones. While the customer may mandate some milestones, there is no reason the project manager cannot add additional milestones to help better track the progress of the project.

It may also be that activity durations are a little too long. If the project manager or other key stakeholders feel they need to track progress on an activity, its duration is probably too long. Once again, the solution is simple: break it up into several smaller activities with shorter durations.

There are no regulations that govern the duration of an activity, but experienced project managers suggest the optimum duration is somewhere between one and two weeks. If the duration is longer than a month, it becomes difficult to measure progress accurately. On the other hand, if it is shorter than a week, it may result in an overly detailed project plan that makes tracking burdensome.

PROJECT REPORTING

Earned Value

Interestingly, the *PMBOK* does not mention "Percent Complete" as a method for measuring progress on project work. Instead, the recommended measure is the project SPI (Schedule Performance Index), a measure derived from Earned Value analysis often referred to as EVM or EVA.

Earned Value is an increasingly popular method for tracking and reporting progress. Because time and cost are interrelated, tracking time and cost separately does not always provide a complete picture of the project's status. Suppose, for example, a project is two weeks ahead of schedule. This is a good thing, right? What if it cost 125 percent of the budgeted cost of the work to get to this point? It may not be so good after all. An accurate estimate of project status requires a measure that combines time and cost information.

Figure 15.1 | Basic Tenets of ANSI/EIE-A Standard (Earned Value)

1. Plan all work for the project to completion.
2. Break down the project work scope into finite pieces that can be assigned to a responsible person or organization for control of technical schedule and cost objectives.
3. Integrate project work scope, schedule, and cost objectives into a performance measurement baseline plan against which accomplishments may be measured.
4. Use actual costs incurred and recorded in accomplishing the work performed.
5. Objectively assess at the work performance level.
6. Analyze significant variances from the plan, forecast impacts, and prepare an estimate at completion based on performance to date and work to be performed.
7. Incorporate Earned Value Management in the company's man-agement processes.

Source: U.S. Department of Emer-gency Preparedness, Office of the Assistant Secretary for Preparedness and Response

The most common method for measuring the joint effect of time and cost is called Earned Value, sometimes abbreviated EVA or EVM. It was developed by the Department of Defense (DOD) in the 1960s primarily as a method to control project costs and schedules. It has since evolved into an overall approach to the management of project work. DOD and the Office of Management and Budget (OMB) now require vendors to report Earned Value metrics. Many large corporations, including Sprint, also use some form of EV for tracking project performance.

Earned Value methods, however, have had a reputation for being conceptually complex and difficult to implement. For this reason, EVM has not been widely used by project managers outside the United States federal government. Interest in EVM, however, has increased significantly in recent years. Two events have facilitated the increased use of EV in business and industry. The first was the inclusion of EV methods in the first edition of PMI's *PMBOK*, published in 1987. The second was the development and adoption of the ANSI/EIA 748-A Standard about 10 years later, which outlines the basic principles of effective EV implementation and use.

In its simplest form, Earned Value involves the use of three basic measures.

Planned Value (PV)
This is simply the estimated labor cost of the work planned. Note that this does not include non-labor costs such as materials and supplies.

Earned Value (EV)
This is the estimated value of the work that has been completed.

Actual Cost (AC)
As its name suggests, actual cost is the actual cost of the work that has been completed.

PROJECT REPORTING

These measures are used to calculate the two basic indices of project status. The first is the Cost Performance Index (CPI). The other is the Schedule Performance Index (SPI). The formulas for calculating SPI and CPI are shown below.

CPI = EV/AC
SPI = PV/EV

The CPI is a ratio of Earned Value and Actual Cost. It is the estimated cost of the work that has been completed divided by the actual cost of completing the work. Ideally, it should be about 1.0. An index greater than 1.0 indicates that the work has been completed for less than the estimated cost, i.e., the work was done efficiently. Conversely, an index of less than 1.0 means that the work has cost more than its estimated value, suggesting a lack of efficiency.

The SPI is a ratio of the Planned Value and the Earned Value. It should also be about 1.0. Measures greater than 1.0 indicate that the project is ahead of schedule, i.e., the value of the work completed is greater than the value of the work scheduled. Conversely, values of less than 1.0 occur when the value of the work completed is less than the value of the work scheduled. In this case, the project is behind schedule.

Ideally CPI and SPI values should be between .95 and 1.05. Values below .90 or above 1.10 should be a cause for concern. For example, if the CPI is well below 1.0, it indicates that the project is over budget, and the actual costs are higher than what was originally planned. This could be due to a variety of factors, such as unexpected expenses, poor budgeting, or inefficient use of resources. In such cases, it's important to identify the root cause of the cost overruns and take corrective action to bring the project back within budget.

If the Cost Performance Index (CPI) is well above 1.0, it indicates the project is under budget, and the actual costs are lower than what was originally planned. This could be due to the efficient use of resources, cost-saving measures, or other factors that have helped to reduce project costs. While this is generally a positive development, it's important to ensure the quality of the work is not being compromised in order to achieve cost savings.

If the SPI is less than .90 the project is significantly behind schedule, and work is not being completed as quickly as originally planned. This could be due to a variety of reasons, such as unexpected delays or poor planning. In such cases, it's important to identify the root cause of the delay and take corrective action to get the project back on track.

A Schedule Performance Index (SPI) above 1.10 indicates that the project is well ahead of schedule and work is being completed at a much faster pace than originally planned. While this may seem like a good thing, it's important to make sure the quality of the work is not being compromised to achieve this speed. Additionally, if the project is completed too far ahead of schedule, it may mean the project team has overestimated the amount of work required, which could result in unused resources and higher costs.

To do an EV analysis, there must be a complete (though not necessarily detailed) enumeration of the work necessary to accomplish the project goals. The WBS provides this list. In addition, estimates for all work activities must be made, and each work activity must have a scheduled start date. These data are used to calculate CPI and SPI.

Let's take a look at a simplified example. Figure 15.2 includes a high-level listing of the work necessary to complete a software development project together with the information needed to calculate the CPI and SPI.

For example, the team members assigned to code the project have just finished their work, and the software is ready for testing and approval. They have also completed the marketing materials. The EV (the estimated value of the work scheduled to be completed) is $47,000. It cost $51,500 to complete this work. Using the cost performance formula, the CPI is .91. The company has paid $51,500 (AC) for work valued at $47,000 (PV). Therefore, the project is significantly over budget.

Figure 15.2 | Earned Value Analysis Table

	Activities	Planned Value	Earned Value	Actual Cost
1	Requirements	$10,000	$10,000	$10,500
2	Design	$12,000	$12,000	$12,500
3	Code	$17,000	$17,000	$21,000
4	Test/Approve	$3,000		
5	Usser Manual	$2,500		
6	Training Materials	$1,500		
7	Marketing Materials	$8,000	$8,000	$7,500
8	Package	$3,500		
9	Ship	$1,000		
		$58,500	$47,000	$51,500

The calculation of the SPI requires the project schedule data. The Gantt chart in Figure 15.3 indicates that Requirements started on time and finished on time. Design started on time but was not completed until one week after its scheduled completion date. This delay pushed back the coding start date by one week. The development of the marketing materials is not dependent on coding and was, therefore, unaffected by this delay.

Earned Value is $47,000. Because testing started two weeks late, Planned Value is $47,000 plus the value of the two weeks of work on testing scheduled but not completed. This makes the Planned Value $47,500 and the SPI .99. The project is slightly behind schedule.

Because the CPI and SPI are snapshots of the project at a single point in time, EV analyses are often calculated at regular intervals beginning at the start of the project. Therefore, the *PMBOK* suggests reporting EV information in the format shown in Figure 15.4. According to the results presented in this chart, it does not look like

ON TIME, ON BUDGET

Figure 15.3 | Tracking Gantt Chart

#	Title	Q1/2023		Q2/2023			Q3/2023
		March	April	May	June	July	
0	**Software Project**						
1	Start						
2	Requirements						
3	Design						
4	Code						
5	Test/Approve						
6	Package						
7	Ship						
8	User manual						
9	Training materials						
10	Marketing materials						
11	Finish						

Figure 15.4 | Earned Value Analysis Report

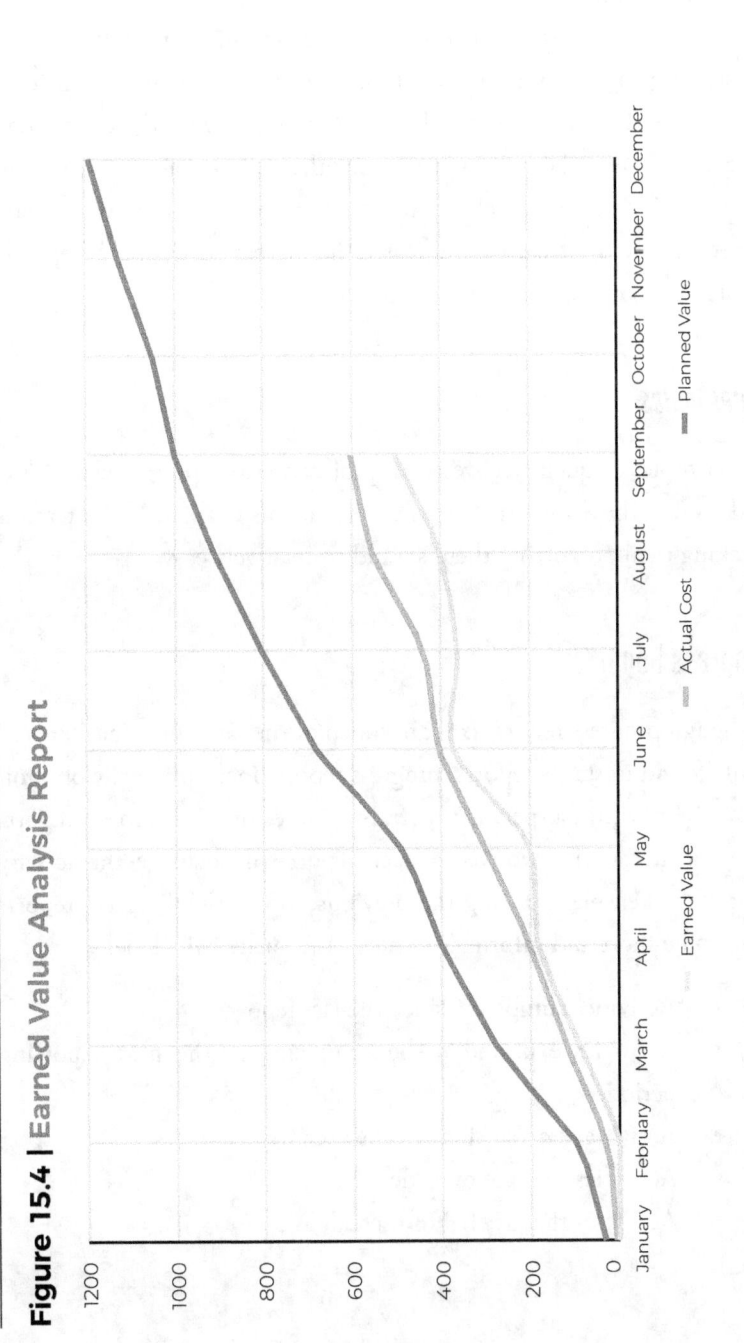

the project will finish within the budget, though it is possible that it may finish on time.

Because many stakeholders may not be familiar with CPI and SPI measures, project managers sometimes translate these numbers using a color-coded system. For example, an SPI between .95 and 1.05 is coded green, indicating the project is on schedule. Values from .90 to .95 and 1.05 to 1.10 are coded yellow, and those below .90 or above 1.10 are coded red. Red, of course, indicates the project is beyond acceptable limits, and corrective action is required.

Other Topics

Other topics frequently covered in project status reports include risks and issues. These were discussed earlier in this chapter. If the team is tracking them, reporting them should be relatively easy.

Progress Reports

Although progress reports contain much of the same information generally found in status reports, progress reports focus primarily on project activity within a specific timeframe. For example, if project reports are generated every two weeks, each report will focus on the activity that has taken place during the previous two weeks. Progress reports tend to be short and informal. As such, they usually include:

- Activities completed since the last report
- Activities expected to be completed in the next reporting period
- Activities started since the last report
- Activities that are overdue
- Activities that are behind schedule

PROJECT REPORTING

Progress reports may also contain some or all of the following financial information:

- Cost of work completed during the reporting period
- Planned cost of work scheduled during the reporting period
- Unplanned costs incurred during the reporting period
- Cost overruns that occurred during the reporting period
- CPI

Other information might include the status of unresolved issues, the emergence of new issues, the status of known risks, and the emergence of new risks.

Some project managers like to use a system in which key project measures are color-coded, where green is "on track," yellow is "at risk" for slippage, and red is "not meeting objectives." One team at a large manufacturing plant used to put the color-coded activity list on the back wall of the team meeting room. They blew it up so it covered most of the back wall. It attracted team members' attention, particularly when the list contained activities colored red. This system can be used with either status reports or progress reports.

Future Status/Forecasting Reports

While the project's current status is important, the ultimate goal is to finish on time and within budget. Future status or forecasting reports estimate completion parameters based on past and current performance.

Estimates of future performance may be based on informal methods such as expert judgments, simple extrapolations, or more formal methods such as time-series analysis, regression, or simulation. An increasingly popular method for forecasting future project performance is Earned Value, as discussed earlier in this chapter.

The primary EV cost forecasting value is Estimate at Completion (EAC). It is the estimated cost of the project based on the current rate of resource utilization. The formula is:

$$EAC = BAC/CPI$$

where BAC (Budget at Completion) is the total Planned Value for all activities included in the WBS.

In the example in Figure 15.2, the CPI is .91, and the BAC is $58,500. Plugging these numbers into the formula above results in an EAC of $64,286. A CPI of .91 indicates that the organization is not using its project resources efficiently. This utilization rate results in a total project cost of $5,786 over the BAC unless measures are taken to cut costs.

Reporting Bad News

When the project is on time and within budget, reporting is relatively easy. However, when the project falls behind schedule, begins to exceed budget estimates, or experiences some other kind of problem, status and progress reporting become more problematic.

Many project managers tend to withhold bad news from customers, hoping the problem will be quickly resolved and the customer will never find out. Unfortunately, it seldom works this way. The situation becomes much more serious if the customer finds out there was a problem and they were not informed.

While customers (internal and external) do not need to know about every problem that occurs during the course of the project, you should report problems that may lead to missed deadlines, cost overruns, and other problems that significantly impact the project. Failure to do so may blindside the customer, undermining the customer's trust in the project manager and the team.

So, what is the best way to communicate bad news? It is never easy, but there are some guidelines to make it a little less difficult. First, be proactive. Customers do not like surprises, particularly negative ones. For example, when it appears you may miss a deadline, inform the customer that the work may not finish on time. It is not necessary to wait until the next scheduled meeting to report bad news. If the situation warrants it, set up a meeting with the customer to discuss the problem. If the customer asks why no one informed them earlier, then you probably waited too long.

If you are going to report bad news at a meeting, be sure to inform key stakeholders in advance so they will not be surprised. Advance notice also gives them a chance to prepare. In particular, key stakeholders and the project sponsor do not like to be blindsided by unexpected bad news.

Second, do not sugarcoat it. Be honest and open with the customer. Most customers appreciate it, and it helps build and maintain trust.

When reporting bad news, be sure to have a plan to get back on track. Customers do not want to hear about problems. They want to hear about solutions. An explanation of how the problem occurred and what is being done to fix it will help maintain the customer's confidence in the project manager and the project team.

Lastly, do not point fingers. The focus of the discussions with the customer is the problem and how to resolve it. Pointing fingers only serves to divert attention from the real issue.

In summary, ". . . your clients expect you to call out issues and risks. It's where the real value of a project manager lies." (Meredith Zehnder, 2015)

Summary

Performance reporting is an important part of the tracking process. Performance reports keep key stakeholders informed of the status of the project. The three most common types of reports are the status report, the progress report, and the future status/forecasting report. While each of these is a distinct type, in practice, most performance reports are a combination of the three.

Percent complete and Earned Value are the two most common methods of reporting the status of the project and the amount of progress since the last report. The use of percent complete to report status or progress is somewhat problematic since it is often difficult to estimate and often subject to political pressures. An increasingly popular method of measuring and reporting progress is Earned Value.

SPI (Schedule Performance Index) and CPI (Cost Performance Index) are measures of status/progress derived from Earned Value Analysis. A healthy project is one in which the SPI and CPI are between 0.95 and 1.05. Another EV measure, EAC (Estimate at Completion), is also an important metric used in future status/forecasting reports. It measures the estimated completion cost of the project based on the current rate of resource utilization.

When the project is not going well, it is important to communicate openly and honestly with key stakeholders quickly. This communication should include information about how you will resolve the problem.

Successful projects do not just happen. They are the result of careful planning based on a clear understanding of what the customer wants. The plan, however, is of little value if it is not effectively executed. Monitoring the project helps make that happen to the extent that discrepancies between the plan and the execution are carefully controlled. The next chapter deals with this issue.

CONTROLLING THE PROJECT

Introduction

Controlling the project consists of those activities that ensure the project proceeds according to plan within the established parameters. This further underscores the importance of a detailed charter and a carefully thought-out plan. Project control can only be achieved when cost, schedule, and scope are clearly documented, realistically estimated, and carefully managed.

Control consists of comparing actual performance with planned performance as outlined in the various project planning documents. When there is a gap between planned and actual performance, the project manager must take some action to resolve the discrepancy. This might involve taking corrective action or adjusting the project plan to bring it into alignment with the changes. Ignoring the discrepancy should not be one of the options.

In order to manage projects successfully, the project manager must be able to manage the change process effectively, as well as manage conflict, issues, risks, and other challenges to the effective implementation of the project plan. Failure to do so increases the likelihood that the project will fail to achieve its intended objectives.

Issues

When a risk event occurs, it is no longer a risk. Risk is about uncertainty. When a risk event happens there is no longer any uncertainty; it has become an *issue*. In most cases, issues require the immediate attention of the project manager and members of the project team. Some issues may also involve other key stakeholders.

Many of the issues that arise during the course of the project can be anticipated by effective risk planning. For example, vendor delays are common on construction projects. Risk planning attempts to identify potential delays and strategies to address them (e.g., mitigation, avoidance, transference, acceptance). If a delay occurs, the project team will execute the appropriate contingency.

In order to ensure that issues are dealt with in a timely manner, teams should report all issues to the project manager or some other designated person as soon as they are discovered. It is important to do this quickly because the damage caused by unexpected issues increases exponentially with time. Failure to deal with them quickly has the potential to increase the cost of the project significantly and extend it well past its expected completion date.

Successful project teams use a systematic process to address these issues when they occur. Such a process is described in the next section on problem-solving.

The issues log (see discussion on page 171 for a review of the issues log) is continually updated throughout the course of the project and archived after the completion of the project. It can be an important source of information for future teams working on similar projects.

Problem-Solving

It is not possible to anticipate all project risks. Most projects are subject to a very high number of risks. Time and resources, on the other hand, are always limited. There just isn't enough time or resources to identify all project risks and develop strategies to deal with them. For this reason, good problem-solving skills are critical to the successful implementation of the project.

Unfortunately, most organizations do little or no risk planning and must, therefore, develop solutions to problems as they arise. Unplanned solutions to unanticipated issues are called "workarounds." Because these issues are unexpected, workarounds are not budgeted nor are they included in the project schedule. As a result, workarounds tend to be "quick fixes," not the kind of solutions that result from careful planning and implementation. Since it is not possible to anticipate all risks, some workarounds are necessary even when the team has done a thorough job of risk planning. Good risk planning keeps the number of workarounds to a minimum.

Although people who engage in project work generally have good problem-solving skills, they are not necessarily proficient in solving problems efficiently. Despite being capable of resolving problems, they may not always choose the most direct approach to the solution.

The problem-solving process depicted in Figure 16.1 is used by Xerox (Xerox, p. 3). Many organizations use a similar process.

The first step is to clearly define the problem that needs to be solved. This involves identifying the cause or causes of the problem. It is important not to confuse symptoms with the underlying cause. While it may be necessary to address the symptoms, doing so does not solve the problem. The problem is solved when the root cause is addressed.

Once the problem has been defined, the next step is to gather as much information as possible about it. This may involve collecting data, conducting research, and consulting with experts.

The next step is to analyze the information. Analysis involves identifying patterns, trends, and potential solutions and may involve using tools like data analysis software, brainstorming sessions, or other problem-solving techniques.

Figure 16.1 | Systematic Problem-solving Process

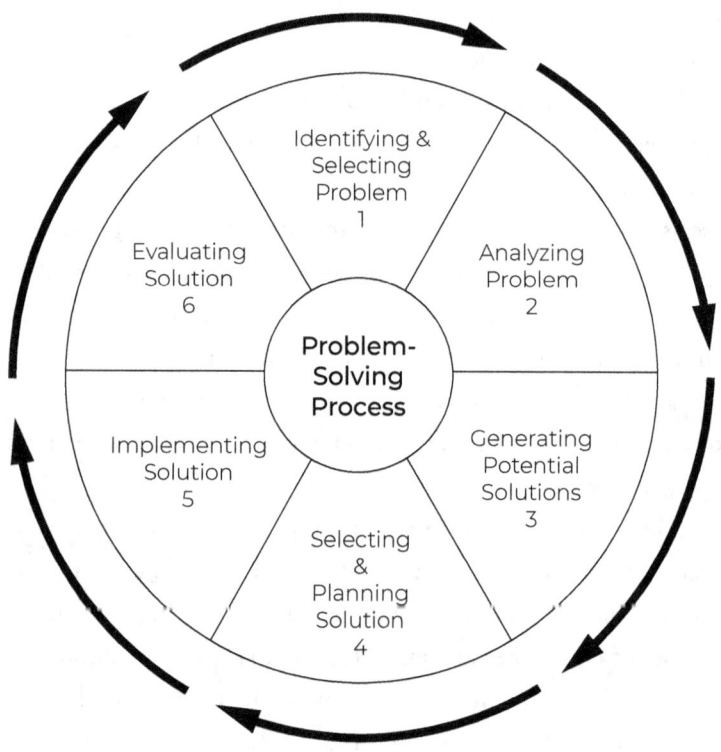

After analyzing the data, it is helpful to generate a list of three to five possible solutions. Evaluate the pros and cons of each solution and consider how likely they are to achieve the desired outcome.

Then, implement the best proposed solution. This means creating a plan of action, allocating resources, and assigning responsibilities. If the proposed solution does not work, return to step three and evaluate the other proposed solutions.

Some of the problems that occur when the project team does not use a systematic process for solving problems include:

- Jumping to conclusions before effectively analyzing all aspects of the problem

- Failing to gather critical data, either about the problem or proposed solutions
- Tackling problems beyond the control or influence of team members
- Working on problems that are too general, too large, or not well defined
- Failing to develop an adequate rationale for a solution
- Failing to involve critical people—especially those outside the group—when looking for solutions
- Failing to plan adequately how to implement and evaluate the recommended solution

Unfortunately, there are many examples of situations in which the problem was not properly defined. One of the classic examples of the failure to apply a structured process to problem-solving is NASA's attempt to develop a zero-gravity pen. This story has been reported on numerous websites over the last ten years. It was mentioned in an episode of NBC's *The West Wing* TV series ("We Killed Yamamoto"; original air date 15 May 2002).

Traditional pens depend on gravity to provide the tip with a continuous flow of ink. There is, of course, no gravity in space. NASA allegedly spent millions of dollars developing a pen that would work in a zero-gravity environment. The Soviets found a very quick and inexpensive solution. They used pencils.

Why didn't NASA come up with this solution? They defined the problem differently. For NASA, the problem was getting a ballpoint pen to work in space. For the Soviets, it was finding a writing implement that would work in a zero-gravity environment. While the difference may seem small, the consequences were significant. The takeaway from this example is that problems should never be defined in terms of a solution.

The space pen is a great example of what happens when the project team fails to use a structured process for solving problems. According to the snopes.com website, however, this account of the zero-gravity pen is not entirely accurate. The pen, which also works in extreme temperatures, was developed by the Fisher Space Pen Company, which sold 400 of the pens to NASA for $2.95 each. It is still a good story and makes the point even if it is not entirely consistent with the facts. In fact, the pens are available on Amazon for between $12 and $41, depending on the model. (See http://www.snopes.com/business/genius/spacepen.asp for more information.)

Change Management Process

Many organizations have a formal change management process designed to address issues. One such process is shown in Figure 16.2.

When the team has identified the change necessary to resolve the issue, the project manager initiates a request for change form, as the proposed solution to the issue must be approved before it can be implemented. The first step is to analyze the impact of the proposed change. If the proposed change impacts the Triple Constraints (time, cost, scope), then the request for change must be approved by the customer, project sponsor, project management office, or some other approving authority. If approved, the team may begin the implementation.

Not all changes require formal approval. Project managers are often empowered to make changes that do not significantly impact the scope, budget, or schedule and these can be made without authorization. Subjecting all changes to a formal authorization process bogs down the process and unnecessarily delays project work.

When changes are made to the scope of the project, corresponding changes must be made to the project budget and timeline. Renegotiating the Triple Constraints is often difficult and may test the project manager's negotiation skills. The success of the project depends on keeping the triple constraint triangle balanced.

Figure 16.2 | Change Management Process

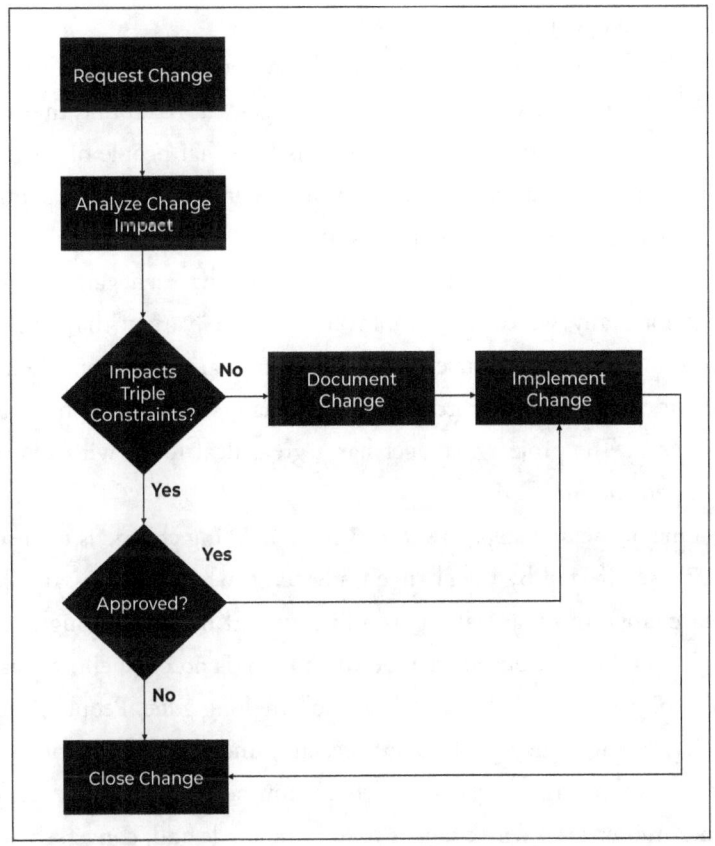

While it may appear from this discussion that change management is a rather mechanical process, it is anything but that. Getting approval for needed changes is often difficult. The project manager often has to deal with stakeholders with big egos who are more dedicated to protecting their turf than the success of the project. Even after the changes have been approved and their impact on the project has been resolved, implementation of the changes may prove difficult.

Stakeholders who have their own agendas may use change orders to gain concessions they were not able to negotiate in the initiation and planning stages of the project. Team members who have not bought into the changes may drag their feet or otherwise undermine the implementation of the changes. For these reasons, the project manager needs to have good people skills.

It is often assumed that most people do not like change, but this is not always true. Research on change management has found that support for change is situational. While it is true that people often resist change, there are situations in which people embrace change, perhaps even actively working to bring it about.

While it is true that the word "change" does have a negative connotation for many, words like "improvement" and "variety" have a positive connotation. Of course, there can be no variety or improvement without change. People's attitude toward change depends on how they perceive it. The project manager has a great deal to do with shaping those perceptions.

One of the first steps in successfully managing change is to ensure that those affected by the change understand why it is necessary. Too often change in organizations is arbitrary and not well thought out. Why should people accept change when there is no compelling reason to do so? The days of "because I said so" are long gone. People seldom support changes they view as unnecessary, undesirable, or capricious. The project manager must ensure that team members and other stakeholders understand why changes need to be made and, conversely why rejected changes cannot or should not be made.

To minimize resistance to change, it is important to involve the people affected by the proposed change in the planning and implementation. Scott Berkun (Berkun, 2005) points out that it is unlikely that project changes will be effectively implemented if those charged with carrying out the change are not involved in the decision-making process. They have, in effect, a veto power over any changes through their ability to undermine the implementation of the change.

It is also important to take resistance to change seriously. This means giving people the opportunity to express their opposition to changes and listening to their reasons for resisting them. This is, in essence, Covey's Third Habit, "Seek first to understand then be understood." Empathetic listening not only provides the project manager with valuable information about how team members and other stakeholders perceive the proposed changes, but resistant stakeholders will also appreciate the fact that the project manager has listened to their concerns and taken them seriously.

In short, successful change management is critical to the success of the project and depends in large part on the project manager's ability to gain the support of those most affected by the change. While there are no magic formulas, good change-management practices can help to minimize resistance and help to gain the support of those critical to the successful implementation of the change.

Change Control Log

Most project managers maintain some kind of change-control log that contains a copy of all approved changes. These are dated with the most recent in the front. This makes it possible to track all changes to the baseline plan.

No project is ever implemented exactly as it was planned. This is not necessarily the result of poor planning. Conditions often change in unanticipated ways that affect project work and for that reason, the details of the project plan may need to change.

Changes in the project plan are formally proposed using a document called a Request for Change. Approved requests are usually called change orders. The typical change request form contains some or all of the following information:

- Date
- Description of the proposed change
- Why the change is needed
- What will happen if the change is not made
- The impact of the change on the budget

- The impact of the change on the schedule
- The impact on existing risks
- New risks that might result from the change
- Disposition (accepted, accepted with specified modifications, rejected, deferred)
- Any other relevant information
- Approving authority
- Date approved, rejected, or deferred

The change-control log becomes the official record for all deviations from the original baseline plan. It can be very useful when there are questions about how the baseline plan has been changed. It can also be very useful in resolving disputes about project work.

When a change request is approved, all relevant project documents (WBS, Gantt Charts, budgets, etc.) must be updated to reflect the changes. Changes must then be communicated in accordance with the project communications plan. Failure to communicate project changes in a timely fashion can lead to confusion potentially causing serious problems.

Communication

As noted earlier, communication skills are among the most critical project management skills. Without communication, there is no monitoring and no control. It is, therefore, not surprising that as much as 90 percent of the project manager's time is spent on communication activities.

Unfortunately, most project managers have little or no formal communications training and many fail to appreciate the critical role it plays in the success or failure of the project.

A survey conducted for the Franklin-Covey organization found that only 17% of workers surveyed felt that the communication in their organization was truly open, candid, and respectful. (Covey, 2006, p. 192) This finding is consistent with many research studies on project teams. It also helps to explain why so many projects fail. Many of the project failure modes are associated with poor communication.

The most under-appreciated aspect of communication is listening. Good listening is at the heart of effective communication. In his book, *The 8th Habit* (Covey, 2006), Covey lists a continuum of listening behaviors. These are:

- Ignoring
- Pretend listening
- Selective listening
- Attentive listening
- Empathetic listening

Truly effective communication happens when the participants in the discussion practice empathetic listening.

Conflict Management

Since project work is carried out by human beings, a certain amount of conflict is inevitable. One of the most critical issues that project managers have to deal with during the course of a project is how to handle this conflict. Unfortunately, many project managers are not well-prepared either by education or experience to effectively manage conflict.

Conflict is a term used to describe human differences when these differences represent an incompatibility between two or more opinions, principles, or interests. It ranges from mild disagreements or differences of opinion between individuals to full-scale war between nations. Among project team members, it can vary considerably both with respect to the source of the conflict and its intensity.

Sources of Conflict

Conflict comes from a variety of sources. The *PMBOK* lists the following:

- Personalities
- Scope of Work
- Work Assignments
- Project priorities
- Cost
- Project Schedule
- Organizational Issues

Some conflicts can be avoided. Project managers who take the time to communicate project constraints such as the scope of work, work assignments, and project priorities to their teams experience fewer conflicts. Involving team members and other key stakeholders in decisions also helps to generate buy-in, avoiding many potential conflicts.

Conflicts can occur at any stage of the project but are most prevalent in the Storming stage of team development. As teams progress to the Norming and Performing stages, team members become more adept at managing internal conflict. Conflicts do not suddenly disappear as the team transitions into the Norming stage. The team just becomes better at managing them.

Unlike most other sources of conflict, personality differences do not lend themselves to a quick or easy solution. There are no right or wrong answers. Moreover, conflicts of this type tend to be more emotional than most other types of conflicts making them among the most difficult types of conflicts to resolve.

Intensity of Conflict

Research has confirmed what most project managers already know: the intensity of various types of conflict varies from one project to another and from one stage to the next within the same project. The effectiveness of the various approaches to managing conflict depends in large part on the type and intensity of the conflict.

Many project managers view conflict as something to be avoided. If it cannot be prevented, it needs to be suppressed. That is a misguided view of conflict and the role it plays in project management. Conflict is an inherent part of all human relationships and, therefore, present in all project interactions. It may not always be visible, but it is always there. As long as people have different needs, values, and goals, there will be conflict. The real issue for the project manager is how to deal with it.

Warren Bennis in *Why Leaders Can't Lead* (Bennis, 1989), wrote, "Leaders do not avoid, repress, or deny conflict, but rather see it as an opportunity." Project managers must also learn to recognize it as an opportunity. One way to do this is to encourage open and honest communication among the project manager, the team, and other key stakeholders. Doing so brings the conflicts out into the open where they can be addressed.

Disagreements are a low-intensity form of conflict and, among team members, can be a sign of a healthy team culture. The project manager should foster a climate in which team members can openly express their disagreements without fear of retribution or ostracism. Open and honest discussions help to forge win-win solutions.

Low levels of conflict can lead to innovation and creativity. If, however, the level of conflict rises above a certain threshold, it becomes dysfunctional. When this happens, the project manager must take action. Delay just aggravates the situation. There are a number of conflict resolution modes available to the project manager to address conflicts.

Conflict Resolution Modes

Research by Thomas and Kilmann (1974) identified five different response modes people use to address conflict. These include:

Accommodation

Accommodation, sometimes referred to as "smoothing," emphasizes areas of agreement while minimizing differences. While it may help to diffuse a tense situation, accommodation is not considered a long-term solution because it does not address the underlying causes of the conflict.

Avoidance

Avoidance or withdrawal is an approach in which the parties in conflict physically or psychologically retreat. This is another short-term solution. Eventually, the source of the conflict must be addressed. Failing to deal with the conflict in its early stages may cause the conflict to escalate making resolution even more difficult. It also tends to undermine the efforts of the project manager to create and maintain a high-performing team.

Competition

This approach, also known as forcing, imposes a solution on the parties in conflict. This solution is a win-lose solution and because it is externally imposed, usually lacks buy-in from the conflicted parties.

Like avoidance, competition is not a long-term solution. It does not address the underlying source of the conflict and may cause some resentment among one or both parties involved in the conflict. There are times, however, when a quick resolution of the conflict, however temporary, may be necessary.

Compromise

Compromise is an approach that seeks a middle ground that is more or less acceptable to all parties in the conflict. It involves some give-and-take, resulting in mutual concessions.

Compromise can be considered a win-win solution in that all parties get at least some of what they want. On the other hand, it is also a lose-lose solution because all parties have to give up something in order to achieve the compromise.

To the extent that one or both parties have compromised strongly held beliefs in order to reach a settlement, the resolution may foster long-lasting resentment. This is not the result of a true win-win solution.

Collaboration

Collaboration is the approach in which the parties in conflict work together to address the issue and seek a resolution. While this is considered the most effective approach, it requires the active cooperation of all the parties involved. Unfortunately, one or more of the parties are often unwilling to deal with the conflict and work toward a mutually satisfactory solution.

Escalation

When an issue arises requiring a solution outside the project manager's comfort zone or beyond his or her authority, the issue must be resolved at a higher level. This is called "escalation."

Some organizations have a standing policy for escalating issues. If not, the project plan should outline the rules for escalation. Most commonly, the project manager is empowered to resolve all issues where the solution does not delay the completion of the project, increase the project budget, or significantly alter the scope of the project. In cases where these requirements are not met, the issue may be escalated to the Project Management Office, a project steering committee, the project sponsor, or to the customer for resolution.

The Covey approach to conflict management outlined in *The Seven Habits of Highly Effective People* (1989) and *The Eighth Habit* (2004) involves the search for what Covey calls the Third Alternative. The Third Alternative is a solution that emerges from the search for a win-win solution. It is an alternative that is better than any of the solutions proposed by any of the individual parties involved in the conflict.

Good conflict management is essential to effective team building. While disagreements are natural and healthy, high levels of unresolved conflict may prevent the team from reaching the Performing stage of team development limiting its ability to execute the project work plan.

When the Project Is Not Going Well

Ideally, projects are terminated when all of the work has been completed. In reality, many projects are prematurely terminated. Premature closure happens for a variety of reasons. In a recent International Institute for Learning white paper, Harold Kerzner wrote that stakeholders' perceptions of failure include:

- The project has become too costly for the expected benefits or value
- The project will be completed too late
- The project will not achieve its targeted benefits or value
- The project no longer satisfies the stakeholders' needs

When a project falls into one of these categories, key stakeholders must decide whether to continue the project or terminate it. This decision is usually a difficult one. The key to successful project management is to know when the project should be terminated and when it can and should be salvaged.

Project Recovery

The decision to terminate a project should be taken very seriously. Failed projects are often very costly. A study commissioned by *PM Solutions*, "Strategies for Project Recovery" (2011), found the average American company manages $200 million in projects each year, with perhaps one-third of those, or $74 million worth, at risk of failing. According to this survey, action strategies can salvage faltering projects about 75%

of the time. What this means is that project recovery efforts have the potential to save substantial amounts of money.

The survey also found that good project management makes a difference. "Project managers not only play a significant role in addressing the root causes of troubled projects, they are the key resource in effectively managing the process to recover them." The obvious conclusion is that recovery efforts should be led by an experienced project manager.

When considering whether or not to rescue a failing project, a number of factors should be considered. First, how important is the project? The more important the project, the more support it is likely to have among key stakeholders. This support is essential because project recovery efforts will almost certainly require additional resources. Without the support of key stakeholders and senior executives, recovery efforts will probably fall short.

Another important factor to consider is the strategic value of the project. Does the project address important strategic goals or business objectives? Organizations are reluctant to kill strategically important projects because doing so can have serious long-term consequences.

Lastly, what is the probability that recovery efforts will be successful given the current level of available resources? If the project is hopelessly over budget or behind schedule, it probably does not make sense to attempt to recover it unless there is a compelling reason to do so.

It is important to identify as early as possible those projects at risk for failure. The earlier problems are detected, the sooner corrective action can be taken. A quick response limits the damage (cost and scope) making it easier to recover.

The first step to project recovery is to recognize that the project is in trouble. While there is consensus on the criteria for project success, there is much less agreement on what constitutes project failure and the point at which the project is beyond recovery.

Because the project manager is much more intimately involved in the day-to-day activities of the project, he or she is more likely than most other stakeholders to notice the small signs indicating the project is beginning to experience problems. Some of these warning signs include:

- sporadic attendance at meetings
- lack of engagement among key stakeholders
- redirection of project resources
- declining project visibility

When the decision has been made to rescue the project, the project manager—together with the team and other key stakeholders—needs to reexamine the project plan. A successful recovery depends on revising the plan so the Triple Constraints are back in balance. For example, if time is the driver, the project manager will need to shorten the critical path. While there are a number of ways to do this (See Figure 7.6), probably the most common is to reduce the scope of work.

This reexamination should also seek to understand how the project got into trouble. If the issues that caused the problems are not addressed, there is no reason to believe they will not continue to plague the project. These issues need to be identified, and steps taken to overcome them.

Project recovery efforts are likely to fail without the active support of key stakeholders, the project sponsor and the project champion in particular. If they do not fully support recovery efforts, it will be very difficult to salvage the project; they must make the project a priority, ensuring it has sufficient resources and that the project manager maintains the cooperation necessary to get the project back on track.

Killing the Project

If the project cannot be salvaged, appropriate action should be taken to bring the project to closure in the most cost-effective manner, with the least possible political damage. Bringing projects to closure is discussed more fully in Chapter 17.

CONTROLLING THE PROJECT

Killing a project is almost always a difficult undertaking. Early in the project, project advocates may argue that there is still sufficient time to get the project back on track. Later in the project, they may argue that the resources expended on the project will have been wasted if the project is terminated. Moreover, project advocates risk looking bad if the project is terminated without meeting its intended objectives.

When a project has been approved for termination, the project manager must do what needs to be done. As Robert Heinlein once said, "When the need arises—and it does—you must be able to shoot your own dog. Don't farm it out. That doesn't make it nicer, it makes it worse." (www.inspiringquotes.us)

The decision to kill a project is much easier when the project manager and the other key stakeholders have negotiated the project "kill points" in advance. These kill points are usually major milestones at which time key stakeholders, usually the project sponsor or the project customer, decide to continue the project or to kill it.

For an organization using Earned Value, the criteria might include an EAC (Estimate at Completion) that is more than an agreed-upon percent above the BAC (Budget at Completion). Some organizations use the CPI to evaluate candidates for termination. For example, any project whose CPI falls below .9 is terminated unless there is a strong reason to believe it can be salvaged.

Keep in mind that some projects cannot be killed. For example, projects mandated by local, state, and federal regulatory agencies must be continued regardless of the time and cost. While there may be some flexibility with respect to schedule and some wiggle room with respect to scope, these projects cannot be killed.

Project Exit Strategy

When the project sponsor, the steering committee, or the customer has decided that recovery is not an option and that the project should be killed, the project manager is authorized to begin the implementation of the exit plan. If there is no plan, the project manager, together with key stakeholders must develop one in order to shut down the project in such a way as to cause the least amount of damage.

Because the decision to kill a project, no matter how strong the case, is likely to create some ill will among some project stakeholders, the project manager must do his or her best to limit the damage. Usually, this means minimizing financial losses. If the organization has invested large sums of money in the project, there will be a temptation to spend more in the hope of recovering the "sunk" costs. The project manager must resist this temptation and limit future expenditures to those items necessary to bring the project to closure.

The project manager must also work to limit any political damage that may result from killing the project. Killing a project often results in blaming and finger-pointing. Although this is a natural response, it is seldom productive.

Another objective is to bring the project to closure without humiliating or embarrassing key stakeholders, and ensuring they do not become scapegoats for the failure of the project. Avoiding blame is particularly important when the customer is external to the organization. Future work may depend on it.

The project manager must also consider that the failure to bring a failing project to a timely closure may have legal implications and jeopardize future business with the client.

Summary

Projects never go exactly according to plan. For this reason, it is important to have a formal problem-solving process. This helps to ensure that the proposed change addresses the issue and not simply the symptoms. The proposed change is implemented using a change-management process. The purpose of this process is to ensure that necessary changes are made quickly and that unnecessary changes are avoided.

CONTROLLING THE PROJECT

The change-management process usually involves the use of change-request forms that are systematically reviewed and acted upon by a change-control board, the project sponsor, or the customer. It is important to update all relevant project management documents (WBS, Gantt charts, budgets, etc.) to reflect project changes.

Effective control depends in large part on the project manager's ability to communicate effectively with key stakeholders. Poor communication is one of the primary causes of project failure.

The most under-appreciated aspect of communication is listening. Lack of good listening skills is the cause of much project miscommunication. Most project managers and other stakeholders, for that matter, are often better at talking than they are at listening.

All projects are subject to risks. Risks and issues must continue to be addressed throughout the project life cycle. During the course of the project, some risks will cease to be relevant while new risks and issues will emerge that require the attention of the project team. For this reason, the risk-management plan must be continually updated to reflect the changes in the project environment.

Like risk, conflict is an issue throughout the project life cycle. Conflict among key stakeholders is inevitable. While differing perspectives on the project and how it should be conducted are a source of new ideas, differences between stakeholders can become dysfunctional if these differences grow too large.

Conflict management is one of the project manager's primary responsibilities. However, most project managers tend to be conflict-averse. They are reluctant to address conflict until it escalates to the point that it can no longer be ignored. Effective conflict management requires quick and appropriate action on the part of the project manager.

The most common modes of conflict resolution are accommodation, avoidance, competition, compromise, and collaboration. Collaboration is ultimately the best method of resolving conflicts because it results in win-win outcomes.

Regardless of how well planned or executed, some projects experience delays and cost overruns. When these delays and overruns become excessive, the project manager and other key stakeholders must decide whether to continue the project or kill it. Ideally, the project is reviewed periodically and go/no go decisions are made at "kill points" usually placed at major milestones.

When the decision has been made to kill the project, the project manager must seek to bring the project to closure with the least amount of damage. That usually means limiting financial loss and minimizing political damage to the key stakeholders.

PROJECT CLOSURE

Introduction

As Yogi Berra famously once said, "It's not over until it's over." In project management, the project is not over until it is brought to closure. Closure is the final phase of the project life cycle. Ideally, this occurs when the work of the project has been completed, the customer has formally accepted the final project deliverable, and all the administrative tasks have been completed.

Unfortunately, some projects never seem to reach that point. The problem often occurs when the project is about 95% complete. Most of the work has been completed. The remaining tasks are largely administrative. With other projects competing for attention, these tasks tend to get delayed or forgotten. Often projects just peter out without any formal closure. It is the responsibility of the project manager to bring the project to a formal closure in a timely manner, ensuring all closeout activities are satisfactorily completed.

Project Closure Methods

There are four methods by which projects are brought to closure. These are:

Addition

Addition occurs when the deliverable evolves into an ongoing operational unit. Because it is ongoing, i.e., does not have a start date and a finish date, it no longer qualifies as a project. A project designed to develop an online degree program is an example of addition if it becomes a new, ongoing process with its own facilities, staff, and students. At this point, it ceases to be a project.

Starvation

Starvation refers to the incremental withdrawal of resources from a project. The gradual death of the project is usually the result of cost overruns and the failure of the project to meet its goals and objectives. It reflects the reluctance of upper management to continue to put resources into a project that appears to be failing. Since the project dies a slow death, there are usually no announcements allowing supporters to avoid the embarrassment associated with a failed project brought to formal closure.

Integration

Integration occurs when a completed project deliverable is integrated into the ongoing operation of the organization. For example, the development of a new employee evaluation system would be an example of integration. The deliverable was integrated into the organization's human resources management system.

Extinction

Extinction refers to the situation in which all resources are withdrawn from the project. Ideally, this occurs because the project has been completed and the resources are no longer needed. The customer has accepted the deliverable(s), and the resources have been reassigned. The project is over.

Figure 17.1 | Closure Methods and Project Success

Closure Methods	Successful	Not Successful
Addition	√	
Integration	√	
Extinction	√	√
Starvation		√

Resources may be withdrawn, however, because the project has failed to meet its goals and objectives and has therefore lost the support of upper management. In this case, the project is prematurely terminated. It is considered a failed project. Although integration and extinction both result in the withdrawal of resources, they differ in that integration refers to the termination of internal projects while extinction may apply to either internal or external projects. And, projects terminated by integration are almost always successful while extinction may be used to terminate any project.

Figure 17.1 lists the methods of closure by project result. Successful projects are terminated by addition, integration, or extinction. Unsuccessful projects are brought to closure by extinction or starvation.

The project closure process establishes the procedures to coordinate the activities needed to verify and document the project deliverables and to coordinate and facilitate formal acceptance of project deliverables by the customer or sponsor. It also establishes procedures for investigating and documenting actions taken when a project is terminated prior to completion.

It is common to distinguish between two types of closure:

- contract closure
- adminitrative closure

Contract closure has to do with the completion of the terms of the contract and the formal acceptance of the project deliverables. Contract closure must be completed before administrative closure can be completed.

Administrative closure has to do with wrapping up the loose ends of the project. It involves, as its name would suggest, a number of administrative activities such as documenting lessons learned, archiving records, releasing project personnel, etc. These activities are described in some detail in the section on administrative closure.

The processes involved in both contract and administrative closure are described in the project acceptance plan developed by the project manager and the customer at the beginning of the project. Many organizations have a standard acceptance plan which may be modified to meet the needs of each individual project.

Contract Closure

Contract closure is a necessary first step in closing out the project. The project is not finished until all contracts have been closed out. If the contract or charter clearly describes the requirements of the deliverable, contract closure is generally rather straightforward. If the requirements are not spelled out in sufficient detail, contract closure can become quite contentious.

There are several steps necessary to close out a contract. First, the project team must ensure the terms of the contract have been met. Second, the customer must acknowledge in writing that the work has been completed to specifications.

The project cannot be closed out until the terms of the contract have been met—all of the contractual work is completed and the project outputs have been delivered to the customer. The project manager should ensure that all work is completed and meets the requirements of the contract. Ideally, this will be done by the project deadline.

Figure 17.2 | Contracts and Charters

Not all projects involve the use of legal contracts. This is true for many small projects and most internal projects. In such cases, the project charter serves as a de facto contract. The fact that there are no formal contracts does not mean that that contract closure can be skipped.

Some project managers hold a team meeting to prepare for closure. The primary purpose is to review the project acceptance plan, contracts, and all other relevant project documents, and work to ensure that it is completed and meets specifications.

Because contracts are legal documents, some organizations prefer to administer contracts in a contract or procurement office that is separate from the project itself. They may do a procurement audit to verify the work has been completed.

As a part of contract closure, all remaining payments that need to be made to the suppliers or partners should be paid.

Customer Acceptance

The second purpose of contract closure is to obtain formal acceptance of the project deliverables by the customer. This acknowledgment must be in the form of a written document. Sometimes the acceptance process is spelled out in the contract itself if there is one.

Customer acceptance comes when the customer receives the deliverables and acknowledges that they meet their requirements—i.e., the deliverables meet the acceptance criteria listed in the contract, project acceptance plan, project charter, or some other project document.

In some types of projects, the project manager may have to demonstrate that the output meets the requirements. It is common in the building trades, for example, to do a walk-through as a part of contract closure. The project manager and the customer walk through the building to verify that the work conforms to requirements. Items that do not meet the requirements are added to a "punch list," a list of deficiencies that must be corrected in order to close out the contract. When the deficiencies have been corrected, the customer signs off on the project and takes possession of the building.

When the requirements are clearly described in the contract and the project team completes the work, project acceptance is generally routine. There are a number of reasons, however, why customers do not accept project deliverables. These include:

Missing work

Not all of the work described in the contract has been completed. Presumably, the customer accepts the deliverables when the missing work has been completed.

Work not done to specification

Some of the work, though completed, does not meet the requirements of the contract. This may be the result of poor workmanship, faulty design, substandard materials, or any one of a number of other issues.

Misunderstanding over requirements

In this situation, the project manager and the customer have a different understanding of the requirements. These differences need to be resolved in order to close out the contract.

The best way to ensure customer acceptance is to make sure that there is a mutual understanding of the project requirements. It also helps to engage the customer in the project. Be sure that change orders that could potentially affect project acceptance are reviewed and approved by the customer.

Premature Closure

Contract closure is more problematic when the project ends prematurely, such as when a project is terminated before it has reached its intended goals or completion date. This can happen for a variety of reasons, for example, changes in the project's priorities, lack of funding or resources, poor project planning, or unforeseen external circumstances. As a result, the acceptance conditions must be renegotiated.

Premature project closure can have several negative consequences, including wasted time, resources, and money, decreased morale and motivation among project team members, and a loss of potential benefits that the project could have delivered. To avoid premature project closure, it is important to have a well-defined project plan with clear objectives, timelines, and resource requirements. Regular monitoring and evaluation of project progress can help identify potential issues early on and allow for corrective action to be taken to keep the project on track. Additionally, maintaining open communication channels with project stakeholders can help ensure that everyone is aligned on the project's goals and priorities, and can help prevent surprises that could lead to premature closure.

Administrative Closure

Administrative closeout takes place when contract closeout has been completed, though some administrative closeout activities may have begun before the contract closeout phase finishes. Like contract closeout, administrative closeout is usually rather straightforward but may be much more difficult when the acceptance of the project deliverables is contentious.

Although the customer considers the project complete when they receive the final deliverable(s), it is not finished until the completion of all administrative closure activities. It is the responsibility of the project manager to ensure that these activities are completed in a timely manner.

Completing Administrative Closure in a Timely Manner

One of the reasons why administrative closeout does not always finish in a timely manner is that there is often not sufficient pressure to do so. The customer has received their deliverables. For them, the project is over. Senior leaders within the organization have shifted their focus to other projects, making the completion of administrative activities a low priority. As a result, team members and other stakeholders may not view administrative activities with any sense of urgency.

The project manager must impress upon team members and other stakeholders who are involved in administrative closure the importance of wrapping up the project quickly so they can all move on. Typically, administrative closure involves the following activities:

- Evaluating the project
- Identifying, documenting, and sharing lessons learned
- Archiving project records
- Releasing project resources
- Recognizing and rewarding team members
- Celebrating closure
- Writing a final report

Evaluating the Project

The primary purpose of project evaluation is to identify opportunities for improvement. Most organizations are continually looking for ways to conduct projects better, faster, and more inexpensively. Evaluation is an important first step in this process.

Evaluation involves assessing the project against a set of performance standards. Project performance is determined by how well it meets these standards, with the most common criteria being team effectiveness and stakeholder satisfaction. From this perspective, a successful project is one that produces deliverables that satisfy key stakeholders in the most efficient and effective manner.

The most common approach to measuring stakeholder satisfaction is to administer a post-project questionnaire to key stakeholders. Some organizations have a standard survey they send to customers shortly after the completion of the project. They may also send a modified form of this survey to other key stakeholders.

Some organizations conduct their own customer satisfaction surveys; Survey Monkey, for example, makes this easy to do. Using an online survey tool like Survey Monkey is an attractive option for smaller organizations due to the high cost of contracting this work out. Unless the organization possesses sufficient research skills, however, it is probably better to contract out.

Projects are considered successful when the customer is satisfied. Customer satisfaction, however, is not sufficient to guarantee a successful project. To be successful, the project must also be effectively and efficiently carried out. Project performance, however, is somewhat more difficult to measure than customer satisfaction.

Some organizations use a team effectiveness survey to measure the success of the execution. These surveys, based on best practices, measure such things as clarity of goals, understanding and acceptance of roles and responsibilities, management support, etc. These surveys can provide a great deal of insight into the execution of the project, but be aware that the results only represent the team's perspective.

A somewhat broader approach involves the use of a set of standards derived from best practices in project management. Project performance is measured by assessing team performance against these standards.

The U.S. Air Force developed such a set of performance standards in the early 1990s for use in the Air Force Team Quality Award competitions. The American Society for Quality (ASQ) Team Excellence Award and several state quality award programs currently use variations of these standards.

The 2013/2014 ASQ Team Excellence Criteria consist of the following categories:

- Project and Team Selection
- Current Situation and Root Cause/Improvement Opportunity Analysis
- Solution/Improvement Development
- Implementation and Results Verification
- Preservation and Stakeholder Communication

Scores are given for each category based on the extent to which the team's performance meets Category requirements. A total score can be obtained by adding up the category scores. For the ASQ standards, the maximum score is 28.

The biggest advantage of this approach is that it not only provides a more comprehensive evaluation of the project, but makes it possible to identify strengths and opportunities for improvement in the definition, planning, and execution of the project.

Examples of project evaluation instruments can be found in Appendix C.

Identifying and Documenting Lessons Learned

Documenting lessons learned is an important closure function. It serves as the basis for the organization's project improvement efforts.

While project evaluations suggest areas where the project could have been more effectively and efficiently carried out, lessons learned has more to do with what the team learned during each stage of the project life cycle that will help them or others in their organization improve future project performance.

The most important source of information about improvements comes from team members, those who are most involved in the day-to-day work of the project. The project manager should solicit their suggestions on a regular basis. Some project managers do this as a part of their regularly scheduled team meetings.

It is important to capture this learning throughout the course of the project. By the end of the project, much of this information may be forgotten or lost. It is usually the responsibility of the project manager, though he or she may delegate this to a team member.

Many organizations hold "Lessons Learned" meetings as part of the closure process, where information collected during the course of the project is reviewed discussed and analyzed. Potential best practices are identified and shared with the organization.

The PMO often serves as the clearinghouse for lessons learned. The PMO reviews and analyzes project performance data and disseminates information about best practices. Some organizations have established a database to facilitate the sharing of lessons learned. One example is The Mistake Bank. While this is a good forum for the sharing of mistakes, some organizations are reluctant to acknowledge that their performance was less than perfect.

Archiving Project Records

The organization should have a systematic process for archiving project records. Archiving project records is important because these records are a rich source of information about past project performance.

So, what documents need to be archived? The answer is simple: all important project documents. This includes:

- Scope planning documents (the Project Concept Document, the Project Charter, the Project Scope Statement, the WBS, WBS dictionary, the stakeholder analysis document, and all risk management and planning documents)
- Staffing documents (skills audit, team skills inventory, and RAM/RACI form
- Execution documents (planned and actual schedules, change orders, status reports, financial records, meeting notes, and changes to planning documents)
- Closure documents (acceptance documents, customer satisfaction results, project reviews, and evaluations.

Contracts, amendments to contracts, and all communications with outside vendors should also be archived. The purpose of archiving these records is to provide a knowledge base for future projects, but they can only serve this purpose if they are easily accessible. How they are archive (and where), and how they are accessed, are all important questions.

Project records are also archived to satisfy financial and legal regulatory requirements. Projects may be subject to internal or external audits. In such cases, these records are essential.

The most common method for archiving project records is to consolidate them on a shared hard drive using SharePoint or some similar type of software. A central repository keeps them secure yet easy to access. When all project records have been archived, the originals should be deleted.

Releasing Project Resources

Resources assigned to a project are committed to the project until officially released. Team members are usually not released until administrative closure is complete, though it is possible that some members may be released earlier.

If the organization is using MS Project Server or some other portfolio management software, formally releasing project personnel returns them to the pool, making them available to other projects. They are not available for reassignment until they have been officially released.

It is also important to release any materials, facilities, and equipment that may have been assigned to the project so they may also be freed up for use by other projects.

Recognizing and Rewarding Team Members

Upon completion of the project, it is important to recognize team members and others who have contributed to the project. One should not overlook the importance of recognizing the team for their hard work. Many organizations, even some very good ones, do not do enough to recognize team members for their efforts.

Some project managers view recognition as a form of compensation. Compensation is not recognition. We compensate people for doing their work. We recognize people for their contributions above and beyond the requirements of the job. Recognition is much more motivating than compensation.

There has been significant research on the subject of recognition over the years. From this research we know that recognition is most effective when it is:

Immediate

Animal researchers have found that positive reinforcement is most effective when it immediately follows the desired action.

The attention span of most animals is sufficiently short that if it is more than a few seconds, the animal does not make the connection between the behavior and the reward. While people have longer attention spans, rewards or recognition are still more effective when they are immediate.

While it is important to recognize team members for their contributions at project closure, rewards and recognition should not be put off until the end of the project.

Specific

Research has also found that positive reinforcement is more effective when it is specific to the desired behavior. Telling people they have done a good job is certainly good for morale but it does not increase the likelihood that the behavior will be repeated because the person may not know what aspect of their performance is being praised. For example, thanking a team member for identifying a potential problem in a vendor bid is much more effective than simply thanking him or her for doing a good job.

Sincere

Lastly, recognition must be sincere. Insincere praise may be worse than no praise at all. It has little effect on the behavior to which it is connected and tends to undermine the praise of other behaviors.

It is also important, as we noted earlier, to reward team effort as well as individual effort. You cannot expect people to work well as a team when they are only rewarded for their individual efforts.

When recognizing people for their efforts to help make the project successful, do not overlook support personnel. While they may not be directly involved in the work of the project, without their efforts, the project probably would not have been as successful. Failure to recognize those who support the project can and often does lead to resentment on the part of support personnel and undermines future project support.

Celebrating Closure

One of the most important closeout activities is to celebrate the team's success. There are many ways in which this can be accomplished. Many project managers like to wrap up the project with an informal celebration with team members and other stakeholders. Often these celebrations, like the kick-off meeting, are held off-site. Such a celebration gives the project manager an opportunity to thank team members and other stakeholders for their contributions and to recognize those who have made a major contribution.

During the course of the project, the team has presumably progressed through the Forming, Storming, Norming, and perhaps the Performing stages of team development. The end of the project marks the beginning of the dissolution of the team. Tuckman called this the adjourning phase. The celebration helps to bring closure to team members.

What if the project was less than completely successful? Does this mean you should forgo the celebration? Probably not. Many projects fail despite the best efforts of the project manager and the team members. In this case, while it may not be appropriate to celebrate the success of the project, it is still important to celebrate the efforts of the team. Failure to recognize hardworking team members has consequences.

As we noted earlier, most projects fail due to factors beyond the team's control. The fact that a project was less than fully successful should not detract from the team's effort. They need to be recognized for that effort.

Post-Project Report

Administrative closure often includes a final project report written for upper management. Its content may vary somewhat, but it almost always focuses on what the project has accomplished, i.e., how the project has created value for the organization.

It may also include some or all of the following:

- Recommendations for changes in future projects of a similar nature
- Best practices identified in the planning and execution of the project
- Observations/recommendations regarding team personnel performance
- Future considerations

Most organizations have a standard form used for the post-project report, which is usually written by the project manager with input from key stakeholders. He or she then sends a copy to the people on the distribution list, and a copy is archived with the other project documents.

Closeout Meetings

There are at least two types of closeout meetings.

- customer closeout meeting
- stakeholder closeout meeting.

These are different types of meetings with distinctly different purposes.

Customer Closeout Meetings

When the customer is external to the organization, it is customary to finish out the project with a customer closeout meeting. This meeting is the final meeting with the customer. The primary purpose of this meeting is to formally close out the project.

A typical customer closeout meeting agenda includes the following items:

PROJECT CLOSURE

Project overview
The project manager, or someone delegated by the project manager, usually gives the overview. In some instances, the project sponsor may take on this role. The overview should focus on the Triple Constraints: schedule, budget, and deliverables.

Review of deliverables
The review should include information about the deliverables, such as who received them and who acknowledged acceptance. Any non-conformance issues should be noted.

Project acceptance
It is possible that the project acceptance documents have already been signed. If not, the customer should sign them now. If there are outstanding issues preventing this, they need to be identified. A common practice in this situation is to attach an amendment to the acceptance document(s) indicating that the project has been accepted pending the resolution of these issues.

Project evaluation
This is an opportunity to obtain feedback from the customer concerning all aspects of the project. This information should become a part of the formal evaluation that takes place during the administrative closeout.

Next steps
When the customer is an external organization, there may be opportunities for additional projects or work associated with the project being brought to closure. The closeout meeting is an opportunity to explore such possibilities.

The agenda for such meetings should be sent to the customer and other stakeholders who will attend well in advance of the meeting to allow time for preparation, as well as additions or changes.

Typically, the customer closeout meeting is attended by the project manager, the customer, and anyone else the customer designates to attend.

Stakeholder Closeout Meetings

The second type of meeting is the stakeholder closeout meeting. The stakeholder closeout meeting is a crucial final step in completing the project. It focuses on the work that needs to be done to complete administrative closure. This work includes project evaluation, identifying lessons learned, evaluating the project and recognizing, and rewarding those who contributed to the success of the project. This meeting also provides team members an opportunity to share their experiences, identify areas for improvement in future projects, and sometimes air grievances.

The stakeholder closeout meeting typically involves the key stakeholders who have been involved in the project, include any or all of the following:

- Project manager and the project team
- Key stakeholders (internal and external)
- Senior management
- Support personnel

The following is a suggested agenda for a project closeout meeting with key stakeholders:

1. Introductions: Begin by introducing everyone in attendance and thanking them for their participation in the project.
2. Project Overview: Provide an overview of the project, including the objectives, scope, timeline, and budget.
3. Project Performance: Discuss the project's overall performance, including any successes and challenges encountered throughout the project lifecycle. Review the metrics and key

performance indicators established at the start of the project and assess how well the project performed against those goals.
4. Lessons Learned: Discuss the key lessons learned throughout the project. Highlight areas of success and opportunities for improvement in future projects.
5. Project Deliverables: Review all the deliverables completed during the project and ensure that all stakeholders agree that the project is complete.
6. Budget and Expenses: Review the project budget and expenses, ensuring all expenses are accounted for and that the project was completed within budget.
7. Outstanding Issues: Discuss any outstanding issues or tasks that need to be addressed after the project has officially closed. Ensure all stakeholders are aware of these issues and have a plan to address them.
8. Next Steps: Discuss the next steps for the project, including any follow-up activities or ongoing maintenance that may be required.
9. Thank You: Finally, thank everyone for their participation in the project and for their contributions to its success.

One of the problems that project managers often face is getting team members and other stakeholders to attend the closeout meeting. This is because work on the deliverables has been completed and the only work left to do is the administrative wrap-up. This work is a low priority for most stakeholders. Most team members have moved on to other projects and work on those projects has a much higher priority.

Getting stakeholders to the meeting is only half the battle. Closeout meetings are not always easy. According to Elizabeth Harrin (2009), the main problem project managers encounter with running this type of end-of-project review meeting are:

- People feel unable to express their true interpretations of the project

- People are unwilling to contribute if their manager is there as they don't want to appear negative
- People mix up the person and the act and feedback becomes picky and personal
- People don't care about what happened in the past; they are focused on the future
- Everyone says the project went like a dream and there is nothing constructive raised about areas to improve
- The area of the project whose personnel cannot make it to the meeting is targeted and all the failings are blamed on them.

Many of the items discussed at the closeout meeting are sensitive. It is often difficult to have an open and forthright conversation about these issues, particularly if senior members of the organization attend the meeting. It is even more difficult if the project did not go well. For this reason, many organizations prefer to obtain feedback from team members and other stakeholders through a written questionnaire or online survey rather than at the closeout meeting. This allows team members some degree of anonymity, increasing the likelihood that they will provide honest and candid feedback. (See Appendix C for some diagnostic surveys that might be helpful in assessing the project and the team's performance.)

There may be additional meetings as a part of the administrative closure process. For internal projects, for example, there may be a meeting with upper management to discuss the project. Such a meeting would cover much of the same topics that would be included in the final project report.

Some project managers hold a post-closeout meeting that is largely a social function designed to facilitate team members bringing social and psychological closure to the project. (See the discussion on the stages of team development starting on page 268.) This meeting, often held off-site, gives the project manager an opportunity to recognize and reward team members for their contributions to the project and to celebrate the completion of the project.

Completing the project on a positive note is important. Project managers who treat team members well will find it easier to staff future projects than those who have a reputation for being difficult to work with. We also know that team members who have had good experiences on teams are more engaged and productive.

Summary

There are a variety of ways in which projects come to an end. These include addition, starvation, integration, and extinction. Successful projects are usually completed by addition, integration, or extinction. Unsuccessful projects are brought to closure by one of two means: integration and starvation.

There are two types of closeout: contract and administrative. Contract closeout has to do with completing the terms of the contract or agreement and obtaining customer acceptance of the deliverables. Administrative closeout has to do with the administrative work necessary to bring the project to closure.

Contract closure is usually rather straightforward. All project work is completed and verified. The customers sign the acceptance documents and, from the perspective of the customer, the project is over.

Many organizations use a formal acceptance form as a part of the contract closeout. Closeout has been achieved when those who signed the project charter sign the acceptance document.

Contract closeout may become problematic when the project is prematurely terminated. In such cases, decisions have to be made about how to bring it to closure and how to distribute the finished and unfinished deliverables to the various parties.

When contract closure has been achieved, the team works to complete any remaining administrative activities. These may include:

- evaluating the project
- identifying, documenting, and sharing lessons learned
- archiving project records
- releasing project resources
- recognizing and rewarding team members
- celebrating closure
- writing a final report

Evaluating project performance, identifying, documenting, sharing lessons learned, and archiving the records all have to do with improving project performance. These activities are all designed to help conduct future projects faster, better, and more inexpensively.

Recognizing and rewarding team members and celebrating the completion of the project are primarily team-building activities. They are designed to build morale and motivation.

Failure to complete administrative closeout in a timely manner usually has negative consequences for the project manager and the organization.

An important part of administrative closeout is the closeout meeting, the purpose of which is to bring the project to contract closure. It is also an opportunity to obtain feedback from the customer and lay the groundwork for future work with the customer and his/her organization.

The stakeholder meeting is likewise designed to facilitate the wrap-up of the remaining administrative work. This includes administering a project evaluation, identifying lessons learned, evaluating the project, and recognizing and rewarding those who contributed to the success of the project.

Some project managers like to hold an off-site, post-closeout meeting to give them the opportunity to recognize and reward team members for their contributions and to celebrate the completion of the project.

APPENDICES

APPENDIX A
Bibliography

Allen, David, *Getting Things Done: The Art of Stress-Free Productivity*, Penguin Books, New York, 2001.

Baca, Claudia, *Project Manager's Spotlight on Change Management*, Harbor Light Press, SYBEX, Inc., Alameda, Calif., 2005.

Barkley, Bruce T. and Saylor, James H., *Customer-Driven Project Management*, 2nd ed., McGraw-Hill, New York, 2001.

Belasco, James A. and Stayer, Ralph C., *Flight of the Buffalo: Soaring into Excellence, Learning to Let Employees Lead*, Warner Books, Inc., New York, 1993.

Bennis, Warren, *Why Leaders Can't Lead*, Jossey-Bass, Inc., San Francisco, 1989.

Berkun, Scott, *The Art of Project Management*, O'Reilly Media, Sebastopol, California, 2005.

Berkun, Scott, *Making Things Happen*, O'Reilly Media, Sebastopol, California, 2008.

Christian Bisson, "Risks Aren't Always Negative," *PMNetwork*, August, 2014, pp. 24–25.

Bossidy, Larry, Charan, Ram and Burck, Charles, *Execution: The Discipline of Getting Things Done*, Crown Business, New York, 2002.

Brooks, Jr., Frederick P., *The Mythical Man-Month*, Addison-Wesley Publishing Co., 1995.

Buchhilz, Steve and Thomas Roth, *Creating the High-Performance Team*, Wilson Learning Corporation, 1987.

Buchtik, Liliana, *Secrets to Managing the WBS in Real-World Projects*, Project Management Institute, Newtown, Pa., 2nd ed., 2013.

Buzan, Tony, *How to Mind Map*, HarperCollins, New York, 2002.

Buzan, Tony and Barry Buzan, *The Mind Map Book: How to Use Radiant Thinking to Maximize Your Brain's Untapped Potential*, Plume, 1996.

Calipari, John, John, and Michael Sokolove, *Success Is the Only Option: The Art of Coaching Extreme Talent*, Harper Collins, New York, 2016.

Campbell, G. Michael, Project Management (Idiot's Guides), Sixth Ed., Alpha, 2014.

Chatfield, Carl and Timothy Johnson, *Microsoft Project 2013*, Microsoft Press, Redmond, Washington, 2013.

Cirillo, Francesco, *The Pomodoro Technique: The Acclaimed Time-Management System That Has Transformed How We Work*, Currency, 2018.

Cleland, David I. and Lewis R. Ireland, *Project Management*, 3rd ed., McGraw-Hill, New York, 1999.

Cook, Helen and Karen Tate, *Project Management* [electronic resource], 2nd ed., McGraw-Hill, New York, 2011.

Covey, Steven R., *The 8th Habit*, Free Press, New York, 2004.

Covey, Steven R., *The Seven Habits of Highly Effective People*, Simon & Schuster, New York, 1989.

Crawford, J. Kent, *Strategies for Project Recovery*, http://www.ihrim.org/Pubonline/Wire/July11/StrategiesforProjectRecovery2011.pdf

Croft, Chris, *Project Management QuickStart Guide: The Simplified Beginner's Guide to Precise Planning, Strategic Resource Management, and Delivering World Class Results*, ClydeBook Media LLC, Albany, New York, 2022.

Crosby, Philip, *Quality Is Free*, McGraw-Hill, New York, 1979.

Davis, Seth, *Getting to Us: How Great Coaches Make Great Teams*, Penguin Press, New York, 2018.

APPENDIX A

de Rond, Mark, "Why Less is More in Teams," *Harvard Business Review*, August 6, 2012.

DeMarco, Tom and Timothy Lister, *Waltzing with Bears: Managing Risk on Software Projects*, Dorset House, 2003.

DeMarco, Tom and Timothy Lister, *Peopleware*, Dorset House, 2003.

DeMarco, Tom, *Slack: Getting Past Burnout*, Busywork, and the Myth of Total Efficiency, Dorset House, 2001.

Dionisio, Cynthia Snyder, *A Project Managers Book of Forms*, 3rd. ed., John Wiley & Sons, Hoboken, N.J., 2017.

DeWeaver, Mary Feeherry and Lori Ciprian Gillespie, *Real World Project Management*, Quality Resources, New York, 1997.

Dinsmore, Paul C., *Human Factors in Project Management*, New York, AMACOM/American Management Association; Revised edition, 1990.

Dobson, Michael, *Practical Project Management*, SkillPath Publications, Mission, Kansas, 1996.

Dow, William and Brice Taylor, *Project Management Communications Bible*, Wiley Publishing Inc. Indianapolis, Indiana, 2008.

Doyle, Michael and David Straus, *How to Make Meetings Work*, Jove Books, New York, 1976.

Frame, J. Davidson, *The New Project Management: Tools for an Age of Rapid Change, Complexity and Other Business Realities*, Jossey-Bass, Inc., San Francisco, 1994.

Frohnhoefer, Ray W., *Accidental Project Manager: From Zero to Hero in Seven Days*, PPC Group, San Diego, CA, 2018-2020.

Fry, Ron, *We've Got to Start Meeting This Way*, Career Press, Franklin Lakes, NJ, 1999.

Gardner, Reich, *How to Manage Projects - Reich Gardner - 6 Cassette Tape Seminar*, SkillPath Publications, Mission, Kansas, 1990.

George, Michael L., *Lean Six Sigma for Service*, McGraw-Hill, New York, 2003.

Gerschel, Antoine and Lawrence Polsky, "Meeting with a Mission," *PMNetwork*, January, 2015, p. 70.

Gido, Jack and James P. Clements, *Successful Project Management*, South-Western College Publishing, Cincinnati, Ohio, 1999.

Goleman, Daniel, *Working with Emotional Intelligence*, New York: Bantam Books, 1998.

Goldratt, Elihu M., *Critical Chain*, The North River Press, Great Barrington, Massachusetts, 1997.

Graham, Nick, *Project Management Checklists for Dummies*, John Wiley & Sons, Chichester, West Sussex, 2014.

Harbour, Jerry L., *The Process Reengineering Workbook*, Quality Resources, New York, 1994.

Harrin, Elizabeth, "Mistakes Matter: Post Project Reviews," http://pmtips.net/mistakes-matter-postproject-reviews," May 10, 2009.

Harrin, Elizabeth, *Social Media for Project Managers*, Project Management Institute, Inc., Newtown Square, Pa., 2010.

Harrin, Elizabeth, Managing Multiple Projects: How Project Managers Can Balance Priorities, Manage Expectations and Increase Productivity, Kogan Page, London, 2022.

Heagney, Joseph, *Fundamentals of Project Management*, 6th ed., American Management Association, New York, 2016.

Heldman, Kim, *Project Management Jumpstart*, 4th ed., SYBEX, San Francisco, 2018.

Heldman, Kim, *Project Management Professional Study Guide*, John Wiley & Sons, New York, 2020.

Heldman, Kim, *Risk Management*, Harbor Light Press, SYBEX, Inc., Alameda, Calif., 2005.

Hinde, David, *The Project Manager and the Pyramid: How to Manage Any Project, Any Place, Any Time: Learn Project Management Skills: How to Manage Any Project, Any Place, Any Time*, Orgtopia, 2016.

Jarvis, Mike with Chad Bonham, *Everybody Needs a Head Coach*, Cross Training Publishing, Omaha, Nebraska, 2015.

Johnson, David W. and Frank P. Johnson, *Joining Together Group Theory and Dynamics*, 12th ed., Allyn and Bacon, Boston, 2016.

APPENDIX A

Josephs, Adam and Brad Rubinstein, *Risk Up Front: Managing Projects in a Complex World*, Celebrity Consulting Group, San Francisco, 2018.

Juran, J.M., *Juran on Leadership for Quality*, Free Press, New York, 1989.

Karten, Barbara, *Project Management Simplified: A Step-by-Step Process* (Systems Innovation Book Series) 1st Edition, Kindle Edition, 2018.

Katzenbach, Jon R. and Douglas K. Smith, *The Wisdom of Teams*, HarperCollins Publishers, New York, 2006.

Kendrixk, Thomas, *Identifying and Managing Project Risk: Essential Tools for Failure-Proofing Your Project*, 3rd ed., AMACON, New York, 2015.

Kerzner, Harold, *Project Management*, 13th ed., John Wiley & Sons, New York, 2022.

Kerzner, Harold, *Project Management Best Practices*, John Wiley & Sons, Hoboken, N.J., 2018.

Kerzner, Harold, *Project Management Metrics, KPIs and Dashboards*, John Wiley & Sons, 3rd ed., New York, 2017.

Kiersey, David and Marilyn Bates, *Please Understand Me*, 5th ed., Prometheus Nemesis Book Co., Del Mar, Calif., 1984

Kilmann, Ralph and Kenneth W. Thomas (1977). "Developing a Forced-Choice Measure of Conflict-Handling Behavior: The "MODE" Instrument." Educational and Psychological Measurement 37: 309.

Kogan, Kory, Suzette Blakemore, and James Wood, Project Management for the Unofficial Project Manager, BenBella Books, Inc., Dallas, Texas, 2015.

Kuzes, James and Barry Posner, *The Leadership Challenge*, 6th ed., Jossey-Bass, San Francisco, 2017.

Lange, Erik, *Streetsmart Project Management: The Art of Getting Things Done*, Self-Published, 2021.

Larson, Carl E. and Frank M.J. LaFasto, *Teamwork What Must Go Right/What Can Go Wrong*, Sage Publications, Newbury Park, California, 1989.

Larson, Erik W. and Clifford F. Gray, *Project Management: The Managerial Process*, 8th ed., McGraw-Hill Education, New York, 2020.

Leach, Lawrence P., *Critical Chain Project Management*, 3rd ed., Artech House, 2014.

Lencioni, Patrick, *Death by Meeting: A leadership Fable*, Jossey-Bass, San Francisco, 2004.

Lencioni, Patrick, *Overcoming the Five Dysfunctions of a Team: A Field Guide for Leaders, Managers, and Facilitators*, Jossey-Bass, San Francisco, 2005.

Lencioni, Patrick, *The Five Dysfunctions of a Team: A Leadership Fable*, Jossey-Bass, San Francisco, 2002.

Lewis, James P., *Fundamentals of Project Management*, 3rd ed., AMACON, New York, 2007.

Lewis, James P., *Project Planning, Scheduling, and Control*, 5th ed., McGraw-Hill, New York, 2011.

Madsen, Susanne, *The Power of Project Leadership*, 2nd ed., Kogan Page Limited, London, 2019.

Malooley, Jake, "If Only I'd Known", *PMNetwork*, January, 2015, pp. 48–53.

Mehrabian, A. and M. Wiener, "Decoding of inconsistent communications", *Journal of Personality and Social Psychology*, 1971, 6, 109–114.

Mehrabian, A. and S.R. Ferris, "Inference of Attitudes from Nonverbal Communication in Two Channels," *Journal of Consulting Psychology*, 1967, 31, 3, 48–258

Maurer, Rick, *Beyond the Wall of Resistance*, Bard Books, Inc., Austin, Texas, 1996.

Maylor, Harvey and Neil Turner, *Project Management*, 5th ed., Pearson Education Limited, Upper Saddle River, NJ, 2022.

APPENDIX A

McConnell, Steve, *Software Project Survival Guide*, Microsoft Press, Redmond, Washington, 1998.

Meredith, Jack R., Scott M. Shafer, Samuel J. Mantel, Jr., Margaret M. Sutton, *Project Management*, 7th ed., John Wiley & Sons, New York, 2020.

Miller, Dennis P., *Building a Project Work Breakdown Structure: Visualizing Objectives, Deliverables, Activities, and Schedules*, Auerbach Publications, Boca Raton, Florida, 2009.

Mersino, Anthony C., *Emotional Intelligence for Project Managers: The People Skills You Need to Achieve Outstanding Results*, American Management Association, New York, 2007.

Mulcahy, Rita, *Risk Management: Tricks of the Trade for Project Managers*, RMC Publications, Minneapolis, Minnesota, 2003.

Newton, Richard, *Brilliant Checklists for Project Managers: Your Shortcut to Success*, Ft Pr., 2nd edition 2011.

Newton, Richard, *The Project Manager's Book of Checklists: How To Complete A Project Successfully, Smoothly And On Time*, 1st Edition, Kindle Edition, 2013.

Newton, Richard, *The Project Management Book: How to Manage Your Projects to Deliver Outstanding Results*, 1st Edition, Kindle Edition, 2014.

Newton, Richard, *Project Management Step by Step: How to Plan and Manage a Highly Successful Project*, 2nd Ed., Pearson Education Limited, Harlow, UK, 2016.

Nieto-Rodriguez, Antonio, *Harvard Business Review Project Management Handbook: How to Launch, Lead, and Sponsor Successful Projects*, Harvard Business School Publishing Corporation, Boston, 2021.

Nizhebtskyi, Dmytro, *Practical Project Management: Proven Framework That Great Project Managers Use In the Real World*, Independently published, March 11, 2022.

Pham, Anh Dao, *Glue: How Project Leaders Create Cohesive, Engaged, High-Performing Teams*, G&D Media, 2022.

Leadership Through Quality: Problem-Solving Process User's Manual, Xerox Corporation, Rochester, New York, 1986.

Engaging sponsors (2014). *PM Network, 28*(11), 18–20.

PM Solutions, "Strategies for Project Recovery" Project Management Solutions, Inc., 2011.

Pitino, Rick, *Success is a Choice: Ten Steps to Overachieving in Business and Life*, Broadway Books, New York, 1997.

Portny, Jonathon and Stanley Portny, *Project Management for Dummies*, 6th ed., John Wiley & Sons, Hoboken, N.J., 2022.

Project Management Institute, *Practice Standard for Work Breakdown Structures*, 2nd ed., Newtown Square, PA, 2006.

Project Management Institute, *PMBOK Guide*, 7th ed., Newtown Square, PA, 2021.

Project Management Institute, *Process Groups: A Practice Guide*, Newtown Square, PA, 2022

Rehman, Navaid Ur, Project Management Book of Templates, Independently published, March 16, 2021.

Ressler, Cali and Jody Thompson, *Why Work Sucks and How to Fix It: The Results-Only Revolution*, Penguin Group, New York, 2008.

Riley, Pat, *The Winner Within: A Life Plan for Team Players*, The Berkeley Publishing Group, New York, 1994.

Rubinstein, Brad and Joseph Adam, *Risk Up Front: Managing Projects in a Complex World*, Celebrity Consulting Group, San Francisco, 2018.

Shentar, Aaron J. and Dov Dvir, *Reinventing Project Management*, Harvard Business School Press, Boston, 2007.

Schmidt, Terry Dean, *Strategic Project Management Made Simple*, 2nd ed., Wiley, 2021.

Scholtes, Peter, Brian Joiner and Barbara Streibel, *The Team Handbook*, 3rd ed., Oriel, Inc., Madison, Wisconsin, 2018.

Schwalbe, Kathy, *An Introduction to Project Management*, 7th ed., Schwalbe Publishing, Minneapolis, MN, 2021.

APPENDIX A

Schwalbe, Kathryn, *Project Management for IT Professionals*, 3rd ed., Thomson Learning, Inc., Boston, 2004.

Shula, Don and Ken Blanchard, *Everyone's a Coach: Five Business Secrets for High-Performance Coaching*, Zondervan Publishing House, Grand Rapids, Michigan, 1995.

Simon, Phil, Project Management in the Hybrid Workplace, Racket Publishing, Gilbert, AZ, 2022.

Summitt, Pat, *Reach for the Summit: The Definite Dozen System for Succeeding at Whatever You Do*, Broadway Books, New York, 1998.

Surowiecki, James, *The Wisdom of Crowds*, Anchor Books, New York, 2004.

Tate, Karen and Paula Martin, *Project Management Memory Jogger*, 2nd ed., GOAL/QPC, Salem, New Hampshire, 2020.

Thomas, Kenneth W. and Ralph H. Kilmann, *Thomas-Kilmann Conflict Mode Instrument* (Tuxedo NY: Xicom, 1974)

Tomczyk, Catherine, *Project Manager's Spotlight on Planning*, SYBEX, San Francisco, 2005.

Tuckman, Bruce W., *Developmental Sequence in Small Groups*, Psychological Bulletin, 1965, vol. 63, No. 6, 384-399.

Tuckwood, Vincent, *Project Management for Human Resources: The structure and art of getting things done in HR*, View Beyond LLC, Waterford, CT., 2020.

Vance, Mike and Diane Deacon, *Think Out of the Box*, Career Press, Franklin Lakes, N.J., 1995.

Versuh, Eric, *The Fast Forward MBA in Project Management*, 6th ed., John Wiley & Sons, Inc., 2021.

Vibrant Publishers and Kalpesh Asher, *Project Management Essentials You Always Wanted to Know*, 4th ed., Vibrant Publishers, Colorado, USA, 2019.

Wiegers, Karl E., *Practical Project Initiation*, Microsoft Press, Redmond, Washington, 2007.

Wysocki, Robert K., *Effective Software Project Management*, Wiley Publishing, Inc., Indianapolis, Indiana, 2006.

Wysocki, Robert K., *Effective Project Management: Traditional, Agile, Extreme, Hybrid*, Wiley Publishing, Inc., 8th ed., Hoboken, NJ, 2019.

Zehnder, Meredith, "Delivering Bad News," *PMNetwork*, January, 2015, pp. 22–23.

APPENDIX B
Project Tools

In this section, the various project management tools referenced throughout the book are listed together with a recommendation for their use. Several caveats go with these recommendations. First, they represent the opinion of the author. Others may have a different perspective.

Second, projects are by definition unique. That means that no recommendation will be appropriate for all projects even within the same project type. These recommendations should, therefore, be taken as guidelines. They are not intended to substitute for common sense.

With that in mind, tools are recommended for use by type of project. The recommendations are optional, recommended, and required.

- **Optional**

   Optional means that the tools may or may not be useful, depending on the nature of the project. Since project managers are busy people not looking for additional work, it is expected that most project managers will not use an optional tool unless there is a specific reason to do so.

- **Recommended**

   A recommended tool is one that should be used (for its intended purpose) unless there is a specific reason not to.

- **Required**

    A required tool is one that should be used in all appropriate situations. Of course, there will always be exceptions, but those are rare. A decision not to use a required tool should only be made after careful consideration.

Tools are designed to make work easier. When a tool does not do this, it becomes counterproductive. This is usually the result of not using it correctly or trying to use it in a situation that it was not designed for. Effective project management requires the use of the right tools in the right situation.

Brainstorming	X	X	X
Change Log	√	X	X
Change Order	√	X	X
Communications Plan	O	O	√
Control Chart	X	√	√
Delphi Method	O	O	O
Earned Value Report	O	O	O
Flexibility Diagram	O	O	O
Gantt Chart	X	X	X
Issues Log	√	X	X
Mind Map	O	O	O
Network Diagram	O	O	O
Office Productivity Software	√	√	√
Progress/Status Report	√	X	X
PICK Chart	O	O	O
Project Charter	X	X	X
Project Concept Document	O	O	√
Project Forecast	√	√	√
Project Management Software	O	√	X

APPENDIX C

Diagnostic Surveys

Teamwork Survey

Objective: To identify the stage of team development.

Directions: This questionnaire contains statements about teamwork. Next to each question, indicate how often your team displays each behavior by using the following scoring system:

1. Almost never
2. Seldom
3. Occasionally
4. Frequently
5. Almost always

Questionnaire:

1.	_____	We try to have set procedures or protocols to ensure that things are orderly and run smoothly (e.g. minimize interruptions, everyone gets the opportunity to have their say).
2.	_____	We are quick to get on with the task on hand and do not spend too much time in the planning stage.
3.	_____	Our team feels that we are all in it together and shares responsibilities for the team's success or failure.

4.	_____	We have thorough procedures for agreeing on our objectives and planning the way we will perform our tasks.
5.	_____	Team members are afraid or do not like to ask others for help.
6.	_____	We take our team's goals and objectives literally, and assume a shared understanding.
7.	_____	The team leader tries to keep order and contributes to the task at hand.
8.	_____	We do not have fixed procedures. We make them up as the task or project progresses.
9.	_____	We generate lots of ideals, but we do not use many because we fail to listen to them and reject them without fully understanding them.
10.	_____	Team members do not fully trust the other members and closely monitor others who are working on a specific task.
11.	_____	The team leader ensures that we follow the procedures, do not argue, do not interrupt, and keep to the point.
12.	_____	We enjoy working together; we have a fun and productive time.
13.	_____	We have accepted each other as members of the team.
14.	_____	The team leader is democratic and collaborative.
15.	_____	We are trying to define the goal and what tasks need to be accomplished.
16.	_____	Many of the team members have their own ideas about the process and personal agendas are rampant.
17.	_____	We fully accept each other's strengths and weaknesses.

APPENDIX C

18.	_____	We assign specific roles to team members (team leader, facilitator, time keeper, note taker, etc.).
19.	_____	We try to achieve harmony by avoiding conflict.
20.	_____	The tasks are very different from what we imagined and seem very difficult to accomplish.
21.	_____	There are many abstract discussions of the concepts and issues, which make some members impatient with these discussions.
22.	_____	We are able to work through group problems.
23.	_____	We argue a lot even though we agree on the real issues.
24.	_____	The team is often tempted to go above the original scope of the project.
25.	_____	We express criticism of others constructively.
26.	_____	There is a close attachment to the team.
27.	_____	It seems as if little is being accomplished with the project's goals.
28.	_____	The goals we have established seem unrealistic.
29.	_____	Although we are not fully sure of the project's goals and issues, we are excited and proud to be on the team.
30.	_____	We often share personal problems with each other.
31.	_____	There is a lot of resisting of the tasks on hand and quality improvement approaches.
32.	_____	We get a lot of work done.

Scoring:

Next to each survey item number below, transfer the score that you give that item on the questionnaire. For example, if you scored item 1 with a 3 (Occasionally), then enter a 3 next to item one below. When you have entered all the scores for each question, total each of the four columns.

Item Score	Item Score	Item Score	Item Score
1. ___	2. ___	4. ___	3. ___
5. ___	7. ___	6. ___	8. ___
10. ___	9. ___	11. ___	12. ___
15. ___	16. ___	13. ___	14. ___
18. ___	20. ___	19. ___	17. ___
21. ___	23. ___	24. ___	22. ___
27. ___	28. ___	25. ___	26. ___
29. ___	31. ___	30. ___	32. ___
Total ___	Total ___	Total ___	Total ___
Forming Stage	Storming Stage	Norming Stage	Performing Stage

This purpose of this questionnaire is to help you assess the stage at which your team normally operates. It is based on the "Tuckman" model of Forming, Storming, Norming, and Performing. The lowest score possible for a stage is 8 (Almost never) while the highest score possible for a stage is 40 (Almost always).

The highest of the four scores indicates which stage you perceive your team normally operates in. If your highest score is 32 or more, it is a strong indicator of the stage your team is in.

The lowest of the three scores is an indicator of the stage your team is least like. If your lowest score is 16 or less, it is a strong indicator that your team does not operate this way.

If two of the scores are close to the same, you are probably going through a transition phase, except:

- If you score high in both the Forming and Storming phases, then you are in the Storming phase.
- If you score high in both the Norming and Performing phases, then you are in the Performing stage.
- If there is only a small difference between three or four scores, then this indicates that you have no clear perception of the way your team operates, the team's performance is highly variable, or that you are in the Storming phase (this phase can be extremely volatile with high and low points).

Reliability and Validity:

Since this survey is a training tool, it has not been formally checked for reliability or validity. However, since the author has received feedback from various sources, he believes it is fairly accurate.

Copyright 2004 by Donald Clark
Reprinted with Permission
Created January 1, 1998
Source: http://www.nwlink.com/~donclark/leader/teamsuv.html

Project Diagnostic Survey

Note: Please rate questions with scores between 1-3 (3-the best). In situations where it is not applicable mark: "N/A"

A. Objectives Rank

1.	_____	Were the objectives for the project clearly defined?
2.	_____	Were the objectives for your particular work on the project clearly defined?
3.	_____	Were all objectives met?

B. Project Planning Rank

1.	_____	Was the project plan clear and easy to follow? If not, how could it be improved?
2.	_____	Were the time estimates for all your tasks accurate?
3.	_____	Was the entire team committed to the project schedule?
4.	_____	Did you have to do any unexpected significant rework?
5.	_____	Did you overestimate the amount of time you would have each week to work on this project?
6.	_____	Was the project significantly delayed or hampered by dependencies outside the project?
7.	_____	Were you diverted to work on another project?
8.	_____	How would you estimate and schedule the project differently next time to avoid any problems noted above?

C. Issue Management Rank

1.	_____	Were issues identified and managed effectively?
2.	_____	Did team members act proactively to identify, investigate and resolve issues?

D. Risk Management Rank

1.	_____	Were risks adequately assessed and managed'?

E. Communication Management Rank

1.	_____	Was progress reporting adequately defined (when, how and who) during project planning?
2.	_____	Was progress reporting done efficiently and effectively?
3.	_____	Was the quality and timing of communication across the team effective?
4.	_____	Were there any problems encountered in the relationships between different work streams of the project?
5.	_____	Did the Integration Sessions add value to the overall process?

F. Roles and Responsibilities Rank

1.	_____	Were the roles clearly defined and the responsibilities appropriately assigned at the start of the project?
2.	_____	Should roles and responsibilities be redefined, added or eliminated in the future?
3.	_____	Were the tasks assigned to the appropriate people?
4.	_____	Were you adequately included in project decisions?

| 5. | _____ | Were you appreciated, recognized, and rewarded for your efforts? |

G. Team productivity Rank

1.	_____	Was the team productive as a group?
2.	_____	Did the team encounter any organizational and/or structural problems?
3.	_____	Were there any major bottlenecks in the project?
4.	_____	Was the project team's physical working environment suitable?
5.	_____	Was the extent and quality of training for the team (induction and ongoing) sufficient?
6.	_____	Was conflict managed appropriately?

Total Score _____

Source: http://www.allpm.com/modules.php?op=modload&name=News&file=article&sid=1135&mode=thread&order=0&thold=0 (This link no longer appears to be active. A search of the site yielded no results.)

Published on July 28, 2004

APPENDIX C

Team Effectiveness Checklist

The following checklist can be used as a resource either as part of a team-building workshop or at one of your regular team meetings. The checklist is a quick means to take a temperature check of the team's effectiveness.

Depending on trust levels within your team – the checklist can be talked through as a team or completed on an individual basis first. If going with the latter approach, each team member completes the scoring individually and scores are then collated anonymously or openly on a flip chart.

Overall scores reveal:

- how much consensus or variance there is for each statement
- the team's view of their biggest strengths and areas for development

There are no right or wrong answers. The idea is to use the results to start a discussion. How far do you agree with the statements made below?

Mark each statement on a scale of 1 (disagree strongly) to 10 (agree strongly).

1. We have mutually agreed and understood aims and objectives.
   1   2   3   4   5   6   7   8   9   10

2. We have well-balanced roles that complement each other.
   1   2   3   4   5   6   7   8   9   10

3. We have good decision-making processes, information systems, and coordinate resources.

    1   2   3   4   5   6   7   8   9   10

4. We have productive meetings and good communication within the team and the organization.

    1   2   3   4   5   6   7   8   9   10

5. There is positive team leadership.

    1   2   3   4   5   6   7   8   9   10

6. There is a high level of support and trust.

    1   2   3   4   5   6   7   8   9   10

7. People express themselves openly and honestly and deal with difficult situations

    1   2   3   4   5   6   7   8   9   10

8. Team members work together cooperatively.

    1   2   3   4   5   6   7   8   9   10

9. There is scope for individual learning and development.

    1   2   3   4   5   6   7   8   9   10

10. Relations with other groups are sound.

    1   2   3   4   5   6   7   8   9   10

Source: University College Dublin
https://www.ucd.ie/t4cms/Team%20Effectiveness%20Checklist.pdf

APPENDIX C

Project Meeting Effectiveness Survey

There are a number of surveys floating around the internet that are designed to measure the effectiveness of project team meetings and team members' satisfaction with these meetings. The following was developed by the author based on his experience as a project manager.

Indicate your agreement or disagreement with each of the following statements.

1 = Strongly agree
2 = Agree
3 = Neither agree nor disagree
4 = Disagree
5 = Strongly disagree
NA = Not applicable

Pre-meeting

1. _____ Meeting materials were sent out in sufficient time for participants to prepare for the meeting.
2. _____ The agenda was sent out in advance of the meeting.
3. _____ It was not entirely clear what needed to be accomplished at this meeting.

Meeting

1. _____ The meeting started on time.
2. _____ Not all the right people were at the meeting.
3. _____ The project manager/facilitator kept the discussion on topic.
4. _____ Not all participants participated in the discussions.
5. _____ The project manager handled conflict among team members well.

6. _____ The meeting did not accomplish all of its objectives.
7. _____ The meeting finished on time.

Post-meeting

1. _____ Meeting minutes were not sent out in a timely manner following the meeting.
2. _____ This meeting was worth the time spent.

APPENDIX C

Team Performance Criteria

As teams are pressured to do more with less, it is important to continuously evaluate and improve team performance. The team performance criteria listed in this section is one method for doing this. The team addresses the criteria and they are evaluated against a set of scoring guidelines. The feedback from this exercise helps teams to understand their strengths and opportunities for improvement.

The American Society for Quality Team Excellence Award is a proprietary set of standards that can be purchased directly from ASQ. The following standards were developed by the author and are patterned after the Secretary of the Air Force Team Quality Award and various other state quality award criteria.

The Criteria

Standard 1 - Selecting the Opportunity (20 points)
a. How and why was this opportunity selected? How does the opportunity support achievement of your organization's objectives?
   1. What process/method was used to determine why this opportunity was an important task for a team effort? What were the reasons leading up to the opportunity?
   2. How was the decision reached to undertake this opportunity?
   3. How will the expected outcome(s) impact the achievement of the organization's objectives?
b. How does the opportunity support achievement of your organization's objectives?
   1. How will the expected outcome(s) impact the achievement of the organization's objectives?
c. What are the objectives of the selected opportunity?
   1. What are the expected outcomes?

2. What boundary conditions existed for this opportunity, such as limitations on budget expenditures, personnel assignments in the completed actions, or authority to implement results?
3. What is the specific scope of the opportunity, including where the team was to begin and where its task was to end?

d. Who are the stakeholders of the opportunity?
1. Who would be impacted by the results of the team activity, and why?

Definitions

Opportunity: A generic term to describe the various types of team tasks, including, but not limited to, problem-solving, project implementation, process improvement, and team operations, which contribute to achieving organizational or community objectives.

Stakeholders: A term that refers to individuals and/or groups impacted by the team's activity. Stakeholders could be, for example, external or internal customers, users of the process/product/service, owners of the process, members of the community, and/or team sponsors.

Notes

1. Explain the decision methodology used to determine that this opportunity should take precedence over others identified by the organization. Include a description of what additional guidance or direction the team received to fully understand the scope, responsibilities, and timeframe of its activity.
2. In showing how achievement of the objectives of this opportunity will contribute to the accomplishment of organizational goals/objectives, including why this is significant to the organization and was influential in the opportunity selection.

APPENDIX C

3. In addition to identifying appropriate stakeholders, your response should also include how these stakeholders will be involved in the team process, or how stakeholder needs will be met, based on the goals set forth for the opportunity.

Standard 2 - Establishing and Developing the Team (15 points)

a. How were team members selected?
   1. What process was used to select team members? Did potential team members participate in the selection process?
   2. How was approval obtained for team member assignments?
b. What were the roles and responsibilities of team members?
   1. What were the specific roles of the team members, as appropriate? For example, the team consisted of John Jones, a process analyst, responsible for drawing the flow charts, Marilyn Smith, a skilled communications specialist, responsible for networking with other organizations on their process, etc. This component could also include more traditional team roles, such as facilitator, timekeeper, etc., as appropriate.
   2. How did team members' roles and responsibilities ensure effective interactions between team members?
c. How was team building achieved?
   1. What actions were taken to help the team work effectively together? Examples of such mechanisms could include attendance at training on team dynamics, conducting personality profiles for team members, establishing team "ground rules", or other mechanisms suitable to the organization's culture.

Notes

1. Explain how the team selection process ensures that the team will be well balanced, knowledgeable and experienced enough to complete the task at hand.

2. Your response should also include areas such as whether team performance reviews were conducted and what change, if any, occurred as a result of such reviews. In addition, discuss how member knowledge and experience in team activities impacted the team building process.

Standard 3 - Analyzing the Situation (15 points)

a. What approach was used to determine what data/information the team would collect?
   1. How did the team decide what data/information was needed to determine how well the existing process was working?
   2. How did the team determine what data-gathering techniques should be used?
b. How did the team gather data, and how was it summarized?
   1. What data-gathering techniques were used?
   2. What information was collected?
   3. How/by whom was stakeholder input obtained, if applicable?
   4. If measurements were obtained, what did the team measure and how?
   5. If benchmark or comparative data were obtained from external sources, how did the team obtain this information?
c. What analysis techniques were used to understand the existing situation?
   1. What approach was used to determine how to analyze the data gathered?
   2. What analyses were conducted to gain an understanding of the scope of the situation?
   3. What conclusions were reached about the existing situation?

Notes

1. Discuss how the team ensured the validity of the data it collected. Explain how the team determined what type of benchmark/comparative data to collect.

2. In discussing the analyses that were conducted, provide a brief explanation of why certain tools were selected.

Standard 4 - Selecting Alternatives or Potential Solutions (15 points)

a. What activities or tasks did the team determine to have the greatest influence on the process or operation?
   1. From the analysis conducted, what did the team determine to be the key activities or tasks within the process, or those factors having the greatest impact on the situation?
   2. How were these activities/tasks/factors chosen?
b. How did the team develop alternatives or potential solutions?
   1. What methods were used to develop alternatives or potential solutions to address the situation?
   2. What alternatives or potential solutions were identified?
c. What process did the team use to determine the best alternative or solution?
   1. How did the team analyze the options and select the best alternatives or solutions?
   2. How were constraints of the opportunity considered in arriving at this decision?
   3. How were the opportunity objectives considered in the decision process?
   4. What outside sources, if any, did the team consult in reaching its decision?

Notes

1. Describe how the key activities/tasks/factors selected were linked to the expected outcomes for the team process.
2. Explain to what extent all team members were involved in the options analysis process. Explain the process used to establish the linkage between the various (what word goes here?)

Standard 5 - Implementing Alternatives/Solutions (15 points)

a. How was the action plan developed to implement the alternative or solution?
   1. What method was used to develop the action plan?
   2. How did the team go about developing a methodology to implement the chosen action plan?
   3. What factors were considered in deciding how to implement the chosen action plan?
   4. What did the team do to ensure that implementation would go smoothly?
   5. What approvals, if any, were needed before beginning implementation?
b. How is progress being/How will progress be monitored?
   1. What steps have been taken to ensure the effectiveness or continuing effectiveness of the solution?
   2. What measures and/or indicators are being/will be employed to monitor the progress, and how were these selected?
c. How did the team obtain agreement from stakeholders, and how did it share information with them?
   1. How did the team determine that the proposed action plan would be of value?
   2. How were stakeholders not involved in the approval chain informed of the proposed action plan and its potential impact on them?

Notes

1. Explain the decision-making process used by the team to establish the appropriate action plan(s). Explain how the team weighed the constraints of the opportunity in implementing the action plan.
2. Discuss how the measurement and/or indicators link back to the original opportunity objectives.

Standard 6 - Monitoring Progress (20 points)

a. What is the status of the implementation process?
    1. What are the key milestones that indicate significant team activity to date, progress thus far, and any future plans?
    2. What was or is being done to monitor the success of the implementation?
b. What are the advantages/benefits that have been achieved by the team's actions and/or those that are anticipated?
    1. If appropriate, what comparisons has the team made of the process performance at the start of the activity with that currently observed?
    2. If the solution has yet to produce documented improvements, or has yet to be implemented, what improvements are anticipated, and how were those improvements determined?
c. What ongoing communication is the team conducting with stakeholders?
    1. What actions have been taken to communicate results to stakeholders, as appropriate?
d. How are/will overall improvement efforts (be) incorporated into ongoing activities?
    1. What plans, if any, does the team have to continue improving the process? If plans are to continue, what are the next steps for the team?
    2. Has the team or will the team be disbanded?

Notes

1. Describe the method(s) used to inform stakeholders of progress/results, and how the feedback is used to reinforce efforts.

Scoring Guidelines

1 Selecting the Opportunity

1a. How and why was this opportunity selected?

1. No description provided of how or why the opportunity was selected.
2. Unclear or partial description of how or why opportunity was selected.
3. Adequate description of how and/or why the opportunity was selected.
4. Description of how and why includes indication that the organization has determined it is capable of accomplishing objective; evidence exists that efforts have been made to improve the selection process.
5. Description of how and why indicates a systematic approach; defined process steps include cost/benefit review, timelines, identification of the "vital few" opportunities, and evaluation and improvement cycles.

1b. How does the opportunity support achievement of your organization's objectives?
1. Linkage between expected outcomes and organizational objectives is not addressed.
2. Linkage between expected outcomes and organizational objectives is vague or unclear.
3. There is clear linkage between expected outcomes and organizational objectives.
4. Linkage between team activities and organizational objectives is a factor in selecting opportunities.
5. There is indication that the organization has defined the linkage between team activities and organizational goals and that this linkage is a driver of the decision to select the opportunity.

1c. What are the objectives of the selected opportunity?
1. Objectives are not determined at the outset.
2. There is vague reference to implied outcome; no guidelines or scope identified.
3. Adequate explanation of expected outcome is provided; clear understanding of guidelines and scope demonstrated.

4. Expected outcomes include statement of goals and timelines; guidelines include definition of resources available, responsibility and authority to make change.
5. Requirements, scope, and expectations are fully defined, such as a team charter, which details the problem, opportunity to improve, expected outcome, team members, and appropriate authorization.

1d. Who are the stakeholders of the project?
1. Stakeholders are not identified.
2. Major stakeholders are identified.
3. Multiple stakeholders are identified.
4. Many stakeholders are identified, including some internal and external customers of the improvement process.
5. Stakeholders are not only identified, but are involved as part of the team process; stakeholders' needs are identified and considered in the team objectives.

2 Selecting and Developing the Team

2a. How were team members selected?
1. No process of team member selection is described.
2. Process used to select team members is not defined, but there is some consideration of team member qualifications.
3. Process is defined and includes identification of skills and experience needed based upon the opportunity.
4. A well-defined process is described that includes interactions between potential team members and their supervision in the selection process.
5. A well-defined process is described that ensures a well-balanced team with the skills, knowledge, and experience to accomplish the objectives; buy-in is obtained from supervision.

2b. What were the roles and responsibilities of team members?
1. Roles and responsibilities are not described.
2. Roles and responsibilities are vaguely identified.

3. Individual roles and responsibilities are identified for team members; responsibilities of team members in working together are described in general terms.
   4. All roles and responsibilities are identified as appropriate; interaction roles and responsibilities are described in detail.
   5. All team member rules and responsibilities are identified, as appropriate; team interaction roles and responsibilities are defined in detail.

2c. How was team building achieved?
   1. No team building initiatives are described.
   2. A few team-building activities have been accomplished, but no defined approach is described.
   3. A defined team building process is outlined that takes into account member knowledge and experience in team activities.
   4. A well-defined process is described that takes into account member knowledge and experience in team activities; the team defines how it will work and handle conflict.
   5. A well-defined process is described that fully considers member knowledge and experience in team activities; the team defines how they will work and handle conflict; team performance reviews are conducted.

3 Analyzing the Situation

3a. What approach was used to determine what data/information the team would collect?
   1. How it was decided what data/information to collect is not described.
   2. Brief description of the decision process for data/information collection is provided.
   3. A systematic process was used to decide what data/information to collect.
   4. An especially thorough process was used to decide what data/information to collect.

APPENDIX C

    5. A robust process was used that encompassed all facets of importance to the project and involved appropriate stakeholders.

3b. How did the team gather data, and how was it summarized?
1. The data/information collection methodology is not described.
2. A brief description is provided of the data/information collection methodology.
3. A clear explanation of the data/information collection methodology is described with indication of what was collected and how.
4. Data/information collection was accomplished from multiple sources with confirmation of data/information validity.
5. Multiple data/information internal sources are supplemented with comparative/benchmark data/information; how it was obtained is explained.

3c. What analysis techniques were used to understand the existing situation?
1. No process to understand the situation is described; team immediately jumps to resolving the situation.
2. Some basic analysis techniques, such as brainstorming, are used to understand the situation.
3. Analysis techniques are used to basically understand the scope of the situation and how to proceed.
4. Multiple analyses are conducted to understand the situation and how to proceed.
5. Multiple analyses are conducted that yield a full understanding of the situation and are used to establish a fact-based approach.

4 Selecting Alternatives or Potential Solutions

4a. What activities or tasks did the team determine to have the greatest influence on the process or operation?
1. Key activities or tasks having influence on the process/operation are not identified.

2. Key activities or tasks are identified, but there is little or no explanation as to why they were chosen.
3. Key activities or tasks are identified and clear rationale for their selection is provided.
4. Linkage is established between key activities/tasks and the expected outcomes or operation of the process.
5. Linkage is established between key activities/tasks and the expected outcomes or operation of the process, and there is clear explanation of how the link was established.

4b. How did the team develop alternatives or potential solutions?
1. No planning was conducted; the team jumped immediately to conclusion about what to do.
2. Some suggestions or pieces of actions were identified; no systematic process is evident; there was limited involvement of the entire team.
3. An adequate action planning process was used that identified several alternatives/ solutions; most of the team was involved.
4. An adequate action planning process was used that identified multiple alternatives/ solutions that link to the opportunity objectives.
5. The entire team participated in developing a comprehensive set of alternatives/solutions that have a strong linkage to the opportunity objectives; stakeholders were involved in the process; comparative/benchmark data have been obtained.

4c. What process did the team use to determine the best alternative or solution?
1. No process is described; it is unclear how team chose the best plan.
2. There is a brief description of the method used to choose the best plan; no systematic process is evident; it is unclear how the analysis of options was accomplished.

3. A systematic process was used to select best plan; adequate analysis of options was accomplished; most of the team participated.
4. An especially thorough process was used to select the best plan; multiple analyses were conducted, involving most of the team.
5. A robust process was used to select the best plan, involving the collection and analysis of comparative/benchmark data; multiple analyses were conducted involving all team members.

5 Implementing Alternatives/Solutions

5a. How was the action plan developed to implement the alternative or solution?
1. No systematic process was used in reaching the decision.
2. The decision was based on the team's alternatives/solutions; there was limited participation by all team members in reaching a decision.
3. Most of the team was involved in making the decision with little consideration of constraints, such as funding, resources, time, etc.
4. A systematic process to determine the best course of action was used; constraints were considered.
5. A dynamic team decision-making process that fully considered boundaries and constraints was used; the impacts of the course of action were fully understood.

5b. How is progress being/How will progress be monitored?
1. There is no indication that a process was put in place to monitor progress or results.
2. A process is in place to obtain some progress and results data, but there is no indication of how measures were selected.
3. A well-defined process is identified to monitor progress or results; measures and/or indicators were identified with a clear explanation as to why they were selected.

4. A well-defined process with clear explanation of measures and/or indicators and their linkage to the opportunity objectives is in place.
  5. A well-defined process with clear explanation of measures and/or indicators that have strong linkage to opportunity objectives is in place.

5c. How did the team obtain agreement from stakeholders, and how did it share information with them?
  1. No systematic process is evident.
  2. Agreement was obtained from some decision makers on the proposed actions.
  3. Through the beginning of a systematic process, agreement was obtained from appropriate decision-makers and appropriate stakeholders were informed.
  4. Through a systematic process, agreement was obtained from appropriate decision-makers, and buy-in from appropriate stakeholders was obtained.
  5. Through a proactive approach, key decision makers and stakeholders were actively involved in arriving at the proposed action; information on the impact of the team's actions was clearly conveyed.

6 Monitoring Progress
6a. What is the status of the implementation process?
  1. No progress has been reported; there is no indication that future plans have been developed.
  2. Some progress has been made, but it falls short of the schedule; there is a brief description of future plans.
  3. Progress has been made in all appropriate areas; most targets have been met; there is a good description of future plans.
  4. Progress is ahead of plan in a few areas; most targets have been met and some exceeded; there is a complete description of future plans.

5. Progress is significantly ahead of plan; all targets have been met and many have been exceeded; the description of future plans is complete and provides options to expedite implementation.

6b. What are the advantages/benefits that have been achieved by the team's actions and/or those that are anticipated?
1. There is no indication that advantages or benefits have been identified.
2. There is some description provided of advantages or benefits attained or anticipated.
3. Descriptions of advantages or benefits achieved or anticipated is provided; there is clear indication that some have occurred or there is a likelihood they will occur.
4. There is a complete description of advantages or benefits achieved or anticipated; some exceed or are expected to exceed expectations.
5. There is a complete description of advantages or benefits achieved or anticipated; many exceed or are expected to exceed expectations.

6c. What ongoing communication is the team conducting with stakeholders?
1. No plans for continuing communication of progress or results are evident.
2. A description of how results have been/will be communicated, including specific action taken/to be taken by the team, is provided.
3. A clear definition of how results have been/will be communicated, including specific action taken/to be taken by the team, is described.
4. A clear definition of a communications plan with identification of communication to key stakeholders and plans for next steps is described; there is clear communication of the impact of the action(s) taken.

5. Proactive communications plan is described with interactive communication to all stakeholders and appropriate milestones and follow-on reinforcement efforts.

6d. How are/will overall improvement efforts (be) incorporated into ongoing activities?
1. No identification of plans for continuing improvement is evident.
2. The team has identified a rough plan for its next stages or for follow on activities by another team.
3. The team has planned out its next steps in some detail; if disbanded, improvement activity to continue enhancement of the process performance has been identified.
4. The team has a well-defined plan for its next steps; if disbanded, the team has captured lessons learned from the process and additional improvement opportunities have been identified.
5. A well-defined plan for the next steps that integrates continuing monitoring of performance and continuous improvement is described; other teams have adopted the team methodology.

APPENDIX D

Exercises

Lost on the Moon Exercise

This training exercise developed by NASA can be used to demonstrate a number of concepts. These include:

- The importance of group decision-making
- The value of diversity
- The role of leadership in small groups
- The nature of conflict in groups facing a competitive task

In addition to using this as a training exercise, psychologists at the Danish Defense's Center for Leadership use it to evaluate cadets' abilities as group members in a decision process. Some companies use a variation of this exercise as a part of their job interviews.

Human Synergistics International publishes a series of similar, though slightly more sophisticated, exercises. These include *Cascades Survival*, *Arctic Survival*, and *Desert Survival*. Human Synergistics also produces additional training materials and videos to support these exercises.

The *Lost on the Moon* exercise is in the public domain and is therefore free to use.

Scenario

Your spaceship has just crashed on the moon. You were scheduled to rendezvous with a mother ship 200 miles away on the lighted surface of the moon, but the rough landing has ruined your ship and destroyed all the equipment on board except for the 15 items listed below.

Your crew's survival depends on reaching the mother ship, so you must choose the most critical items available for the 200-mile trip.

Your task is to rank the 15 items in terms of their importance for survival. Place a number 1 by the most important item, number 2 by the second most important, and so on, through number 15, the least important.

Score Sheet

_____ Box of matches
_____ Food concentrate
_____ 50 feet of nylon rope
_____ Parachute silk
_____ Solar-powered portable heating unit
_____ Two .45 caliber pistols
_____ One case of dehydrated milk
_____ Two 100-pound tanks of oxygen
_____ Stellar map (of the moon's constellations)
_____ Self-inflating life raft
_____ Magnetic compass
_____ 5 gallons of water
_____ Signal flares
_____ First-aid kit containing injection needles
_____ Solar-powered FM receiver-transmitter

APPENDIX D

Solution

Items	Explanation	NASA Rank
Box of matches	No oxygen to sustain flame, virtually worthless	15
Food concentrate	Efficient means of supplying energy requirements	4
Fifty feet of nylon rope	Useful in scaling cliffs, tying injured together	6
Parachute silk	Protection from sun's rays	8
Solar-powered portable heating unit	Not needed on dark side	13
Two .45 caliber pistols	Possible means of self-propulsion	11
One case of Pet milk	Bulkier duplication of food concentrate	12
Two 100-pound tanks of oxygen	Most pressing survival need	1
Stellar map (of the moon's constellations)	Primary means of navigation	3
Self-inflating life raft	CO_2 bottle in military raft may be used for propulsion	9
Magnetic compass	Magnetic field on the moon is not polarized; worthless for navigation	14
5 gallons of water	Replacement for tremendous loss on lighted side	2
Signal flares	Distress signal when mother ship is sighted	10

Items	Explanation	NASA Rank
First-aid kit containing injection needles	Needles for vitamins, medications, etc. will fit special aperture on NASA space suits.	7
Solar-powered FM receiver-transmitter	For communication with mother ship; but FM requires line-of-sight transmission and short ranges	5

Instructions

Participants are divided into teams of 4 to 6 members. They are instructed to do the exercise individually. This takes about 20 minutes. Next, each team has 20 to 30 minutes to reach consensus on the order of the items. Columns 4 and 5 represent the difference between the individual ranks, the team ranks, and the experts at NASA.

		1	2	3	4	5
	Item	Your Rank	Team Rank	NASA Rank	1-3*	2-3*
1	Box of matches					
2	Food concentrate					
3	Fifty feet of nylon rope					
4	Parachute silk					
5	Solar-powered portable heating unit					
6	Two .45 caliber pistols					

APPENDIX D

	Item	1 Your Rank	2 Team Rank	3 NASA Rank	4 1-3*	5 2-3*
7	One case of Pet milk					
8	Two 100-pound tanks of oxygen					
9	Stellar map (of the moon's constellations)					
10	Self-inflating life raft					
11	Magnetic compass					
12	5 gallons of water					
13	Signal flares					
14	First-aid kit containing injection needles					
15	Solar-powered FM receiver-transmitter					
*Absolute difference				Totals		

Scores

0–25 excellent

26–32 good

33–45 average

46–55 fair

56–70 poor—suggests use of Earth-bound logic

71–112 very poor—you're one of the casualties of the space program!

The average team scores are almost always lower (better) than the average individual scores demonstrating the value of teamwork. The percentage improvement is an indicator of team effectiveness.

Myers-Briggs Type Indicator

The Myers-Briggs Type Indicator is a proprietary psychological test. As such, it is not in the public domain. There are, however, a number of websites that offer a scaled-down version at no cost. One that I have used is the HumanMetrics version called The Jung Typology Test, which is based on the work of Carl Jung and Isabel Briggs. You can take this test at http://www.humanmetrics.com/cgi-win/jtypes2.asp.

APPENDIX D

Multitasking Exercise

The purpose of this exercise is to demonstrate the impact of multitasking on performance.

Step 1: As quickly as you can, copy the letters from A to Z in column 1. Then copy the numbers from 1 to 26 in column 3. Using a stopwatch, time your performance.

Step 2: Repeat the exercise filling in the blanks one row at a time starting with A and 1, then B, and 2, etc. Time your performance and compare to Step 1.

	1	2		3	4
A	__	__	1	__	__
B	__	__	2	__	__
C	__	__	3	__	__
D	__	__	4	__	__
E	__	__	5	__	__
F	__	__	6	__	__
G	__	__	7	__	__
H	__	__	8	__	__
I	__	__	9	__	__
J	__	__	10	__	__
K	__	__	11	__	__
L	__	__	12	__	__
M	__	__	13	__	__
N	__	__	14	__	__
O	__	__	15	__	__
P	__	__	16	__	__
Q	__	__	17	__	__
R	__	__	18	__	__

ON TIME, ON BUDGET

S _____ _____   19 _____ _____
T _____ _____   20 _____ _____
U _____ _____   21 _____ _____
V _____ _____   22 _____ _____
W _____ _____   23 _____ _____
X _____ _____   24 _____ _____
Y _____ _____   25 _____ _____
Z _____ _____   26 _____ _____

APPENDIX E

Miscellaneous

A Project Manager's Lessons Learned

by Jerry Madden, retired Associate Director at the U.S. National Aeronautical and Space Administration (NASA)

None of these are original--It's just that we don't know where they were stolen from!

There is no such thing as previously flown hardware, i.e., the people who build the next unit probably never saw the previous unit; there are probably minor changes; the operational environment has probably changed; and the people who check the unit out will in most cases not understand the unit or the test equipment.

- Most equipment works "as built," i.e., not as the designer planned. This is due to layout of the design, poor understanding on the designer's part, or poor understanding of component specifications.
- The source of most problems is people but damned if they will admit it. Know the people working on your project, so you know what the real weak spots are.
- Most managers succeed on the strength and skill of their staff.
- A manager who is his own systems engineer or financial manager is one who will probably try to do open heart surgery on himself.

- One must pay attention to workaholics—if they get going in the wrong direction, they can do a lot of damage in a short time. It is possible to overload them, causing premature burn-out, but hard to determine if the load is too much, since much of it is self-generated. It is important to make sure such people take enough time off and that the workload does not exceed 1-1/4 to 1-1/2 times what is normal.
- NASA programs compete for budget funds—they do not compete with each other, i.e., you never attack any other program or NASA work with the idea you should get their funding. Sell what you have on its own merit.
- Contractors respond well to the customer who pays attention to what they are doing, but not too well to the customer that continually second-guesses their activity. The basic rule is: a customer is always right, but the cost will escalate if a customer always has things done his way, instead of the way the contractor had planned. The ground rule is never change a contractor's plans unless they are flawed or too costly, i.e., the old saying, "Better is the enemy of good."
- Never undercut your staff in public, i.e., don't make decisions on work that you have given them to do in public meetings. Even if you direct a change, never take the responsibility for implementing away from your staff.
- The project has many resources within itself. There probably are five to 10 system engineers considering all the contractors and instrument developers. This is a powerful resource that can be used to attack problems.
- Know who the decision makers on the program are. It may be someone on the outside who has the ear of Congress, or the Administrator, or the Associate Administrator, or one of the scientists—or someone in the chain of command—whoever they are, try to get a line of communication to them on a formal or informal basis.

APPENDIX E

- You and the program manager should work as a team. The program manager is your advocate at NASA HQ and must be tied in to the decision making and should aid your efforts to be tied in too.
- A project manager should visit everyone who is building anything for his project at least once, should know all the managers on his project (both government and contractor), and know the integration team members. People like to know that the project manager is interested in their work, and the best proof is for the manager to visit them and see first-hand what they are doing.
- Never ask management to make a decision that you can make. Assume you have the authority to make decisions unless you know there is a document that states unequivocally that you cannot.
- Wrong decisions made early can be salvaged, but "right" decisions made late cannot.
- Never make excuses; instead, present plans of actions to be taken.
- Never try to get even for some slight by another project. It is not good form—it puts you on the same level as the other person—and often ends up hindering the project getting done.
- If you cultivate too much egotism, you may find it difficult to change your position—especially if your personnel tell you that you are wrong. You should instill an attitude on the project whereby your personnel know they can tell you of wrong decisions.
- One of the advantages of NASA in the early days was the fact that everyone knew that the facts that we were absolutely sure of could be wrong.
- Managers who rely on the paperwork to do the reporting of activities are known failures.

- Not all successful managers are competent and not all failed managers are incompetent. Luck still plays a part in success or failure, but luck favors the competent, hard-working manager.
- If you have a problem that requires the addition of people to solve, you should approach recruiting people like a cook who has under-salted, i.e., a little at a time.
- A project manager must know what motivates the project contractors, i.e., their award system, their fiscal system, their policies, and their company culture.
- Other than original budget information prior to the President's submittal to Congress, there is probably no secret information on the project--so don't treat anything like it is secret. Everyone does better if they can see the whole picture, so don't hide any of it from anyone.
- Know the resources of your center and if possible other centers. Other centers, if they have the resources, are normally happy to help. It is always surprising how much good help one can get by just asking.
- Contractors tend to size up their government counterparts, and staff their part of the project accordingly. If they think yours are clunkers, they will take their poorer people to put on your project.
- Documentation does not take the place of knowledge. There is a great difference in what is supposed to be, what is thought to have been, and what the reality is. Documents are normally a static picture in time which is outdated rapidly.
- Remember who the customer is and what his objectives are, i.e., check with him when you go to change anything of significance.
- In case of a failure:
  a. Make a timeline of events and include everything that is known;
  b. Put down known facts—check every theory against them;

APPENDIX E

    c. Don't beat the data until it confesses, i.e., know when to stop trying to force-fit a scenario;

    d. Do not arrive at a conclusion too rapidly. Make sure any deviation from the norm is explained—remember the wrong conclusion is prologue to the next failure;

    e. Know when to stop.

- Remember the boss has the right to make decisions, even if you think they are wrong. Tell the boss what you think but, if he still wants it done his way, do your best to make sure the outcome is successful.
- Redundancy in hardware can be a fiction. We are adept at building things to be identical so that if one fails, the other will also fail. Make sure all hardware is treated in a build as if it were one of a kind and needed for mission success.
- Don't be afraid to fail or you will not succeed, but always work at your skill to recover. Part of that skill is knowing who can help.
- Experience may be fine but testing is better. Knowing something will work never takes the place of proving that it will.
- People have reasons for doing things the way they do them. Most people want to do a good job, and if they don't, the problem is they probably don't know how or exactly what is expected.
- The boss may not know how to do the work, but he has to know what he wants. The boss had better find out what he expects and wants, if he doesn't know. A blind leader tends to go in circles.
- A puzzle is hard to discern from just one piece, so don't be surprised if team members deprived of information reach the wrong conclusion.
- Reviews are for the reviewed and not the reviewer. The review is a failure if the reviewed learn nothing from it.

- The amount of reviews and reports are proportional to management's understanding, i.e., the less management knows or understands the activities, the more it requires reviews and reports. It is necessary in this type of environment to make sure the data is presented so that the average person, slightly familiar with activities, can understand it. Keeping the data simple and clear never insults anyone's intelligence.
- In olden times, engineers had hands-on experience, technicians understood how the electronics worked and what it was supposed to do, and layout technicians knew too-but today only the computer knows for sure, and it's not talking.
- Not using modern techniques like computer systems is a great mistake, but forgetting the computer simulates thinking is still greater.
- Management principles are still the same. It is just the tools that have changed. You still should find the right people to do the work and get out of the way so they can do it.
- It is mainly the incompetent that don't like to show off their work.
- Whoever you deal with, deal fairly. Space is not a big playing field. You may be surprised how often you have to work with the same people. Better they respect you than carry a grudge.
- Mistakes are all right, but failure is not. Failure is just a mistake you can't recover from; therefore, try to create contingency plans and alternate approaches for the items or plans that have high risk.
- You cannot be ignorant of the language of the area you manage or with that of areas with which you interface. Education is a must for the modern manager. There are simple courses available to learn computerese, communicationese, and all the rest of the modern "eses" of the world. You can't manage if you don't understand what is being said or written.

APPENDIX E

- Most international meetings are held in English, which may be a foreign language to some participants. It is important to have adequate discussions so that there are no misinterpretations of what is said.
- NASA Management Instructions (NMI's) are written by another NASA employee like yourself; therefore, challenge them if they don't make sense. It is possible another NASA employee will rewrite them or waive them for you.
- A working meeting has about six people attending. Meetings larger than this are for information transfer.
- Being friendly with a contractor is fine—being a friend of a contractor is dangerous to your objectivity.
- The old NASA pushed the limits of technology and science; therefore, it did not worry about "requirements creep" or overruns. The new NASA has to work as if all are fixed price; therefore, "requirements creep" has become a deadly sin.
- Many managers, just because they have the scientists under contract on their project, forget that the scientists are their customers and many times have easier access to top management than the managers do.
- Most scientists are rational unless you endanger their chance to do their experiment. They will work with you if they believe you are telling them the truth. This includes reducing their own plans.
- Cooperative efforts require good communications and early warning systems. A project manager should try to keep his partners aware of what is going on and should be the one who tells them first of any rumor or actual changes in plan. The partners should be consulted before things are put in final form, even if they only have a small piece of the action. A project manager who blindsides his partners will be treated in kind and will be considered a person of no integrity.

- All problems are solvable in time, so make sure you have enough schedule contingency-- if you don't, the next project manager that takes your place will.
- The number of reviews is increasing but the knowledge transfer remains the same; therefore, all your charts and presentation material should be constructed with this fact in mind. This means you should be able to construct a set of slides that only needs to be shuffled from presentation to presentation.
- Just because you give monthly reports, don't think that you can abbreviate anything in a yearly report. If management understood the monthlies, they wouldn't need a yearly.
- Abbreviations are getting to be a pain. Each project now has a few thousand. This calls on senior management to know a couple hundred thousand. Use them sparingly in presentations unless your objective is to confuse.
- Occasionally things go right—the lesson learned here is: Try to duplicate that which works.
- Running does not take the place of thinking. For yourself, you must take time to smell the roses. For your work, you must take time to understand the consequences of your actions.
- Sometimes the best thing to do is nothing. It is also occasionally the best help you can give. Just listening is all that is needed on many occasions. You may be the boss but, if you constantly have to solve someone's problems, you are working for him.
- We have developed a set of people whose self-interest is more paramount than the work or at least it appears so to older managers. It appears to the older managers that the newer ones are more interested in form than in substance. The question is, are old managers right or just old.
- One problem new managers face is that everyone wants to solve their problems. Old managers were told by senior

APPENDIX E

management "solve your damn problems; that is what we hired you to do."

- Remember, it is often easier to do foolish paperwork than to fight the need for it. Fight only if it is a global issue which will save much future work.
- Know your management—some like a good joke; others only like a joke if they tell it.
- Integrity means your subordinates trust you.
- You cannot watch everything. What you can watch is the people. They have to know you will not accept a poor job.
- Next year is always the year with adequate funding and schedule—next year arrives on the 50th year of your career.
- The first sign of trouble comes from the schedule or the cost curve. Engineers are the last to know they are in trouble. Engineers are born optimists.
- External reviews are scheduled at the worst possible time: therefore, keep an up-to-date set of technical data so that you can rapidly respond. Having to update business data should be cause for dismissal.
- Hide nothing from the reviewers. Their reputation and yours is on the line. Expose all the warts and pimples. Don't offer excuses—just state facts.
- NASA is establishing a set of reviewers and a set of reviews. Once firmly established, the system will fight to stay alive, so make the most of it. Try to find a way for the reviews to work for you.
- Knowledge is often confounded by test. Computer models have hidden flaws, not the least of which is poor input data.
- Today one must push the state of the art: be within budget, take risks, not fail, and be on time. Strangely, all these are consistent as long as the ground rules, such as funding profile and schedule, are established up front and maintained.

- Most of yesteryear's projects overran because of poor estimates and not because of mistakes. Getting better estimates may not lower cost but will improve NASA's business reputation. Actually, there is a high probability that the cost of getting better estimates will increase cost and assure a higher profit to industry, unless the fee is reduced to reflect lower risk on the part of industry. A better reputation is necessary in the present environment.

- A scientific proposal takes about nine months to put together. It takes NASA HQ about nine months to a year to select the winning proposals. Then, it takes three to four years to sell the program. This means five to six years after the initial thoughts, the real work starts. Managers, for some strange reason, do not understand why a scientist wants to build something different than proposed. Managers are strange people.

- There are rare times when only one man can do the job. These are in technical areas that are more art and skill than normal. Cherish these people and employ their services when necessary as soon as possible. Getting the work done by someone else takes two to three times longer, and the product is normally below standard.

- Software now has taken on all the parameters of hardware, i.e., requirement creep, high percentage of flight mission cost, need for quality control, need for validation procedures, etc. It has the added feature that it is hard as hell to determine it is not flawed. Get the basic system working and then add the bells and whistles. Never throw away a version that works even if you have all the confidence in the world the newer version works. It is necessary to have contingency plans for software.

- History is prologue. There has not been a project yet that has not had a parts problem despite all the qualification and testing done on parts. Time and being prepared to react are the only safeguards.

APPENDIX E

- Award fee is a good tool that puts discipline both on the contractor and the government. The score given represents the status of the project as well as the management skills of both parties. The Performance Measurement System (PMS) should be used to verify the scores. Consistent poor scores require senior management intervention to determine the reason. Consistent good scores, which are consistent with PMS, reflect a well-run project, but if these scores are not consistent with the PMS, senior management must take action to find out why.
- A project manager is not the monitor of the work but is to be the driver. In award fee situations, the government personnel should be making every effort possible to make sure the contractor gets a high score, i.e., be on schedule and produce good work. Contractors don't fail, NASA does, and that is why one must be proactive in support. This is also why a low score damages the government project manager as much as the contractor's manager because it means he is not doing his job.
- There is no greater motivation than giving a good person his piece of the puzzle to control but a pat on the back or an award helps.
- Morale of the contractor's personnel is important to a government manager. Just as you don't want to buy a car built by disgruntled employees, you don't want to buy flight hardware built by them. You should take an active role in motivating all personnel on the project.
- People who monitor work and don't help get it done, never seem to know exactly what is going on.
- Never assume someone knows something or has done something unless you have asked them. Even the obvious is overlooked or ignored on occasion—especially in a high-stress activity.

- Don't assume you know why senior management has done something. If you feel you need to know, ask. You get some amazing answers that will dumbfound you.
- If you have someone who doesn't look, ask, and analyze, ask them to transfer.
- Bastards, gentlemen, and ladies can be project managers. Lost souls, procrastinators, and wishy-washers cannot.
- A person's time is very important. You must be careful as a manager that you realize the value of other people's time, i.e., work you hand out and meetings should be necessary. You must, where possible, shield your staff from unnecessary work, i.e., some requests should be ignored or a refusal sent to the requester.
- A good technician, quality inspector, and strawboss are more important in obtaining a good product than all the paper and reviews.
- The seeds of problems are laid down early. Initial planning is the most vital part of a project. Review of most failed projects or of project problems indicates that the disasters were well planned to happen from the start.
- A comfortable project manager is one waiting for his next assignment or one on the verge of failure. Security is not normal to project management.
- Remember, the President, Congress, OMB, NASA HQ, senior center management, and your customers all have jobs to do. All you have to do is keep them all happy.
- Always try to negotiate your internal support at the lowest level. What you want is the support of the person doing the work, and the closer you can get to him in negotiations the better.
- Whoever said beggars can't be choosers doesn't understand project management. Many times it is better to trust to luck than to get known poor support.

APPENDIX E

- Remember your contractor has a tendency to have a one-to-one interface with your staff; so every member of your staff costs you at least one person (about a 1/4 of million) on the contract per year.
- There is only one solution to a weak project manager in industry—get rid of him fast. The main job of a project manager in industry is to keep the customer happy. Make sure the one working with you knows that "on schedule, on cost, and a good product"—not flattery—is all that makes you happy.
- Talk is not cheap. The best way to understand a personnel or technical problem is to talk to the right people. Lack of talk at the right levels is deadly.
- Projects require teamwork to succeed. Remember most teams have a coach and not a boss, but the coach still has to call some of the plays.
- In the rush to get things done, it is always important to remember who you work for. Blindsiding the boss will not be to your benefit in the long run.
- Over-engineering is common. Engineers like puzzles and mazes—try to make them keep their designs simple.
- Never make a decision from a cartoon. Look at the actual hardware or what real information is available, such as layouts. Too much time is wasted by people trying to cure a cartoon whose function is to explain the principle.
- An Agency's age can be estimated by the number of reports and meetings it has. The older it gets, the more the paperwork increases and the less product is delivered per dollar. Many people have suggested that an Agency self-destruct every 25 years and be reborn starting from scratch.
- False starts are normal in today's environment. More than ever, in this type of environment, one must keep an ear open for the starting gun and be prepared to move out in quick and orderly fashion once it is sounded. In the past, too many false

starts have resulted in the project not hearing the real starting gun or jumping off and falling on its face.

- The pioneering phase of NASA is mostly done, if not actually by fiat. This means the difficult and more important work has started. This work requires more discipline, but there should still be room for innovation.
- There are still some individuals who think important decisions are made in meetings. This is rarely the case. Normally, the decision-makers meet over lunch or have a brief meeting to decide the issue and then (at a meeting called to discuss the issue) make it appear that the decision is made as a result of this discussion.
- In political decisions, do not look for logic—look for politics.
- Interagency agreements are hard to make even if there is no conflict in the responsibilities and the requirements do satisfy both parties. Conflict in these areas normally leads to failure no matter how hard the people involved try to make an agreement.
- In dealing with international partners, the usual strategy is to go one day early, meet with your counterpart, discuss all issues to be brought up at a meeting, arrive at an agreeable response (or a decision to table the issue for later discussion), and agree not to take any firm positions on any new issues brought up at the meeting. This makes it appear to the rest of the world that you and your counterpart are of one mind and that the work is in good hands. All disputes are held behind closed doors with the minimum number of participants.
- Gentlemen and ladies can get things done just as well as bastards. What is needed is a strong will and respect—not "strong arm" tactics. It must be admitted that the latter does work but leaves a residue that has to be cleaned up.
- Though most of us in our youth have heard the poem that states "for want of a nail the race was lost," few of us realize

that most space failures have a similar origin. It is the common place items that tend to be overlooked and thus do us in. The tough and difficult tasks are normally done well. The simple and easy tasks seem to be the ones done sloppily.

- In the "old NASA," a job done within schedule and cost was deemed to be simple. The present NASA wants to push the start of the art, be innovative, and be a risk taker but stay on schedule and cost. One gets the feeling that either the new jobs will be simple or that the reign of saints has finally occurred.
- Meetings, meetings. A Projects Manager's staff meeting should last five minutes— minimum/1 hour max. Less than five minutes and you probably didn't need the meeting; longer than one hour, it becomes a bull session.
- Taking too many people to visit a contractor or other government agency puts them in the entertainment business, not the space hardware or software business.
- Too many engineers get in the habit of supporting support contractors and of using them as a crutch. In many cases it is getting to the point where one has to wonder who is who.
- Reviews, meetings, and reality have little in common.
- You should always check to see how long a change or action takes to get to the implementor—this time should be measured in hours and not days.
- Let your staff argue you into doing something even if you intended to do it anyway. It gives them the feeling that they won one! There are a lot of advantages to gamesmanship as long as no one detects the game.
- Some contractors are good, some are bad, but they seem to change places over time, making the past no guarantee of the future; thus, constant vigilance is a project requirement.
- It is rare that a contractor or instrumentor does not know your budget and does not intend to get every bit of it from you. This is why you have to constantly pay attention to the manpower

- they use and to judge their activities in order to assure that they are not overloading the system.
- People tend to ask for what they think they can get and not what they need. On GRO the specs for photomultiplier tubes were based on the engineering unit's performance on all parameters. One parameter, though made in the engineering tubes, was difficult to obtain in the flight tubes. It was a meaningless parameter put in only because the engineering tubes met it. Finally, after about nine months of sweat and tears, this was recognized and deleted so we could get the flight tubes.
- Today one must get an honest bid, one which is accurate to 15 percent. On GRO, with TRW the only bidder and with them knowing it, we all got what we believed to be an honest bid that was off by about 18 to 20 percent at the finish. The main area of overrun was the structure. TRW had never built one this large or heavy before. We estimated that the structure would require 600 drawings, multiplied this by 1.25 to get 750 and rounded to 800 to estimate the cost. It took 1,186 drawings. It is normally not the complex systems that get you, so beware when you estimate the cost, especially if there is no experience base.
- Too much cost data on a proposal can blind you to the real risks or forgotten items. On a project we thoroughly knew, we spent six months of government and contractor time validating the cost, had rooms full of data, and presented our findings to Headquarters. Two weeks later, the contractor found an "Oh, I forgot" that costs $30 million. One should look at how past programs spent their money to try to avoid these traps.
- On GRO we sort of estimated we needed about 20 percent contingency on previously flown subsystems and about 40 percent to 50 percent on new ones. The ratio was about right except the order was reversed.

APPENDIX E

- There are some small companies that make the same subsystem correctly every time because the same people do it. There are some large companies that can never make the same unit correctly every time because different people do the work each time. Heritage should be questioned when the people doing the work all have peach fuzz on their faces.
- Too many project managers think a spoken agreement carries the same weight as one put in writing. It doesn't. People vanish and change positions. Important decisions must be documented.
- Make sure everyone knows what the requirements are and understands them. Much easier to say than do. On GRO we stated quite clearly that the scientific instruments had to take 18g in a specific axis. Everyone understood the requirement but until the mechanical test on EGRET no one stood up and said it was impossible to meet it. The thermal specification for the momentum wheels required that they run five degrees colder than normal limits to make the spacecraft thermal engineer's life easier. No one stood up until after nine months of failure in the test program to say that the grease used changes state if taken that cold, and would not recover when brought back to higher temperature. You have to have the right people look at requirements. A bunch of managers and salesmen nodding agreement to requirements should not make you feel safe.
- Too many people at Headquarters believe the myth that you can reduce the food to the horse every day till you get a horse that requires no food. They try to do the same with projects which eventually end up as dead as the horse.
- The project manager who is the smartest man on his project has done a lousy job of recruitment.

APPENDIX F

Project Forms

Project Selection Form

Project Title	
Customer	
Rate each factor from 1 to 10 with 1 representing the lowest score and 10 the highest.	

Factor	Score	Comments
Alignment with vision and mission		
Likelihood of winning the bid		
Expected ROI		
Risk		
Availability of personnel		
Total Score		
Strengths		
Weaknesses		

ON TIME, ON BUDGET

Stakeholder Register

#	Name	Organization	Phone	E-mail	Role	Level of Support	Must Do	Must Not Do	Notes
1									
2									
3									
4									
5									
6									
7									
8									
9									
10									
11									
12									
13									
14									
15									
16									
17									
18									
19									
20									

APPENDIX F

Project Charter

Project name
Version
Date

Project Team Name

Project Name:	
Sponsor/Customer:	
Project Manager:	
Customer(s):	
1. Business Problem: (What is the problem that requires this project?)	
2. Solution: (What will be done to fix this problem?)	
3. Primary Project Goals:	
4. How is this project aligned with the organization's strategic goals and objectives?	
5. Return on Investment: (Why should the organization undertake this project?)	
6. Key Assumptions: (What assumptions does the success of the project depend on?)	

APPENDIX F

7. Key Risks: (What events might cause the project to fail?)		
8. Exclusions: (What deliverables are not included in this project?)		
9. Constraints		
	Driver:	
	Middle Constraint:	
	Weak Constraint:	
10. Parameters		
	Estimated Project Cost:	
	Estimated Project Duration:	
11. Signatures	**Signature**	**Date**
Project Manager		
Sponsor/Customer		
Stakeholders		
Other Stakeholders		

Attachments:

Scope Statement Template

Project Scope Statement	
Project Name	
Project Manager	
Date	
Project Overview: (What is the problem that requires the project and what will be done to fix it?)	
Key Deliverables: (What products/services must be produced to meet project goals?)	
Key Characteristics and Requirements: (What are the key characteristics and requirements of the deliverables listed above?)	
Exclusions: (What deliverables or requirements are outside the scope of the project?)	
Time and Cost Estimates: (List approved timeframe and cost estimate)	

APPENDIX F

Roles and Responsibilities: (List team members and their roles and responsibilities for the project)
Risks: (What events or circumstances might cause great damage to the project or cause it to fail?)
Assumptions: (What assumptions does the success of the project depend on?)
Constraints: (List other constraints)

Approvals	Name	Signature	Date

RAM/RACI Example

Project Name: Website Development Project

Activity ID	WBS	Project Manager RACI	Project Manager Effort	Team Member 1 RACI	Team Member 1 Effort	Team Member 2 RACI	Team Member 2 Effort	Team Member 3 RACI	Team Member 3 Effort	Total
0	Web Project		2		43.5		49		20	114.5
1.0	Requirements		1		8		6		1	16
1.1	Review charter	AR	1	R	1	R	1	R	1	4
1.2	Verify requirements	A		R	4	R	2			6
1.3	Develop SOW	A		R	3	R	3			6
2.0	Contents		0		0		18		0	18
2.1	Identify required content	AI				R	5			5
2.2	Acquire/develop content	A				R	10			10
2.3	Transfer content to vendor	A				R	3			3
3.0	Vendor		0		9.5		2		0	11.5
3.1	Bidding		0		5		0			5
3.1.1	Develop bidding list	A		R	3					3

APPENDIX F

Project Budget Template

WBS	Name	Type of Cost				Total
		Labor	Equipment	Materials	Facility	

ON TIME, ON BUDGET

APPENDIX F

Project Control Chart

WBS #	Name	Budgeted Cost	Actual Cost	Difference	Estimated Duration	Actual Duration	Difference

APPENDIX F

APPENDIX F

Change Order Request

Request number	
Request date	
Project name	
Project sponsor	
Change requested by	
Description of requested change	
Why is this change necessary? What will happen if the request change is not made?	
How will the proposed change impact......?	
Scope	
Schedule	
Cost	
Risk	
Quality	
Other	
Potential risks	

Approvals		
Name	**Signatures**	**Date**
Project Manager		
Sponsor		
Customer		

Change Control Log

#	Date	Description	Rational	Consequences	Budget Impact	Schedule Impact	New Risks	Disposition	Date	Approving Authority	Notes

APPENDIX F

Risk Register Template

#	Risk Event	P	I	Cost Increase	CRE	Delay (Days)	SRE	Action	Cost
1									
2									
3									
4									
5									
6									
7									
8									
9									
10									
11									
12									
13									
14									
15									
16									
17									

APPENDIX F

18													
19													
20													
21													
22													
23													
24													
25													
26													
27													
28													
29													
30													
												Totals	

P = Probability
I = Impact
Cost Increase = The additional cost of the project if the event occurs
CRE = Cost Risk Exposure
Delay = The number of additional days it will take to complete the project if the event occurs
SRE = Schedule Risk Exposure
Action = Avoid, Mitigate, Transfer, Accept for risks or Exploit, Enhance, Share, Accept for opportunities
Cost = Cost of the action taken

APPENDIX F

Issues Log

#	Description	Potential Impact	Priority	Date Opened	Date Closed	Issue Owner	Department	Status	Notes

APPENDIX F

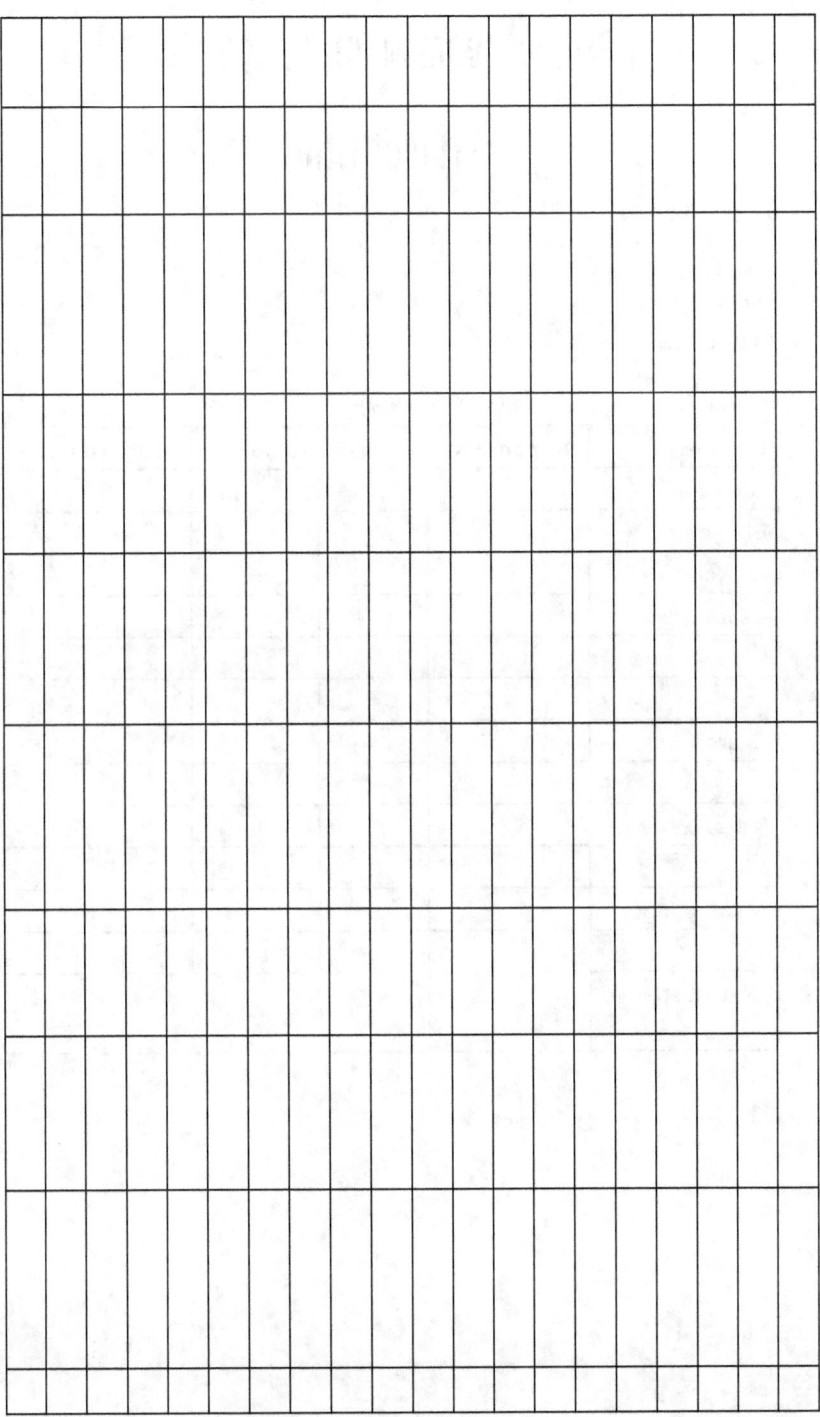

ON TIME, ON BUDGET

Project Team Meeting Agenda

Project Title

Date:

Attendance:

Vision Statement (*or Project Objective*):

Updates	Responsible	Status	Action	Assigned to:
Timeline				
Budget				
Deliverables				
Issues				
Challenges				
Risks				
Assumptions				
Next Meeting Topics				

ABOUT THE AUTHOR

John Shoemaker holds a B.A. from Pacific Lutheran University and an M.A. from Western Washington University. He received his Ph.D. at the University of Kentucky after completing his doctoral research at the University of Copenhagen in Copenhagen, Denmark.

John has taught courses in project management, public administration, quality management systems, statistics, research methodology, and marketing research at a number of colleges and universities including Kansas State University and the University of Kansas.

Since leaving full-time academic employment, he has held a number of positions in the private, public, and not-for-profit sectors. He is currently an associate faculty member in the MBA program at City University of Seattle. He has also worked at CETYS Universidad in Baja California, Mexico, and the University of International Business and Economics in Beijing, China where he taught project management.

John has extensive practical experience in project management. For over 20 years, he managed projects in the advertising, marketing, and marketing research industries. He also worked as a corporate trainer for over 15 years. In this capacity, he conducted more than 200 project management seminars throughout the U.S., Canada, Puerto Rico, the United Kingdom, and the United Arab Emirates. His client list includes many Fortune 500 companies.

In addition to project management seminars, he does contract project management, project management consulting, and Merlin-based project management software training and consulting.

He has been a senior member of the American Society for Quality and the Project Management Institute and is retired from the Kansas Air National Guard. He lives in Gig Harbor, Washington.

John may be contacted through his website at www.pmprof.online.

INDEX

Acceptance, 12, 221, 236, 245, 291, 293, 347-353, 356, 361, 365
Actual Cost (AC), 286, 311-313, 315, 317
Addition, 346, 347
Adjourning, 268, 270, 280, 298, 359
Agile project management, 3, 16, 128
Allen, David, 274
American Society for Quality, 238, 354, 393, 456
Assumptions, 49, 52-54, 169, 171, 225, 282, 291, 292, 304, 308, 438, 441, 454
Audits, 235, 252, 253, 290, 291, 304, 349, 356
Avoidance, 205, 207-209, 211, 293, 336, 343
Backward pass, 153, 157-159
Barnitz, Andy, 247
Berkun, Scott, xvii, 251, 330
Booz, Allen and Hamilton, 2, 127
Brainstorming, 74-76, 192, 193, 325, 380, 403
Budget at Completion (BAC), 320, 341
Change log, 222, 224, 227, 380
Change request, 218, 219, 221, 224, 225, 331, 332, 447
Conflict resolution modes, 335-338

Cost Performance Index (CPI), 313, 314, 322
Cost Risk Exposure, 196, 202, 451
Covey, Steven, 249, 250, 257, 274, 280, 331-333, 337
Critical path, 1, 2, 113, 140, 143, 145-147, 154-157, 159, 162, 191, 285
Crosby, Philip, 230
DeMarco, Tom, xvii, 132, 277
Delphi Method, 74, 77, 78, 128, 140, 194, 380
Dependencies, 2, 124, 134-138, 143, 144, 148, 152, 154, 156, 161, 162, 285
Dow, William, 167
Driver, 43, 56, 58, 113, 116, 117, 123, 145, 199, 340, 400, 427, 439
Dupont Corporation, 2
Duration, 4, 15, 51, 55, 56, 60, 74, 75, 78-80, 87, 91-95, 100, 107-109, 112, 124-133, 136, 138, 140, 141, 143, 145, 147, 148, 152-155, 157, 159, 160-162, 192, 202, 203, 309, 310, 439, 445
Earned Value (EV), 2, 308, 309, 311-313, 315, 317, 319, 321, 322, 341, 380
Earned Value Method, 2, 308, 309, 311-313, 315, 317, 319, 341, 380

INDEX

Effort, 91-95, 101, 102, 104, 115, 124
Eisenhower Method, 66, 274, 275
Elapsed duration, 130, 131
Emotional intelligence, 246, 247
Employee engagement, 250, 251, 257
Event-driven Scheduling, 140
Execution stage, 10-13, 20, 21, 65-67, 85, 243, 244, 262, 266, 281, 292
Five Dysfunctions of a Team, 271
Float (See Slack), 112, 113, 145, 147, 148, 156-159, 162, 163, 192, 277
Forming, 268-271, 359, 384
Forward pass, 152, 157-159
Gantt chart, 1, 135, 136, 145, 148, 161, 244, 278, 283, 285, 286, 315, 316, 332, 380
Getting Things Done, 274, 275
Goleman, Daniel, 246, 247
Heldman, Kim, xvii
Initiation stage, 10-13, 20, 21, 35, 41, 45-47, 54, 63, 65, 70, 114, 172, 179, 209, 210, 243, 260, 265, 266, 281, 329
Integration, 20, 346, 347, 365, 387
Juran, Joseph, 230, 231
Kennedy, John F., 255
Kerzner, Harold, 8, 338
Kick-off meeting, 279, 359
Kouzes, James, 254, 255
Lencioni, Patrick, 271
Lewis, James, xvii, 21, 71
Lister, Tim, xvii, 132,
Lost on the Moon exercise, 272, 409
Madden, Jerry, 417
Malcolm Baldrige National Quality Award, 26, 232
Management reserve, 120, 121, 141
McConnell, Steve, 224, 239, 270, 271
Middle constraint, 43, 439
Milestones, 100, 134, 160-162, 308, 310, 341, 344, 399, 408
Mind map, 76, 77, 380
Mitigation, 195, 203-208, 211, 293, 324, 451
Multitasking, 276-278-280, 415
Myers-Briggs Type Indicator (MBTI), 272, 414
Norming, 268, 269, 280, 334, 359, 384, 385
Padding, 130-132, 155, 182, 203, 204
Percent Complete, 308-311
Performing, 268, 270, 271, 280, 334.338.359, 384, 385
Planned Value (PV), 312, 313-315, 317, 320
Planning Poker, 126, 128, 129
PMBOK, 6, 8-10, 19, 48, 52, 68, 70, 90, 110, 188, 190, 199, 208, 210, 230, 231, 236-238, 244, 262, 265, 311, 312, 334
Portfolio Management, 8, 25, 26, 34
Posner, Barry, 254, 255
Performance Domains, 9, 19
Problem-solving, 23, 296, 324-327, 343, 394
Program, 2, 7, 8, 14, 418
Program Management, 7, 14, 81
Program Evaluation and Review Technique (PERT), 1, 2, 70, 134
Progress Reports, 169, 172, 307, 318, 319

INDEX

Project Acceptance, 221, 291, 348-351, 361

Project budget, 61, 71, 108, 116, 118-121, 202, 207, 208, 220, 286, 328, 337, 363, 443

Project charter, 11, 46, 47-63, 65, 66, 68-70, 85, 114-117, 160, 171, 187, 189, 213, 219, 231, 236, 260, 265, 281, 287, 291, 292, 307, 323, 349, 356, 365, 380, 437

Project closure, 11-13, 20, 338, 345-352, 355-359, 360-364

Project Management Definition, 6-9

Project Management Institute, 6, 9, 20, 48, 70, 220, 238, 273, 276, 312, 456

Project Management Office, 62, 98, 99, 221, 265, 266, 328, 337, 355

Project manager, xvii, xviii, 2, 3, 5, 8-10, 16, 17, 21, 25, 30, 31, 34-37, 39, 40, 42-45, 37-49, 52-56, 58-63, 66-71, 75-78, 80-82, 85, 86, 89, 90, 91, 96-102, 104-110, 112-115, 117, 120-124, 128, 131-134, 137, 140, 143, 147, 148, 153, 154, 157, 160, 162, 166, 168-172, 174, 175, 178, 180-184, 187, 194, 196, 203, 204, 206, 211, 213, 218, 220, 224-226, 229, 230, 234, 235, 238, 240, 243-249, 252-257, 259-270, 272-274, 276, 279-282, 285-287, 292, 293, 298-304, 307, 309, 310, 312, 318-321, 323, 324, 328-337, 339-343, 345, 348-350, 352, 355, 357, 359-366, 379, 391, 417-433, 438-440, 442, 447

Project recovery, 338-340

Project Scope Statement, 68, 69, 86, 189, 356, 440

Project selection, 23-34, 48, 400, 435

Project Status Report, 82, 169, 170, 182, 184, 245, 299, 301, 307, 308, 318, 319, 321, 356, 380,

Project support personnel, 259, 264, 358, 362

Qualitative Risk Analysis, 198-201

Quality assurance, 68, 231, 240, 245

Quality control, 231, 235, 240, 287, 290, 426

Quality improvement, 5, 240, 383

Quantitative risk analysis, 198, 200-203

Rand Corporation, 2, 77

Resource Assignment Matrix, 100-105, 115

Resource-driven scheduling, 124, 140

Resource leveling, 110-114

Resource over-allocation, 110, 113, 122, 153,

Ringlemann Effect, 267

Risk, 10, 12, 14, 15, 23, 31, 33, 41, 45, 49, 52, 54-56, 59, 60, 65, 66, 80, 101, 107, 117, 121, 123, 132, 133, 148, 155, 159, 167, 169, 170, 182, 187-213, 218, 219, 225-227, 239, 245, 256, 261, 282, 287, 292, 293, 301, 304, 308, 319, 321, 323-325, 332, 338, 339, 341, 343, 356, 387, 422, 425, 426, 431, 432, 435, 439, 441, 447, 448, 450, 451, 454

INDEX

Risk acceptance, 203, 206, 207, 211, 324
Risk appetite, 208
Risk acceptance, 203, 206
Risk tolerance, 203
Risk triggers, 200, 292, 293
Schedule Performance Index (SPI), 308, 311, 313, 314, 315, 322
Schedule Risk Exposure (SRE), 197, 202, 450, 451
Scope creep, 51, 71, 195, 287
Skills audit, 90, 106, 119, 252, 253, 356
Slack, 112, 113, 145, 147, 148, 156-159, 162, 163, 192, 277
Stakeholders, 9, 10, 11, 16, 34-40, 45, 47, 49-55, 58-61, 63, 69, 77, 78, 85, 86, 100, 104, 106, 117, 123, 124, 155, 159, 160, 165-173, 175, 177-184, 189, 190, 192, 194, 195, 206, 214, 220-223, 225-227, 229, 230, 233, 234, 240, 244, 246, 247, 255, 257, 259-267, 269, 287, 293, 299, 304, 307, 310, 318, 321, 324, 329, 331, 334, 335, 338-344, 351-354, 356, 359-364, 394-396, 398, 399, 401, 403, 404, 406-408, 436, 439
Stakeholder closeout meeting, 360, 362
Standish Group, 4, 5, 55
Starvation, 346, 347, 365
Status Reports, 82, 169, 170, 182, 184, 245, 299, 301, 307, 308, 318, 319, 321, 356
Storming, 268-270, 280, 334, 359, 384, 385
Team Building, 181, 250, 268, 270, 272, 280, 338, 395, 396, 402

Team contract, 267
Team Effectiveness, 353, 389, 414
Team Performance Criteria, 354, 393, 402
Team selection, 252, 265, 266, 354, 395
Team size, 266
Team Skills Inventory, 90, 106, 121, 356
The Leadership Challenge, 254
The Wisdom of Crowds, 129-130
The Wisdom of Teams, 268
Three-point estimate, 126-128, 130
Time management, 274-276, 296
Transference, 203-206, 208, 227, 293, 324, 451
Triple Constraints, 41, 55, 71, 91, 98, 117, 160, 218, 221, 229, 287, 304, 328, 340, 361
Tuckman Model of Team Development, 268, 280, 359, 384
Waterfall Method, 2, 3
Workarounds, 210, 211, 220, 225, 325
WBS dictionary, 68, 356
Weak constraint, 43, 439
Work Breakdown Structure, 2, 68-86, 99, 102, 117, 120-123, 132, 155, 160, 189, 193, 194, 202, 203, 219, 234-236, 252, 286, 287, 291, 314, 320, 332, 343, 356, 442, 443, 445
Work contours, 108, 109, 153
Work package, 73-75, 79, 81, 82, 86, 87, 90, 91, 100, 104, 114, 115, 119, 193, 286

www.ingramcontent.com/pod-product-compliance
Lightning Source LLC
Chambersburg PA
CBHW070123080526
44586CB00015B/1540